T0355022

DIVINE MUSINGS

Reflections on the Word of God

GEORGE THOMAS YAPUNCICH

WESTBOW
PRESS®
A DIVISION OF THOMAS NELSON
& ZONDERVAN

WestBow Press books may be ordered through booksellers or by contacting:

WestBow Press
A Division of Thomas Nelson & Zondervan
1663 Liberty Drive
Bloomington, IN 47403
www.westbowpress.com
844-714-3454

ISBN: 978-1-6642-4728-4 (sc)
ISBN: 978-1-6642-4729-1 (hc)
ISBN: 978-1-6642-4727-7 (e)

Library of Congress Control Number: 2021921020

Print information available on the last page.

WestBow Press rev. date: 11/01/2021

CONTENTS

Preface ix

Introduction xi

Full List of Entries in This Book xv

Reflections on Key Biblical Terms and Concepts 1

Index to Scriptural References 301

About the Author 309

PREFACE

To Understand the Bible Is to Be Reborn

As a pastor, missionary, teacher, mentor, husband, father, and international businessman, I've met many people—both Christian and non-Christian—who know the Bible inside out but do not understand its message. I particularly remember working with a ministry in Florida where many of my students had large portions of the Bible memorized and could quote them with dazzling speed and accuracy. I was amazed and humbled by my own limited recall powers. But I soon came to realize that they knew only the words, not the message behind them. They did not know how to apply the Word to their lives; they were rather more intent on impressing others. Along with other volunteers, I was responsible for opening the verses to these students and teaching them to apply the scriptures not only to their present lives, but to their eternal lives.

I know many people in church pews who read their Bibles daily, but they read only words; they do not mine the Bible's message. I have friends who know of the Bible and have read many of its popular passages but have no idea what the Bible is saying to them.

The Bible conveys a beautiful message that deserves not just to be read but also to be understood, applied, and lived out. It is rich in history—starting at creation and ending with a taste of eternity. To fully understand this wonderful book takes a lifetime. Only by grasping its many nuances can one begin to appreciate its message.

In this book, *Divine Musings*, I've attempted to reveal deeper meanings for many key biblical terms, thereby opening up a fuller understanding of the Bible's message. To understand the Bible is to experience a whole new life. It is to be reborn.

My objective here is to assist the reader in discovering that although the

Bible addresses many basic issues of life and death, and of the present and the future, its chief message is in its wonderful presentation of salvation. The good news of salvation in Jesus Christ is the fundamental message of the scripture.

"For God so loved the world, that he gave his only Son, that whoever believes in him should not perish but have eternal life. For God did not send his Son into the world to condemn the world, but in order that the world might be saved through him" (John 3:16–17).

INTRODUCTION

About the Bible—and This Book

"The Word"—whenever one hears that phase, recognition of it is immediate. "The Word" refers to a single book, the one book that has survived intact and unchanged over the millennia. "The Word" refers to one book only: the Holy Bible. Nothing else is comparable to it for wisdom, instruction, reproof, and training in righteousness. This book is a lamp to our feet and a light to our path. It stands forever, unchanging, with nothing being added to it or subtracted from it. This book is not the word of humanity but the Word of God, "God-breathed." It is the key to salvation. It is the key to eternal life.

The Bible is a title that comes from Latin and Greek words meaning "book." It's a fitting name, since the Bible is the book for all people, for all time. Its complexity can baffle great minds, yet its simplicity can be understood by children. It is the most widely read, most fiercely debated, and most often quoted book in history. It is the handbook of all true Christians.

The Bible is one book divided into two major divisions. The Old Testament contains thirty-nine separate books, and the New Testament contains twenty-seven books. These sixty-six books are further divided into chapter and verse. They were written by more than forty different authors over a period of about fifteen hundred years. These authors came from a wide range of occupations: kings, governmental officials, priests, fishermen, farmers, shepherds, tentmakers, and doctors.

From all this diversity comes an incredible unity, for the Bible has one common theme woven throughout. This unity is because it ultimately has one author—God Himself. The Bible is truly "God-breathed." The human authors wrote exactly what God wanted them to write, and the result is the perfect and holy Word of God. It is a trinitarian communication to us: God, the Father, speaks all the words through the Son, the eternal Word, and God speaks in the power and means of the Holy Spirit.

The Old and New Testaments stand on two sides of the center point of history, the coming of Christ. The Old Testament sets forth the earlier part of the history of redemption, with growing anticipation of Christ. The New Testament sets forth the later course of history, looking back on Christ's redemption accomplished in His life, death, resurrection, and exaltation. The New Testament encourages Christians by reminding them to live in the light of Christ's present-day reign and in His future return.

The Old Testament lays the foundation for the coming of the Messiah, the Christ, who would sacrifice Himself for the sins of the world. The New Testament records the ministry of Jesus Christ and then looks back on what He did and how we are to respond. Both testaments reveal the same holy, merciful, and righteous God who condemns sin but desires to save sinners through Christ's atoning sacrifice. In both testaments, God reveals Himself to us and shows us how we're to come to Him through faith.

God reveals Himself to us in different ways. Nature, with its vastness and complexity, gives testimony to God and His glory. Our consciences also tells us that God exists. All societies have a certain moral code built into them in which certain acts are universally condemned, and this sense of right and wrong testifies to God's existence. But God has especially revealed Himself to the world through the person of Jesus Christ, who Himself testified that He had come to earth to reveal the will of God, the Father. And the Bible reveals God Himself through the written Word. It is God's revelation of Himself to humankind. It is man's source for the knowledge of God and His plan. As our final authority, the Bible allows us to be certain of what God said and did.

Only through knowing God can we draw close to Him. Eternal life is entering into a personal relationship with God through Jesus Christ. Eternal life begins the moment this relationship starts. Only through the Bible do we learn about this good news, for the Bible testifies about Jesus Christ and His works. And through knowing God we learn the reality of a final judgment to come.

We can love and trust someone only as much as we know them; the more we know about God, the more we can love and obey Him. The more we know God intellectually and experientially, the more we can grow spiritually. Through knowing God, we can better understand ourselves.

We can truly worship God only from an accurate knowledge of Him. The Bible lets us know God, allowing us to build a personal relationship with

Him. This relationship leads us to eternal life with Him. True knowledge of God and of his character is essential for salvation. Reading the Bible affords us this true knowledge. It is our definitive source for the answers to our questions about God. Additionally, by knowing God, the Bible teaches us to imitate Him. It aids us in finding our paths through life. It keeps us from sin. It renews our minds so we can know the will of God. Reading the Bible allows us to receive the desires of our hearts through basking in His Word.

Through reading the Bible, we become courageous, for it teaches that we will never be alone—that God is always at our sides, never forsaking us. And reading the Bible helps us be fruitful in all we do, whether in sharing the gospel, raising a family, or loving one another.

The Bible is our source for answers to life's questions: What is our life's purpose? Where did we come from? Is there life after death? How do we get to heaven? Why is the world full of evil? Why do we struggle to do good? What really matters in life? Additionally, the Bible gives practical advice in many areas, such as how to have a successful marriage, how best to raise our children, and how to be a good friend. It tells us how we can change, how we can deal with difficult situations, and how we can identify and avoid false teachings. We should read the Bible because it is totally reliable and without error.

God desires His people to know and understand His Word—that is why He gave it to us and instructed fathers to teach it to their children in the home. Over the centuries, scholars have identified various methods for understanding the Bible. These interpretative methods center around the literal, allegorical, moral, and anagogical senses. They each follow certain hermeneutic rules or principles to avoid misinterpreting what the Bible says. There is an old Latin rhyme that helps explain the purposes behind each of the four methods:

The literal teaches what God and our ancestors did,
The allegory is where our faith and belief are hid,
The moral meaning gives us the rule of daily life,
The anagogy shows us where we end our strife.

Regardless of how one interprets scripture, one essential guiding principle that holds fast is to let scripture interpret itself. To understand the Bible and apply it to our lives, one cannot just read this sacred text; it demands study.

Only through a proper interpretation of the Bible can we truly understand what our Creator has to say to us.

In many aspects, the Bible is a love letter in which God communicates His love to us. Only through understanding His Word can we be obedient to His commandments. Through obeying God, we bring honor to Him as He guides us in the way of life. By understanding the Bible, we can identity life's problem (sin) and find the solution (faith in Christ). Through an understanding of the Bible, we can obtain the assured hope of eternal life in heaven, where we will see God face to face.

This book, *Divine Musings*, identifies many biblical terms and concepts that are essential to properly understanding the Bible. Each term and its reflection are meant to be read and mediated upon. Do not read this book in a few settings but rather slowly, pensively, meditatively. Keep it by your bedside, next to your Bible, on your breakfast table, or any place where it's easy to pick up. Truly absorb the meaning, implications, and relevance of each term. Through a greater understanding of the Bible, you can obtain a greater understanding of God's message to you and reap His benefits. And what a blessing that is!

George T. Yapuncich

FULL LIST OF ENTRIES IN THIS BOOK

Key Biblical Terms and Concepts

Abraham
Adam
Adultery
Advent
Amen
Ancient of Days
Angels
Angels—Fallen
Anxiety
Apostle
Atonement
Baal
Baptism
Banquet
Beloved
Bethlehem
Birthright
Blessing
Blindness
Blood
Bondservant of Christ
Born Again
Bread of Life
Bread of Presence
Call
Character of God

Cherub
Children of God
Church
Christ
Christ Is Risen
Circumcision
Comfort
Confession
Conquerors (More Than)
Cornerstone
Covenant of Grace
Covenant
Covet
Creation
Cross
Curses
Curtain (of the Temple)
Daily Bread
Darkness
David
Day of Atonement
Deacon
Death (Physical)
Death (Second)
Death (Spiritual)
Debtors

Deserts
Deserving
Deuteronomy
Earth
Elder
Enemy
Enmity
Epistle
Eternal Life
Evil
Exalt
Exodus
Faith
Faithfulness
The Fall
Fasting
Fear
Fear of God
Feast of Tabernacles
Fig Tree
Fire and Brimstone
Firmament
Firstfruits
Flesh (Is Weak)
Forbearance
Foreknowledge

Forgiveness
Fornication
Fortress
Free Will
Fruit of the Spirit
Generosity
Genesis
Gentleness
Glorification
Glory
God
Godhead
Golden Rule
Goodness
Gospel
Great Commission
Green Pastures
Hallowed
Harmony
Heal
Heart of Flesh
Heaven
Heir
Hell
Holy Spirit
Hope
Humility
Hunger for Righteousness
Idolatry
Incarnation
In Christ
Infallible
Inherit the Earth
Inspired (Divinely)
Israel
Jehovah
Jesus
Jesus Christ—Christ Jesus
Jew
John
John the Baptist

Joy
Judges
Judgment
Justice
Justification
Kindness
King
Kingdom of God
Kingdom of Heaven
Know God
Last Days
Law
Leviticus
Lily of the Valley
Lord's Prayer
Lord's Supper
Love the Lord
Love Your Neighbor
Love
Luke
Lust
Majesty
Man
Manna
Mark
Marriage
Mary Magdalene
Matthew
Meek
Melchizedek
Mercy
Messiah
Minor Prophets
Money Changers
Mourn
Names of God
Narrow Gate
Nature of God
Neighbor
Nephilim
New Jerusalem

New Testament
Numbers
Old Testament
Omnipotent
Omnipresent
Omniscient
Original Sin
Parables
Passion of Christ
Passover
Patience
Patriarchs
Paul
Peace
Pentateuch
Pentecost
Persecution
Pestilence
Peter
Poor in Spirit
Praise
Pray
Prayer
Preaching
Predestination
Pride
Priest
Principalities and Powers
Prodigal
Prophecy
Prophets
Prophets, False
Proverbs
Providence
Psalms
Publican
Pure in Heart
Rainbow
Rapture
Rebuke
Redemption

Refuge
Regeneration
Rejoice
Repentance
Rest
Resurrection
Revelation
Revelation (Book of)
Reward in Heaven
Righteousness
Rose of Sharon
Sabbath
Sackcloth
Sacrament
Sacrifice
Salt of the Earth
Sanctification
Satan
Savior
Scripture
Seeing God
Self-control
Seraphim
Sermon on the Mount
Seven Deadly Sins
Shaken
Shepherd, Good
Signs and Wonders
Sin
Six Days
Slave
Sodom and Gomorrah
Son of God
Son of Man
Sons of God
Songs of Ascent
Sovereignty (God's)
Spiritual Gifts
Steadfastness
Stewardship
Tabernacle

Temple (of Herod)
Temple (of Solomon)
Temptation
Transfiguration
Transgressor
Treasures in Heaven
Tree of Good and Evil
Tree of Life
Trinity
Trustworthy
Truth
Unconditional Love
Valley
Vanity
Wait for the Lord
Wilderness
Wisdom
Wisdom Literature
Worship
Worthy
Wrath
Yoke
Zion

REFLECTIONS ON KEY BIBLICAL TERMS AND CONCEPTS

(Arranged Alphabetically)

Abraham

"The LORD had said to Abram, 'Go from your country, your people, and your father's household, and go to the land I will show you. I will make you into a great nation, and I will bless you; I will make your name great, and you will be a blessing. I will bless those who bless you, and whoever curses you I will curse; and all peoples on earth will be blessed through you.'"

(Genesis 12:1–3 NIV)

An obedient man,
Called by God
To leave his homeland
For an unknown destination.
Not a special man
But a man made special
    by God—
A man who laughed at God
When told of a child
Sired by him in old age.
A man who lied about
His wife being his sister,
Yet he was a man who
    trusted God
When most would turn away.

Scripture is filled with stories
Of Abraham's life—
Stories of his failures,
Stories of his faith.
Abraham and his wife, Sarah,
    were
Shamed for no heirs,

1

Yet God promised one
To be born.
But Abraham showed a lack of
    faith,
For a child with Hagar was
    born.
Yet God abounds in grace.
God changed his name from
Abram, meaning "high
    father," to
Abraham, the "father of a
    multitude."
The first of many was Isaac.

Abraham, a man
Of obedience toward God.
Asked to leave his family, he
    left.
Asked to sacrifice Isaac,
He obeyed without hesitation
(Son was saved by
divine intervention).
Yet Abraham had an active
Relationship with God
In questioning His plans,
Interceding for others,
Trusting God's justice,
And submitting to His will.

Twice, the apostle Paul
Uses Abraham as
An example of
Justification by faith alone.
His faith demonstrated that
Faith always has trials, yet
Faith shines through darkness.

Faith, in spite of trials,
Glorifies God.
Abraham's obedience of faith
Earned him the honor,
"Abraham, my friend!"

God made a covenant
With Abraham, including:
The promise of land in
    Canaan,
The promise of numerous
    offspring,
The promise of blessings and
    redemption unto the world.
An unconditional covenant,
Spoken by God
To a man of faith.

"And he believed the LORD, and he counted it to him as righteousness."

(Genesis 15:6)

Adam

"Then the LORD God formed the man of dust from the ground and breathed into his nostrils the breath of life, and the man became a living creature."

(Genesis 2:7)

The first man,
Created by God

In His own image,
Formed out of dust.
God breathed
Into his nostrils
The breath of life,
Gave him dominion
Over all the lower creatures,
Placed him in the garden of
     Eden
To cultivate it and
To enjoy its fruits.
He was husband of Eve,
Father of all mankind.
He received only one
     prohibition:
Eat not of the tree
Of the knowledge of
Good and evil.

Adam—not just a proper
     name.
Yes, he was the first human,
But also a designation
For all humankind.
Made a little lower than angels,
     he was
Crowned with glory,
     honor, and
Commissioned to rule
Over God's creation.
He was blessed beyond
     description.

But this was not enough.
Adam fell from his
Glorious state of innocence,

Disobeyed God's one
     prohibition,
Therefore condemning not only
Himself to death,
But all humankind.
His sin was imputed to all,
For as Adam sinned,
All humans sinned.
As Adam was guilty,
All humans were guilty.
All humans are now depraved,
Holding a sinful nature
Inherited from our
First father, Adam.
Because we all are
Children of Adam,
We all share his sin,
Share his condemnation.

Now, all humans are deserving
Of God's wrath,
Not solely because
Of our actions,
But because of our nature—
The nature inherited
From Adam:
Unable to do good and
Unable to please God.

Give thanks to Jesus,
For through His sacrifice
On the cross,
We can be born again.
Through His blood,
We are new creatures,
Born into God's family and

Given the nature of Christ.
Our sins are forgiven; our
Eternal life is assured.

"Therefore, just as sin came into the world through one man, and death through sin ... so death spread to all men because all sinned."

(Romans 5:12)

Adultery

"And you shall not commit adultery."

(Deuteronomy 5:18)

Conjugal infidelity,
Stepping outside
The bounds of marriage,
Illicit intercourse with one
Not your spouse.
But the definition
Does not stop there.
It also includes
Fornication without marriage,
Lusting after another,
Even without physical contact.
Idolatry, covetousness,
        apostasy—
All spoken as spiritual adultery.

Adultery begins in the heart
Before it ever reaches the bed.
When lust lingers unabated,
It conceives sin, which,
Whether mental or physical,
Is still adultery.
It is being unfaithful to God
And to His glory.

Why is God against adultery?
He created marriage
To be a building block
Of His creation, of society,
Not only for procreation,
But to express the image of
A faithful God.
A holy, faithful marriage
Reflects God's character.
Adultery is the complete
Corruption of God's
Good creation of marriage.

Adultery rips at the
Fabric of society.
It tears apart
Marriages and families.
It stains God's holy image.
The commandment
Forbidding adultery
Is a standard
For true Christian behavior.

"Let there be no sexual immorality, impurity, or greed among you. Such sins have no place among God's people."

(Ephesians 5:3 NLT)

Advent

And the angel said to them, "Fear not, for behold, I bring you good news of great joy that will be for all the people. For unto you is born this day in the city of David a Savior, who is Christ the Lord."

(Luke 2:10–11)

A special season
Meaning "arrival" or "coming,"
It is a time of looking back
And looking forward.
A time of celebrating
Christ's incarnation,
His life on earth.
It is a time of eagerness for
Christ's return in the future.
As Israel longed for their
    Messiah,
Christians long for their Savior
To come again.
A season of two elements:
Remembrance and
    anticipation.

Common to celebrate
With an evergreen wreath.
Inside stand four colored
    candles
Surrounding a white one in the
    center,
All shaped in a never-ending
    circle

Symbolizing the eternity
    of God.
Candles are lit one at a time
On successive Sundays:
Hope, love, joy, and peace.
The white candle, lit on
    Christmas Eve,
Is called the Christ candle.
Reminds us that Christ is the
Light of the world.

Fulfilled promises,
Promises to be filled.
And Christ is the promise of
    both.
He has come;
He will come again—
The essence of Advent.

"So Christ, having been offered once to bear the sins of many, will appear a second time, not to deal with sin but to save those who are eagerly waiting for him."

(Hebrews 9:28)

Amen

"Blessed be the LORD, the God of Israel, from everlasting to everlasting! Then all the people

said, 'Amen!' and praised the
LORD."

(1 Chronicles 16:36)

Amen,
It is so, so be it.
Spoken to express
Solemn ratification,
Spoken in agreement.
Not just a ritualized
Conclusion to prayers.

Used extensively in
Old and New Testaments.
Hebrew root can mean,
"To support, to be loyal,
To be certain, to place faith in."
Translated today as,
"Verily, truly,
Surety, faithfulness,
So be it."
It denotes acceptance as truth
To the preceding message.

To say *amen*, we are saying
Yes before God,
I agree with that,
I accept that
It is established;
I believe that to be true,
I want that to be so.

Implications of saying amen are
    great.
Someone acknowledging what
Has been said

In prayer or statement
As the truth
Promises a solemn oath
To faithfully perform it
In his or her life.
A serious vow.

A right conclusion to our
    prayers,
Confirming our prayers
To be truthful,
That our praises and petitions
Are the truth, only the truth.
It follows the model of
Jesus and the apostles,
As though we are saying,
Please, let it be as
We have prayed.
It shows our confidence
That God hears our prayers,
That God will answer our
    prayers.
Amen.

"He who testifies to these things
says, 'Surely I am coming soon.'
Amen. Come, Lord Jesus! The
grace of the Lord Jesus be with
all. Amen."

(Revelation 22:20–21)

Ancient of Days

"As I looked, thrones were placed, and the Ancient of Days took his seat; his clothing was white as snow, and the hair of his head like pure wool; his throne was fiery flames; its wheels were burning fire."

(Daniel 7:9)

A title from the book of
    Daniel,
Stated in three verses.
Clear reference to deity,
Referring to the
Eternality of God.
As in Psalm 90,
God is from everlasting to
    everlasting.
As in Isaiah 44, where
God is the first and the last.
Eternal, an attribute
Only for the Lord as supreme
    being,
For only God is truly ancient,
Existing before time began.

Prophet Daniel uses the title
"Ancient of Days"
To refer to both
God, the Father, and
God, the Son.
In both cases,
Deity is inferred,

Emphasizing the
Lord eternal.

"As I looked, this horn made war with the saints and prevailed over them, until the Ancient of Days came, and judgment was given for the saints of the Most High, and the time came when the saints possessed the kingdom."

(Daniel 7:21–22)

Angels

"Praise the LORD! Praise the LORD from the heavens; praise him in the heights! Praise him, all his angels; praise him, all his hosts!"

(Psalm 148:1–2)

Part of the divine hierarchy,
Supernatural beings
Created by God,
Have intelligence,
Emotions, and will.
Exuberant witnesses for
    God and
Spiritual beings, they are not
    subject
To limitations of the flesh.
Have one role:
To declare and promote
The will of God.

Angels used by God
For a variety of purposes:
To minister to God's elect,
To deliver messages,
To wage spiritual battles,
To worship God,
To do the Word of God,
To execute judgment,
To convey God's Word.

Some angels appear'
In the form of a human.
Many have wings,
But not all.
Some have multiple faces—
Lion, ox, eagle.
Some are bright, shining, fiery.
Many are invisible,
But their presence is felt,
Their voices heard.

All were created by God
With eternal lives,
Were present at creation.
Too numerous to count.

Angels announced
The birth of Christ.
Angels ministered to Christ.
Angels rejoice in God's
Work of salvation.

A number of them
Did fall in the rebellion,
Chose Satan over God,
Were expelled from heaven
To become demons below.
Unlike humans,
This choice of the angels
Was an eternal choice.
No opportunity for
Repentance, forgiveness.
Demons forever,
Worthy of God's eternal wrath.

Two angels called by
Name in scripture:
Gabriel and Michael.
Lucifer is hinted at.
Some called cherubim,
Others, seraphim.
Mightier in might and power
Than humans,
Yet angels definitely
Not to be worshiped.
Worship is solely reserved
For God,
Creator of all.

"But concerning that day and hour no one knows, not even the angels of heaven, nor the Son, but the Father only."

(Matthew 24:36)

Angels—Fallen

"And the great dragon was thrown down, that ancient serpent, who is called the devil and Satan, the

deceiver of the whole world—he
was thrown down to the earth,
and his angels were thrown down
with him."

(Revelation 12:9)

Synonym: demons.
Angels sided with Satan.
Unable to repent,
Forgiveness was not for them.
Once knew God
In all His glory,
Now living in darkness
Forever.

The angels who God made,
One third of them all
Fell prey to Lucifer's
Prideful deception
Of equality with God.
Hurled together to earth,
A fall from grace,
Caught in the trap of sin.

Some locked in darkness,
Bound with eternal chains.
Others, free to roam.
Powers of this dark world,
Spiritual forces of evil
Following orders of Satan,
Battling faithful angels,
Leading men astray,
Attempting to thwart
God's plan,
Hinder His people.

As with Satan,
All enemies of God—
Defeated enemies they are.
Disarmed by Christ,
Made into public spectacles,
Triumphed over by the cross.
Although potent enemies
Of God's people,
There is no need to fear,
For the Lord's sovereignty
Rules over all creation,
Fallen angels included.

"And the angels who did not
stay within their own position
of authority, but left their proper
dwelling, he has kept in eternal
chains under gloomy darkness
until the judgment of the
great day."

(Jude 6)

Anxiety

"Do not be anxious about
anything, but in everything by
prayer and supplication with
thanksgiving let your requests
be made known to God. And the
peace of God, which surpasses all
understanding, will guard your

hearts and your minds in Christ Jesus."

(Philippians 4:6–7)

Portrayed in scripture
As being inconsistent
With trust in God—
A lack of faith.
Anxiety is all about us,
But is never from God.
It is a stumbling block,
A hindrance to walking
The paths God set before us.
Anxiety is distress
About future uncertainties,
Both real and imagined.
Anxiety reveals what
Is essential to us,
Identifies the items we think
More important than God.
Anxiety is the end of faith.
Faith is the end of anxiety.

Anxiety is a feeling
Of worry, nervousness, unease,
Including apprehension and
    fear—
Usually regarding a pending
    event
Or an uncertain outcome,
Often accompanied by
Undesirable physical symptoms
Such as restlessness, fatigue,
Lack of concentration,
Irritability, headaches,
Insomnia, nausea.

Scripture identifies the
Source of anxiety:
"O you of little faith"—
An unbelief in the
Promises of God.
It is a subtle insinuation
That God is either unable
Or possibly disinclined
To attend to our welfares,
Both of which are falsehoods.
For our God is a faithful God,
One who has a plan
For each of us, and this plan
Is all-wise, all-providing,
All-protecting, ever assisting.

There will always be
Periods of anxiety in our lives.
But there will always exist
Spiritual strategies
For confronting, besting
All temptations of anxiety—
Mainly, casting all our
Anxieties on God,
For He cares for us.
He promises us His peace.

"Casting all your anxieties on him, because he cares for you."

(1 Peter 5:7)

Apostle

"The names of the twelve apostles are these: first, Simon, who is called Peter, and Andrew his brother; James the son of Zebedee, and John his brother; Philip and Bartholomew; Thomas and Matthew the tax collector; James the son of Alphaeus, and Thaddaeus; Simon the Zealot, and Judas Iscariot, who betrayed him."

(Matthew 10:2–4)

Envoy, ambassador, messenger,
Commissioned to carry out
    God's Word.
Threefold criteria for Christ's
    apostle:
—Witness the resurrected
    Christ,
—Explicitly chosen by the
    Holy Spirit,
—Enabled to perform signs
    and wonders.

Jesus Christ, Himself an
    apostle,
Wearing *apostle* as a title,
Sent to earth by the heavenly
    Father,
Carrying God's
Authoritative message.
Selected His twelve apostles
With one ultimate mandate:

Bear witness to His message
By continuing His work.

Every apostle was a disciple,
But not every disciple an
    apostle.
Disciple refers to a learner,
Refers to all Christians.
Essential qualification of an
    apostle:
Called and sent by Christ.

The twelve apostles were
    selected
From among the disciples.
Each was given authority
By the one who sent him.
Whose names are now
Inscribed on the twelve
    foundations
In the walls of the New
    Jerusalem.

The twelve apostles were
    ordinary men
Used by God in an
    extraordinary manner
From all walks of life,
Including fishermen,
Tax collectors, revolutionaries.
After Pentecost, their
Full apostolic vocation was
Empowered by the Holy Spirit.
Although accompanied
By a miraculous sign,
First and foremost

Was their function of
Preaching and teaching.

Judas, after his betrayal,
Replaced with Matthias.
Paul, the Christian oppressor,
Later added by Christ Himself
On the road to Damascus,
Became the apostle to the
Gentiles.

The term *apostle*
Still in use today,
But not in the
Same special sense.
Now refers to select
missionaries
Or entrepreneurial leaders
Always in a more general
manner.

The apostles,
Having direct knowledge
Of the incarnate Word,
Sent out as authorized
Agents of the gospel,
Provided the authentic
interpretation
Of the life and teachings of
Jesus,
Considered normative for the
church.
Regarded as pillars
And foundations of the church,
Whose teachings are the model

For Christian faith and
practice.
Revelations were transmitted
by apostles
Preserved in the New
Testament,
Form the basis of postapostolic
preaching
And teaching in the church.

True ambassadors for Christ,
Witnesses to all nations,
Making disciples of all peoples.

"And he went up on the mountain and called to him those whom he desired, and they came to him. And he appointed twelve (whom he also named apostles) so that they might be with him and he might send them out to preach and have authority to cast out demons."

(Mark 3:13–15)

Atonement

"God presented Christ as a sacrifice of atonement, through the shedding of his blood—to be received by faith. He did this to demonstrate his righteousness, because in his forbearance he had

**left the sins committed beforehand
unpunished."**

(Romans 3:25 NIV)

The Bible's central message:
God provided a way
For humanity to restore its
Harmonious relation,
A reconciliation.
To atone is to make amends,
To repair a wrong.
Biblically, it means to
Remove the guilt of humans.
The atonement is just that—
Christ's death on the cross
Satisfied the law and justice
   of God,
Bringing forgiveness,
Imputing righteousness,
Reconciling people to God.
Christ's death paid
The penalty for sin.
Through faith, we can accept
Christ's substitution
As payment for our sins.

Because every aspect of us—
Mind, will, and emotions—
Has been corrupted by sin.
Hence, we truly are
Spiritually dead,
Totally corrupt,
Unable to repair
Our relationships with God,
Unable to make satisfaction

For our offenses.
Unable to save ourselves.

When we speak
Of the atonement,
We speak of Christ's work
When He
Expiated our sins through
His work of reconciliation
On our behalf,
His act of dying on the cross
As a substitute for sinners.
He substituted Himself for us,
Suffering what we rightly
   deserved.
Christ paid the full price.
His death is the atonement,
The appeasement,
The satisfaction.
His substitutionary death
Pacified the wrath of God.
Through faith in Christ
Our sins are forgiven,
And we are cloaked in
Christ's righteousness,
Guaranteed eternal life
With God.
All through the
Atonement of
Jesus Christ on the cross.

**"He himself bore our sins in his
body on the tree, that we might die**

to sin and live to righteousness. By his wounds you have been healed."

(1 Peter 2:24)

Baal

"They have built the high places of Baal to burn their children in the fire as offerings to Baal—something I did not command or mention, nor did it enter my mind."

(Jeremiah 19:5 NIV)

Pagan god,
Worshiped in ancient
Canaan, Phoenicia.
Infiltrated Jewish life
During the time of Judges.
Name means "lord, master."
The fertility god to them
For land to produce crops,
People to produce children.
Seen as a most
Powerful god.
Adaptable to cultures,
Various form of worship,
Worst being human sacrifice.
Rooted in sensuality,
Involved in temple
Prostitution.

Israel was warned by God:
Avoid worship of any
Canaan gods.
Yet Israel turned to
Idolatry in their ways.
Jezebel was one famous
Worshiper of Baal.
God did not take kindly
To this sin of false gods,
Rained down judgment
Various times
To punish Israel
For this idol worship.

God showed He alone
Controls the rains,
Not some god named Baal.
God caused a drought
Lasting three and a half years.
Elijah called for a face-off
On Mount Carmel
To prove his true God.
Four hundred fifty prophets of
    Baal
Versus one prophet of God.
Prophets of Baal called
Their god to send fire
From heaven to no avail.
Elijah prayed a simple prayer;
God answered immediately
With fire from heaven.
Winner without a doubt,
Crying, "The Lord—He
    is God!
The Lord—He is God!"

"But what is God's reply to him? 'I have kept for myself seven thousand men who have not bowed the knee to Baal.'"

(Romans 11:4)

Baptism

"I baptize you with water for repentance, but he who is coming after me is mightier than I, whose sandals I am not worthy to carry. He will baptize you with the Holy Spirit and fire."

(Matthew 3:11)

One of two sacraments
Instituted by God,
A sign and seal of regeneration,
Whereby through the
Washing with water,
In the name of the Father,
The Son, and the Holy Spirit,
Signifies our ingrafting into
    Christ,
Partaking of the benefits of
The covenant of grace.
Symbolically represents
God's internal purification
Of the elect, according to
His sovereign will.

Baptism is an
Outward testimony
Of the inward change
In a Christian's life,
An act of obedience
To the Lord.
Although closely associated
With salvation,
Not a requirement of salvation.
Christians are not to be
Secret disciples,
Must never be ashamed to
Let people see
Whose we are,
Whom we serve.
We must take up our cross,
Confess our Lord Jesus
Before the world
Through the
Sacrament of baptism.

Baptism signifies
The believer's total trust,
Total reliance, in Christ,
As well as a commitment
To live obediently to Him.
Additionally, expresses
Unity with all believers.
A recognition that we are
Saved by grace
Through faith,
Apart from works.

Christian baptism,
Which has the form
Of a ceremonial washing,
Is a sign from God
Signifying inward cleansing,

The remission of sins.
This Spirit-wrought
Regeneration and new life
With the abiding presence
Of the Holy Spirit
As God's seal,
Testifies and guarantees
That we will be kept safe
In Christ forever.
It signifies union
With Christ
In His death, burial,
And resurrection.
This union is the source
Of every element
In our salvation.
Receiving this sign in faith
Is the assurance of God's
Gift of new life in Christ,
Which is freely given,
And it commits the receiver
To live henceforth
In a new way as a
Committed disciple of
Jesus Christ.

Controversies abound
Within the churches.
Who are the proper
   recipients of
This sacrament—
Infants of believers or
Restricted to confessing
Adult believers?
Total immersion or a
Sprinkle of water?

Many questions,
Many interpretations.
But important to remember:
There is one faith,
One Lord,
One baptism.

"There is one body and one Spirit—just as you were called to the one hope that belongs to your call— one Lord, one faith, one baptism, one God and Father of all, who is over all and through all and in all."

(Ephesians 4:4–6)

Banquet

"Jesus spoke to them again in parables, saying: 'The kingdom of heaven is like a king who prepared a wedding banquet for his son.'"

(Matthew 22:1–2 NIV)

An elaborate meal,
Known also as a feast,
Celebrating weddings,
Passover, homecomings.
Fatted calves and wine,
A joyous occasion.

Implying and displaying
Blessings, prosperity,
Abundance, wealth, and joy.

A symbol of God's faithfulness,
power;
A foretaste of heavenly
Blessings and honor.

An invitation
Extended to all
To enter eternally the
Messianic banquet
With Christ
In the kingdom of heaven.
Each to decide
Whether to accept or not.

"On this mountain the LORD of hosts will make for all peoples a feast of rich food, a feast of well-aged wine, of rich food full of marrow, of aged wine well refined."

(Isaiah 25:6)

Beloved

"Behold, my servant whom I have chosen, my beloved with whom my soul is well pleased. I will put my Spirit upon him, and he will proclaim justice to the Gentiles."

(Matthew 12:18)

One who is dearly loved.
Expression of deep affection.
Israel is often called

"Beloved of God,"
Set apart for His divine love.
God refers to His Son, Jesus:
"My beloved Son, in whom
I am well pleased."

Apostles use this term often,
Addressing fellow Christians.
Beloved implies more than
Mere human affection.
Suggests an esteem for others,
Recognizing their worth
As children of God.
More than just friends,
Brothers and sisters
In Christ,
Thus, highly valued.

A truly beautiful word
Carrying an intimate
connotation.
Not simply "love," but
Of a deeper relationship.
A term of affectionate
endearment.
A love that is rich, infinite,
lavish.
In truth, a love that is
Breathtaking.

All adopted into God's family,
Through faith in Christ,
become
Beloved by the Father.
As God has shed His love
on us,

We are able to reciprocate,
Calling Him our beloved.

"I am my beloved's and my beloved is mine."

(Song of Solomon 6:3)

Bethlehem

"After Jesus was born in Bethlehem in Judea, during the time of King Herod, Magi from the east came to Jerusalem and asked, 'Where is the one who has been born king of the Jews? We saw his star when it rose and have come to worship him.'"

(Matthew 2:1–2)

One of the oldest towns in
    Palestine,
Home of Ruth and David,
Fortified by Rehoboam.
The locale where our Lord and
    Savior,
Jesus Christ, was born.
Visited by the shepherds, the
    Magi also.

Located six miles south by west
Of Jerusalem.
Situated high up with a fine
    view
In every direction.

Surrounding hills terraced,
Clothed with vines, fig trees,
    almonds,
Valleys bore rich crops of grain.

Prophesied in the Old
    Testament,
A birthplace of our Lord.
A humble village,
Not sophisticated as Jerusalem.
Chosen by God to change
The course of history—
For men not to boast on merits,
But only on the glorious mercy
    of God.

"But you, Bethlehem Ephrathah, though you are small among the clans of Judah, out of you will come for me one who will be ruler over Israel, whose origins are from of old, from ancient times."

(Micah 5:2)

Birthright

"He must acknowledge the son of his unloved wife as the firstborn by giving him a double share of all he has. That son is the first sign of his father's strength. The right of the firstborn belongs to him."

(Deuteronomy 21:17)

A powerful word
Denoting special privileges
And advantages belonging
To firstborn sons, who
Received a double portion
Of inheritance.
The eldest son succeeded
To official authority
Of the father.
In all this,
Great respect is given
With birthright.

The firstborn became
Head of the family,
In charge of the family
    property,
Responsible for maintenance of
Younger sons, widows,
And all unmarried daughters.
In the case of a king,
The firstborn's birthright
Included succession
To the throne.

Not always automatic,
For birthrights could be
    altered—
By consent of the eldest son,
By the decision of the father.
Yet always confirmed by
The father's blessing.
At times, obtained deceitfully:
Jacob tricked his father,
And Esau lost out.

This blessing, a type of
Last will and testament.

New Testament Christians
Inherit birthright status
Through Jesus Christ
As the firstborn Son of God.
We are to protect this gift as
Godly, honorable, important.
For through His grace
And our faith,
We are counted as joint heirs.

"The Son is the image of the invisible God, the firstborn over all creation."

(Colossians 1:15)

Blessing

"Blessed is the man who walks not in the counsel of the wicked, nor stands in the way of sinners, nor sits in the seat of scoffers."

(Psalm 1:1)

A word with a history,
Translated from various
Hebrew and Greek words.
Different meanings applied:
"To consecrate with blood;
To praise, worship;
To wish good fortune
    upon one."

Modern usage has two
   applications:
Where God is referred to,
Blessed has the sense of praise;
Where humanity is in mind,
It's used in the sense of
Satisfaction or "to be favored."

Yet God's true blessings
Often come disguised.
Blessed are the poor in spirit,
Blessed are those who mourn,
Blessed are those who remain
Steadfast under trial.
No hint of material prosperity,
No hint of perfect health,
No hint of a pleasant life.
Quite the contrary, biblical
   blessings
Are usually connected with
Poverty and difficult trials,
These being conduits for
The true blessing of
Being fully satisfied in God
   Himself,
Regardless of our
   circumstances.
A blessing can be defined as
Anything God gives
To make us fully satisfied
   in Him,
Anything that draws us closer
   to Jesus,
Anything that assists us
In focusing on the eternal.

Since God is perfect,
How then do we bless God?
We bless Him by praising Him,
Honoring His name.
We add nothing to Him
When we bless Him,
Yet we worship Him
As an appropriate response
To His greatness and love
   for us,
And for the many blessings
He constantly bestows on us.

"Blessed is the man who trusts in the LORD, whose trust is the LORD. He is like a tree planted by water, that sends out its roots by the stream, and does not fear when heat comes, for its leaves remain green, and is not anxious in the year of drought, for it does not cease to bear fruit."

(Jeremiah 17:7–8)

Blindness

"The god of this age has blinded the minds of unbelievers, so that they cannot see the light of the gospel that displays the glory of Christ, who is the image of God."

(2 Corinthians 4:4)

A grievous condition
Experienced by those who
Do not believe in God.
To be blind is to not see Christ,
Hence not to see God.
Referred to as spiritual
blindness,
That state in which a person is
unwilling,
Unable to perceive divine
revelation,
Unable to see the light of the
gospel
Of the glory of Christ,
Who is the image of God.
For the things of God are
perceived
Not by observation or inquiry,
But by revelation, illumination.

This blindness is not forced
on us.
It is not against what we truly
desire
In our natural, fallen state.
For men love the darkness,
Are always looking to things
Other than God.

It is the Lord who
Gives sight to the blind.
God lets the light shine out of
darkness,
To shine in our hearts
To give the light of the
knowledge

Of the glory of God
In the face of Jesus Christ.
He cures our blindness for His
glory.

"The Spirit of the Lord is on me, because he has anointed me to proclaim good news to the poor. He has sent me to proclaim freedom for the prisoners and recovery of sight for the blind, to set the oppressed free."

(Luke 4:18)

Blood

"Indeed, under the law almost everything is purified with blood, and without the shedding of blood there is no forgiveness of sins."

(Hebrews 9:22)

Blood, the sustainer of life,
The life of the flesh.
The term *blood* references
death,
For the loss of this precious
commodity
Results in the loss of life.
Scripture focuses not on
Blood in our veins,
But on shed blood—

Not on blood's chemical
  properties,
But on its symbolic import.

All life belongs to God,
Especially of humanity made
  in His image.
Sin made us guilty before God,
The penalty being death.
And justice must be served.
Blood must be shed.

And shed it was, on the cross
Where Christ's blood freely
  flowed,
Accomplishing what no
Animal sacrifice could.
Those sacrifices, limited in
  effectiveness,
Needed to be repeated again
  and again.
Not so with Christ; His
  sacrifice was
"Once, for all."

A sin against a holy and
  infinite God
Requires a holy and infinite
  sacrifice.
Only the precious blood of
  Jesus,
Lamb without blemish or
  defect,
Paid in full the debt of sin.

Because the blood of Christ
Has redeemed us, we are now
New creations in Christ.
By His blood, we are freed
  from sin
To serve the living God,
To glorify Him,
Enjoying Him forever.

**"In him we have redemption
through his blood, the forgiveness
of our trespasses, according to the
riches of his grace."**

(Ephesians 1:7)

Bondservant of Christ

**"James, a bondservant of God and
of the Lord Jesus Christ."**

(James 1:1 NASB)

Devoted to Christ
With disregard of our own
  interests.
Following Christ to the
  complete
Indifference of our own wills,
Our emotions, our desires.
Complete and utter devotion
  to God,
To His Word, to His will.
A bondservant is to love as
  Christ loved,

To walk as Christ walked,
Seeking God first, above all
    else.

A bondservant of Christ,
More than a slave,
This requires a choice—
A choice till death.
To lead a life of service
As a grateful, dutiful, loving
    response
To God, requires personal
    qualities:
Knowledge, self-control,
    perseverance,
Brotherly kindness, love,
Dedication, and responsibility.
A renouncing of all other
    masters,
Including this world, ourselves,
    and others.
For Christ alone is Lord,
Our allegiance is due to Him
    alone.

"But now that you have been set free from sin and have become slaves of God, the benefit you reap leads to holiness, and the result is eternal life."

(Romans 6:22 NIV)

Born Again

"Since you have been born again, not of perishable seed but of imperishable, through the living and abiding word of God."

(1 Peter 1:23)

Literally means "born from
    above."
An act of God, whereby eternal
    life
Imparted to a believing person.
It is a spiritual transformation,
Adoption into God's family.
A new relationship between
    God and humankind.
A cleansing from God
From all sin, from all idols,
A turning to Jesus as Lord and
    Savior.
A circumcision of the heart.

Not by humanity, but by God.
For who can birth him- or
    herself?
All are spiritually dead;
Only God can breathe new life
Into fallen humanity.
Not just life, but purity also,
For as God is pure and sinless,
None but the pure in heart
Can be His children.

A change so radical,
It speaks of a new creature, a
    new person.
Reborn unto knowledge after
    the image
Of the God who created us.
All old things have passed away
    for us;
Now all is new as sons and
    daughters
Of our heavenly Father.

This new birth, being of
The kingdom of God, makes us
    ultimately
No longer imperfect physical
    beings,
But spiritual beings.
For that which is born of flesh
    is flesh;
That which is born of spirit is
    spirit.
Now believing, accepting Jesus,
Never to perish, having eternal
    life.

No shallow, emotional event,
But one of repentance and
    faith,
Receiving the indwelling of
The Holy Spirit,
Growing in knowledge and
    grace of God,
Guided by His righteous law,
Giving all glory to God.

"Jesus answered him, 'Truly, truly, I say to you, unless one is born again he cannot see the kingdom of God.'"

(John 3:3)

Bread of Life

"Jesus said to them, 'I am the bread of life; whoever comes to me shall not hunger, and whoever believes in me shall never thirst.'"

(John 6:35)

A self-description of Jesus,
Equating Himself with
    bread—
The primary means of
    sustaining life,
A staple food, basic dietary
    item.
So common an item,
Synonymous for food in
    general.
As the bread of life, Jesus is
    saying
He is essential not only for
    physical life,
But spiritual life as well.
Physical bread that perishes
Feeds a life that perishes,
While spiritual bread creates
    a life

Imperishable, enduring to
everlasting life.

We cannot separate Christ,
As the bread of life, from what
He gives.
His personality is the center
Of His gift to the world.
That He should give such bread
is much;
That He should *be* such bread
is far more.
That this bread came down
from heaven
Points to His incarnation,
The Son of God.

Jesus was saying
That all your good works,
All your religious experiences
Cannot feed you.
"Only I, as the bread of life
Can truly sustain you;
Only I am your source of life."

By eating this bread of life,
You become part of Him,
One with Him—
A complete integration
Of His being with ours.

As bread is necessary for
earthly life,
This bread of life is precious for
Eternal life. Jesus did not come
To meet our physical desires,

But to be our treasure
Above everything in this world.
He paid the full penalty for our
sins;
He freely gave His perfect
righteousness
To those who believe in Him
As the true bread of life.

"I am the bread of life. Your fathers ate the manna in the wilderness, and they died. This is the bread that comes down from heaven, so that one may eat of it and not die. I am the living bread that came down from heaven. If anyone eats of this bread, he will live forever."

(John 6:48–51)

Bread of Presence

"Put the bread of the Presence on this table to be before me at all times."

(Exodus 25:30)

Made of fine flour,
Baked in twelve loaves,
Arranged in two piles,
Covered with
frankincense, and
Served as an offering to the
Lord.

Referred to also as
Showbread or *shewbread*.

A special bread, always present
On golden tables in the
    tabernacle.
A bread in which God
Was perpetually present,
This bread of presence
Consumed on the Sabbath.

The bread of presence,
A reminder of God's
    omnipresence
And of His gracious provision.
And, as everything in the Old
    Testament,
A foretaste of Christ,
A whisper of His coming.

Provides a picture of Jesus,
For Jesus is holy before God
As the bread was.
Jesus provides true sustenance
As bread nourishes.
Jesus is always present,
As the bread permanently was.

Jesus declared, "I am the bread
    of life.
"Whoever comes to me
Will never go hungry."

**"This bread is to be set out before
the LORD regularly, Sabbath**
**after Sabbath, on behalf of the
Israelites, as a lasting covenant."**

(Leviticus 24:8)

Call

**"God is faithful, who has called
you into fellowship with his Son,
Jesus Christ our Lord."**

(1 Corinthians 1:9)

Prominent term of scripture,
Used in three manners:
In worship, in election, and in
    vocation.

To call on God
Is to utter His name,
At times as an appeal
To His grace and mercy
In situations of need and
    weakness.
More often connotes
A basic commitment to the
    Lord,
A means of worshiping Him
With divine honors.

Also, closely associated
With election.
In the sense of naming,
Giving an identity to one.
An effective summons
Of people to faith in Christ.

God's sovereign drawing
Of a sinner to salvation.
Synonym: irresistible grace,
An effectual call leading to
	salvation
That is otherwise unattainable.

Due to humanity's fallen
	nature,
This calling denotes a person's
Ultimate destiny in heaven
As a child of God.

The third variation:
This term *call* references
	vocation.
Example of Paul's calling by
	grace,
Referring not only to his
	conversion,
But equally to his
	appointment as
An apostle of Christ. Refers
	also
To exercising gifts received
	by God,
Especially in the realm of
	ministry.

"I therefore, a prisoner for the Lord, urge you to walk in a manner worthy of the calling to which you have been called, with all humility and gentleness, with patience, bearing with one another in love,
eager to maintain the unity of the Spirit in the bond of peace."

(Ephesians 4:1–3)

Character of God

"And they were calling to one another: 'Holy, holy, holy is the LORD Almighty; the whole earth is full of his glory.'"

(Isaiah 6:3)

God's character reflects
His perfection,
For all His characteristics
Are perfect.

His character encompasses
All that is perfect.
God is perfectly just.
God is perfect loving.
God is perfectly truthful.
God is perfectly holy.
God is perfectly merciful.
God is perfectly compassionate.
God is perfect grace.
God judges sin perfectly.
God forgives sin perfectly.

God is holy—not just holy, but
Holy, holy, holy.
People can share many of
God's characteristics—
Never perfectly—

But God's holiness
Is not shared by humanity.
God's holiness is
What separates Him
From all creation and
Makes Him distinct and
    separate
From all else.
More than just His
Perfection or sinless purity,
Holiness is the
Essence of His being.
To recognize God's holiness
Is to beware of our
Own sins and despair.
It causes us to revere Him,
To be awe-inspired by Him.

As God is perfect,
We are to worship Him—
Worship with the right
    understanding,
With the right heart
Of our inner selves.
This worship must be our
    priority,
All the days of our lives,
In our words, thoughts, and
    deeds.

The character of God:
"Holy, holy, holy
Is the Lord Almighty."

"And he said, 'I will make all my goodness pass before you and will proclaim before you my name "The Lord." And I will be gracious to whom I will be gracious, and will show mercy on whom I will show mercy.'"

(Exodus 33:9)

Cherub

"He drove out the man, and at the east of the garden of Eden he placed the cherubim and a flaming sword that turned every way to guard the way to the tree of life."

(Genesis 3:24)

Angelic beings
Involved in the worship
And praise of God.
Frequently mentioned in
    scripture,
Especially in connection
With the worship of God
And being in His presence.
A cherub has hands like
    humans,
Wings of an angel, and
A body similar to humans,
Yet distinct in many ways.
Some armed with flaming
    swords.
Ezekiel describes them with

Four faces, four wings, many
    eyes, and
Straight legs with soles like a
    calf's foot.
Face of a lion,
Representing wild animals;
Face of an ox,
Representing domestic animals;
Another face of a human,
Representing humanity;
And the fourth, an eagle,
Representing winged creatures.
Possibly not true for all
    cherubs.
Whatever their physical shapes,
Clearly important angelic
    beings
Tasked with serving
Directly in God's presence,
Highly involved in the
Worship of the Lord.

One cherub of note, Lucifer
    himself,
Called the anointed cherub.
Created to reside in
The throne room of heaven,
In the very presence of God
    Himself.
Yet pride consumed him
And God cast him out of
    heaven.

"And the four living creatures, each of them with six wings, are full of eyes all around and within, and day and night they never cease to say, 'Holy, holy, holy, is the Lord God Almighty, who was and is and is to come!'"

(Revelations 4:8)

Children of God

"But to all who did receive him, who believed in his name, he gave the right to become children of God."

(John 1:12)

Salvation is much more than
Forgiveness of sins,
Deliverance from
    condemnation.
Salvation includes
Positions of great blessings,
Including becoming a child
    of God.
And all this through faith
    alone.

As children of God,
Christians are assured of
Blessings in this life,
Eternal fellowship
With God in the next.
A gift of divine love,
Promises of nurturing and
    protection,

Knowing we are redeemed
By the blood of Christ Jesus.

By becoming children of God,
We are adopted into
The heavenly family,
Allowing us the honored
    position
As true family members,
Heirs of God,
Joint heirs with Christ.
All that Christ has in the
    Father,
We also have.

As children of God,
We rejoice in the assurance
That God is our Father;
We are His children.
His love is steadfast,
Our destinies are secure.

As children of God,
We live to bring
Honor and glory to Christ,
Paving the way
For this adoption
In God's family.

As children of God,
Share your joy with others,
Proclaim the saving grace
Found only in Christ Jesus.
As children of God,
Remember your position.
You are in the family,

You are God's child;
Live according to the riches
You have received,
Remembering that your
    purpose
Is to glorify God.

Your goal is to be
Conformed to the image
Of Christ. Your mission is
To magnify God, share the
    gospel.
Your destiny is confirmed,
Your life is eternal,
One day being in the
    presence of
The Lord Jesus Christ
    forevermore.

"The Spirit himself bears witness with our spirit that we are children of God, and if children, then heirs—heirs of God and fellow heirs with Christ, provided we suffer with him in order that we may also be glorified with him."

(Romans 8:16–17)

Church

"And I tell you, you are Peter, and on this rock I will build my

church, and the gates of hell shall not prevail against it."

(Matthew 16:18)

The body of Christ:
Greek word translates to
"An assembly, called-out ones,
    gathering."
Not a building, as many
Understand it today,
But the body of believers.
The church is the body of
    Christ,
Of which He is the head.

Universal church consists
Of everyone, everywhere,
Having a personal relationship
With Jesus Christ.
All those who have received
    salvation
Through faith in Jesus
Comprise the universal church.

Local church comprised of
Local body of believers,
Who are also part of the
    universal church:
Any number of denominations,
Various sizes, in homes, in
    buildings,
In the cities, and in the
    countryside.
All members of the universal
    church

Should seek fellowship, seek
    edification,
In a local church.

Movement today toward
"Organic church" of Acts 2
Counters the modern
Evangelical philosophy of
Large programs, large
    buildings,
Professional pastorate,
Complex business model,
Dependence on money.
Focusing instead on small
    groups.
Purpose is for spiritual growth,
Mutual help and comfort,
Bible study, growth in Christ—
All while being led by the Holy
    Spirit.
Analogy is the "simple church."

The church is not a building,
But a group of people.
It is not a denomination,
But everyone having received
The Holy Spirit.
It doesn't grant salvation;
It is people loving and
    glorifying God,
Teaching others the gospel.
It is a group of people
Encouraging, teaching,
Building one another up
In the knowledge and grace
Of the Lord, Jesus Christ.

It is not merely a
Human association,
A gathering of the faithful.
A church is a divinely created
    affair.
It is the people of the kingdom
    of God,
Not the kingdom itself.
Referred to scripturally as
The temple of God
And the bride of Christ.

Described by Jesus in
    Matthew 9,
The church is an assembly
Of imperfect people who
Know they need a Savior,
Working together to
Build relationships,
Help those in need.
They glorify God by
Striving to be like Christ,
Sharing His love.

"Greet also the church in their house. Greet my beloved Epaenetus, who was the first convert to Christ in Asia."

(Romans 16:5)

Christ

"For unto you is born this day in the city of David a Savior, who is Christ the Lord."

(Luke 2:11)

A title meaning "anointed,"
Official title of our Lord, Jesus,
Denoting that He was
Anointed or consecrated for
His great redemptive work
As prophet, king, and priest.
He is Jesus the Christ,
The anointed one.

Used by Christians
Both as a name and title,
Is synonymous with Jesus.
Christ Jesus, meaning
The Messiah, Jesus,
Independently as the Christ.

From the Greek word *Christos*,
Meaning, "anointed one,
    chosen one."
Hebrew equivalent to *Christos*
Is *Mashiach* or Messiah.

This title, *Christ*, signifies
That Jesus was chosen
To deliver God's people.
It means He is the one who
    fulfills
Old Testament prophecies.

He is God's anointed one.
This title dignifies His time
On earth as King of kings and
   Savior.
He came to save sinners,
One day to return to establish
His kingdom on earth.

**"For in Christ all the fullness of
the Deity lives in bodily form, and
in Christ you have been brought
to fullness. He is the head over
every power and authority."**

(Colossians 2:9–10)

Christ Is Risen

**"He is not here, but has risen.
Remember how he told you, while
he was still in Galilee, that the
Son of Man must be delivered
into the hands of sinful men and
be crucified and on the third day
rise."**

(Luke 24:6–7)

Christian faith stands or falls
With the resurrection.
Christ's resurrection
And our salvation—
Inseparably linked to each
   other.

Christ is risen—

Means He can be
Trusted absolutely.
His promise that He would die,
Then rise again,
Means that all His promises
Can be trusted absolutely.

Christ is risen—
Means our sins
Have been forgiven.
Christ's sacrifice
On the cross
Accepted by the Father.
Christ was resurrected
For our justification.

Christ is risen—
Means Satan was defeated,
Death was overcome;
Christ conquered the power of
   darkness,
Disarmed the evil rulers,
Triumphed over them all.

Christ is risen—
Means new life is possible.
Through faith, we are
United to Christ.
We live in Him,
Dependent on His living
   presence,
Drawing on our union
With His glorious person.

Christ is risen—
Guarantees our resurrection.

Death cannot hold us.
Eternity with Christ is
    guaranteed.
A living hope assured.
Despair turned into sunlight.

Hallelujah!
Christ is risen!
He is risen indeed!

"Blessed be the God and Father of our Lord Jesus Christ! According to his great mercy, he has caused us to be born again to a living hope through the resurrection of Jesus Christ from the dead."

(1 Peter 1:3)

Circumcision

"This is my covenant, which you shall keep, between me and you and your offspring after you: Every male among you shall be circumcised."

(Genesis 17:10)

Literally means "to cut
    around."
A surgical removal of the
    prepuce,
Foreskin of a male.
A religious rite

Required of all Abraham's
    descendants
As a sign of covenant
God made with him.
Repeated in the Mosaic law,
Practice continues to this day.
Administered on the
Eighth day of life.

In Mosaic law,
A spiritual interpretation
    included
Circumcision of the heart,
Commanded followers to
Recognize that in addition
To bearing a physical mark,
Also under obligation to
Manifest spiritual qualities
Of commitment and obedience
To the Lord's will.

Circumcision's purpose
Distorted over time.
Thought to be a necessary
Part of salvation
As well as a guarantee.
Under the new covenant,
Gentiles received
The outpouring of the Holy
    Spirit
Without the physical rite
Of circumcision,
Demonstrating salvation
Comes by grace and faith,
Not by works.

While circumcision is of value
For the old covenant,
It now carries no real
    significance
For the converts of promise
Under the new covenant.
Faith through grace,
Apart from which
Circumcision or
    uncircumcision
Are meaningless. For believers,
The matter of circumcision—
Or the lack of it—
A matter of indifference.
More important is faith and
    obedience.

"Was anyone at the time of his call already circumcised? Let him not seek to remove the marks of circumcision. Was anyone at the time of his call uncircumcised? Let him not seek circumcision. For neither circumcision counts for anything nor uncircumcision, but keeping the commandments of God."

(1 Corinthians 7:18–19)

Comfort

"Blessed are those who mourn, for they shall be comforted."

(Matthew 5:4)

Divine comfort,
The peace of God
Fills the heart of believers
With assurance that they are
Cleansed from all sin.

A free, full forgiveness—
Not through works of
    humanity,
Only through the atoning
Blood of Christ.
As a result,
No past, present, or future
Distress can separate us
From the love of God
Through Christ Jesus.

Angels are not in need of
    comfort;
Satan is eternally beyond
    comfort;
Only humans were created to
    receive
This comfort, God's comfort—
A true freedom from guilt.
In His mercy and love,
God is eager to provide
Comfort in all situations,
No matter the trial faced.

In this manner, God offers
Peace, happiness, and blessings.
He is God of all comfort.

This comfort received,
Flows through us to others,
Letting us encourage,
Console, give relief to,
Exhort, aid, and stand
    alongside
Our neighbors in need.
Comfort—a gift not only to be
    received,
But to be shared actively,
Advancing the kingdom
    of God.

Once in eternity,
No need for comfort,
For there will be no more
    death,
No more mourning, crying, or
    pain
For all that has passed away.
We will enjoy the God of all
    comfort
Forever.

**"Blessed be the God and Father
of our Lord Jesus Christ, the
Father of mercies and God of all
comfort, who comforts us in all
our affliction, so that we may
be able to comfort those who
are in any affliction, with the
comfort with which we ourselves
are comforted by God. For as
we share abundantly in Christ's
sufferings, so through Christ we
share abundantly in comfort too."**

(2 Corinthians 1:3–5)

Confession

**"If we confess our sins, he is
faithful and just to forgive us our
sins and to cleanse us from all
unrighteousness."**

(1 John 1:9)

Owning up to something
You know or believe,
Telling it forthrightly to all
Who should hear it.
Synonyms include
    acknowledgment,
Admission, profession, and
    disclosure.

Possible to group under two
    heads:
Confession of faith and
Confession of sin.
Under faith, a public
    acknowledgment
Of one's fidelity to God,
To the truth that God has
    revealed—

Declaration of unqualified
confidence
In Christ, surrender to His
service.
It is agreeing with God
About what Jesus did on the
cross.

Confession of sin,
Acknowledgment of our fallen
nature,
Of our wrongs against God
and neighbors.
The penitent freely
acknowledges
One's guilt against God,
To those whom he or she has
done wrong.
Genuine confession reflects
A genuine change of mind,
A repentance more than mere
words,
For it is active—an actual
Turning from sin. It is to avow
And acknowledge one's faults
Honestly and sincerely.

Not a request for forgiveness,
For we have forgiveness
Through the blood of Christ.
Important to confess sins,
To confess Christ,
Acknowledge, agree, profess,
Declare, and give thanks
to God

For what Christ did on the
cross
For you and me.

**"Whoever confesses that Jesus is
the Son of God, God abides in
him, and he in God."**

(1 John 4:15)

Conquerors
(More Than)

**"No, in all these things we are
more than conquerors through
him who loved us."**

(Romans 8:37)

Satan is our adversary.
His minions are relentless
In life-defeating, joy-stealing
attacks
Threatening our well-being,
Even our faith in God.
Trouble, hardship, persecution,
Famine, nakedness, sword—
The attacks come.

Yet through Jesus Christ,
Who loved us,
We not only achieve victory;
We are overwhelmingly
victorious,
More than conquerors.

We are encouraged to stand
firm
In our faith,
To face our trials with
certainty,
Knowing we are not alone.
We follow Jesus Christ,
Who conquered death itself.

We have the promise of eternal
life.
No sins of ours,
No attempts of the enemy
Can beat us.
For God is with us,
Making us, without doubt,
More than conquerors.
No opposition, no accusation,
No condemnation, no
separation—
We are more than conquerors.

"Even though I walk through the valley of the shadow of death, I will fear no evil, for you are with me; your rod and your staff, they comfort me."

(Psalm 23:4)

Cornerstone

"Therefore thus says the Lord God, 'Behold, I am the one who has laid as a foundation in Zion,

a stone, a tested stone, a precious cornerstone, of a sure foundation: "Whoever believes will not be in haste."'"

(Isaiah 28:16)

Figuratively indicates the stone
At a structure's corner.
Either the foundation stone
Upon which a structure rests
Or possibly the topmost or
capstone,
Which links the last tier
together.
In both cases, it is an
important stone.
Figuratively the Messiah,
Who is the first and the last,
The Alpha and Omega.

Jesus is the cornerstone—
The foundation of all creation,
The foundation of the church,
The foundation of our
individual lives—
To be built upon
In ways pleasing to God:
Faithfully praying,
Sharing the good news,
Living godly lives,
Loving our neighbors.

"So then you are no longer strangers and aliens, but you are fellow citizens with the saints and

38

members of the household of God, built on the foundation of the apostles and prophets, Christ Jesus himself being the cornerstone, in whom the whole structure, being joined together, grows into a holy temple in the Lord."

(Ephesians 2:19–21)

Covenant of Grace

"For God so loved the world, that he gave his only Son, that whoever believes in him should not perish but have eternal life."

(John 3:16)

The establishment of God's
mercy,
His goodwill toward people,
Wherein God freely offers to
sinners
Eternal life and salvation
through
Faith in Jesus Christ.

Conceived in eternity, revealed
in time.
Contains three elements:
The blessings: eternal life,
salvation;
The mediator: Jesus Christ;
The one requirement: faith in
Christ.

Referred to as an unconditional
promise
Given freely on the basis of
God's grace.
Faith may seem like a
condition,
Yet scripture teaches that even
saving faith
Is a gracious gift from God.

Covenant of grace manifested
Throughout time in the
promises:
To Abraham to bless all
nations;
For a Davidic king to rule
eternally
Over God's people;
For the forgiveness of sin—
All fulfilled in Jesus Christ
Himself.

First announced in Genesis
In God's promise of
redemption.
This covenant carries us
through
The history of redemption
Renewed and fulfilled in
Christ.

The fall of Adam necessitated
This covenant, since all
Are dead in trespasses and sin,
Unable to find salvation
But for the covenant of grace.

Summed up in these words:
"I will be their God,
They shall be my people."
Included herein: justification,
Adoption, sanctification, and
glorification.

"But as it is, Christ has obtained a ministry that is as much more excellent than the old as the covenant he mediates is better, since it is enacted on better promises."

(Hebrews 8:6)

Covenant

"Therefore he is the mediator of a new covenant, so that those who are called may receive the promised eternal inheritance, since a death has occurred that redeems them from the transgressions committed under the first covenant."

(Hebrews 9:15)

Literally, a contract, a coming
together.
Promises, stipulations,
Privileges, and responsibilities.
Virtually all covenants contain
both

Conditional and unconditional
elements.
God initiated His covenants;
It is He who determined all
elements.
We are the recipients, not the
contributors,
But usually with obligations
to God.

Remarkable aspects of God's
covenants:
He, being holy,
omniscient, and
Omnipotent, consents to enter
Into covenant with humankind
Being feeble, sinful, and
flawed.

Five major biblical covenants:
Noahic—unconditional
assurance
That He would never again
Destroy the world by flood.
Abrahamic—an unconditional
promise
To bless Abraham's
descendants,
Making them His people.
Mosaic—a conditional promise
Centered around God giving
His divine law to Moses
On Mount Sinai, promised
Blessings for obedience and
Curses for disobedience.

Davidic—an unconditional
blessing
Of David's family,
Assurance of an everlasting
kingdom.
New covenant—promise of
Forgiveness of sin
To all who come to Jesus
Christ in faith.
Jesus Christ is the mediator
Of the new covenant;
His death and resurrection
The basis of the promise.
Fulfilled in this new covenant
All promises made
To Abraham, Moses, and
David.

In dealing with His people,
God uses two simple words:
"I will."
Words of promise, hope, and
Eternal significance.
His promises are faithful and
true,
Just as He is faithful and true.
No ifs, ands, or buts about it.
He makes it abundantly clear:
He shall be our God and
We shall be His people.

"And I will establish my covenant between me and you and your offspring after you throughout their generations for an everlasting covenant, to be God to you and to your offspring after you."

(Genesis 17:7)

Covet

"You shall not covet your neighbor's house; you shall not covet your neighbor's wife, or his male servant, or his female servant, or his ox, or his donkey, or anything that is your neighbor's."

(Exodus 20:17)

A word of desire and envy—
To crave unlawfully, lust after,
Want what is not yours.
A commandment most
Difficult to obey,
Impossible to see;
For a secret kept in the heart
Where only God can see.

The purpose of the law
Is that sin might be shown
as sin.
To covet is to sin.
When we covet, we say to God,
"We are not satisfied
With what we have."
Coveting is discontent
With what one has and
An inordinate desire to possess
That which belongs to another.

The command not to covet
Addresses the inner person,
The location where sin
 originates:
A person's heart.
Covetousness is the
 forerunner of
All manner of sins, including
Theft, embezzlement, and
 adultery.
Its root is found in envy.
Envy leads to covetousness,
Which turns us against our
 neighbors,
Causing feelings of bitterness
 and hatred,
Leading to resentment
Against God Himself,
Questioning His love for us.

To covet is a form of idolatry,
A sin God detests.
It is a tool used by Satan
To shift our focus
From Christ to ourselves,
Pursuing the things of this
 world
And not God Himself.

**"You desire and do not have, so
you murder. You covet and cannot
obtain, so you fight and quarrel.
You do not have, because you do
not ask."**

(James 4:2)

Creation

**"In the beginning, God created
the heavens and the earth."**

(Genesis 1:1)

It started before time,
Started out of nothing.
Ex nihilo.
Accomplished by God,
For only He was there.

Creation includes all things
In heaven and on earth,
Visible and invisible,
The universe complete—
Created by Him and for Him.

Creation includes man and
 woman,
Created in image of God,
The pinnacle of creation,
Appointed to rule
Over the rest of creation.

Creation was for a purpose:
For us to know Him,
For us to love Him,
For us to glorify Him,
For us to enjoy Him.

God exists in a timeless
 manner:
No beginning, no end.
Yet in creation, time was made,

The succession of moments.
Demonstrating God's lordship
    over it.

God, the Father, did not act
    alone.
Both Son and Holy Spirit
    participants.
God created through the Son.
The Spirit's active role in
    creation:
Preserving, sustaining, and
    governing.

Distinct difference between
God, the Creator, and His
    creation.
He is both transcendent and
    immanent;
He is above all creation,
    ruling all,
Yet personally involved
In all of creation.

Six days or six millennia—
The answer not clear.
What is clear:
God is the Creator,
And the heavens declare His
    glory.

**"Ah, Lord GOD! It is you who have
made the heavens and the earth
by your great power and by your
outstretched arm! Nothing is too
hard for you."**

(Jeremiah 32:17)

Cross

**"For the word of the cross is folly
to those who are perishing, but to
us who are being saved it is the
power of God."**

(1 Corinthians 1:18)

Principal symbol of Christian
    religion,
Recalling the crucifixion
Of Jesus Christ,
The redeeming benefits
Of His passion and death.

The cross, a great contradiction.
Simple, upright post
With a traverse bar,
Used for killing men.
Once the cruelest form of
    execution,
Now a symbol of abundant life.

Death and life,
Hate and love,
Violence and peace,
Accusation and forgiveness,
Sin and purity,
Brokenness and wholeness,
All lost, everything gained,

Destruction and restoration,
Defeat and victory.

The cross is where Christ
Died for sinners.
He died for people who
Had lost their way.
A choice by Christ,
A choice made in love,
The cross is the intersection
Of God's love and justice.

Bearing one's cross is not
    meant
To denote an inconvenience or
A bothersome circumstance.
The cross meant only one thing
To early Christians,
And that was death.
It denotes losing one's life
For the sake of Christ
As the way to find it:
Death of the sinful self,
Rising to walk in a
New life through Christ,
Bearing your own cross.

To bear our cross
Demands a death sentence
To our own desires,
Death to sin's passions,
Death to sin's lusts.
Only then do we receive
Life in Christ.

To take up our cross
Is to lose sight
Of our earthly desires,
Have our sights focused
On Christ alone.

"Whoever does not bear his own cross and come after me cannot be my disciple."

(Luke 14:27)

Curses

"Joshua summoned them, and he said to them, 'Why did you deceive us, saying, "We are very far from you," when you dwell among us? Now therefore you are cursed, and some of you shall never be anything but servants, cutters of wood and drawers of water for the house of my God.'"

(Joshua 9:23–24)

Uttered by God—divine.
Uttered by people—human.
The use of powerful words
To invoke supernatural harm,
To bring great evil upon
    another.
The cause of serious injury or
    unhappiness,

That which brings severe
    affliction.

Curses may be spoken or
    written,
Personal or collective,
Binding or conditional.
They are divine maledictions.

Various types of curses
    declared:
Humiliation, barrenness,
Sickness of every kind,
Poverty and failure, defeat,
Being the follower, not the
    leader.

A curse is not always a curse;
It can be a figure of speech.
When Satan was cursed
    by God,
It was actually a judgment:
To eat dust all his days.

Curses may be self-directed:
Job cursed his own life;
David did the same:
"So may God do to me."
Usually given for violating an
    oath.

Many curses are prophetic;
They predict harm or evil to
    come.
As Joshua pronounced upon
    those
Who would rebuild Jericho.

Regardless of its form,
A curse is much more than a
    mere wish.
A curse is considered to possess
Inherent power of carrying
    itself
Into effect.

All humans are cursed;
Doom has been pronounced.
Escape is possible only through
    the cross,
Where Christ endured our
    curse
Of eternal damnation.
The curse loses its power
    when we
Kneel in faith and repentance
    to Christ.

"But the LORD your God would not listen to Balaam; instead the LORD your God turned the curse into a blessing for you, because the LORD your God loved you."

(Deuteronomy 23:5)

Curtain (of the Temple)

"And you shall hang the veil from the clasps, and bring the ark of the testimony in there within the veil. And the veil shall separate for

you the Holy Place from the Most Holy."

(Exodus 26:33)

A barrier to people
From God's presence.
Located in the temple,
Thickness only of a person's
    hand,
With a height of almost sixty
    feet.
A formidable wall in the eyes of
    humans.
Referred to as the temple's
    "inner veil"
Before the Holy of holies.

No simple curtain—
Made of blue, purple, and
    scarlet yarn,
Finely twisted linen.
Cherubim worked into it
By a skilled craftsman.
Hung from gold hooks,
On an acacia wood frame.

Purpose: to separate
The clean from the unclean,
The holy from the profane.
Demonstrating God's
    holiness and
The fallen nature of humanity
Concealed a most sacred
    object:
The ark of the covenant.

Upon the death of Jesus,
With atonement for our sins,
This curtain was not just torn,
But torn in two from top to
    bottom,
Implying that God Himself
Tore this veil.
It could never again perform
Its function. No longer is there
A physical barrier to God.
Reentry into the presence
Of God was once again
    permitted
For the first time since
That fall in the garden.

Through the atoning death
Of Jesus, by His blood,
Believers now have access
To the presence of God.
No longer is there a curtain;
No longer does sin bar our way.
We now enter the Holy of
    holies
With confidence and boldness
Through faith in Jesus
As our Lord and Savior.

"And behold, the curtain of the temple was torn in two, from top to bottom. And the earth shook, and the rocks were split."

(Matthew 27:51)

Daily Bread

"Give us this day our daily bread."
(Matthew 6:11)

Physical provision,
That which we need daily
To sustain our lives:
Food, clothes, protection.

Daily, in acknowledgment of
Our dependence on the
Providence of God,
Sustaining us day by day.

Bread, a staple in the diet,
A symbol of God's provision
For His people,
Including spiritual
     nourishment.

This daily bread
Satisfies our spiritual hunger.
Christ is to be the daily staple
Of our spiritual lives.

Daily bread therefore includes
Not only our physical needs,
But our spiritual, relational,
And emotional needs.

God cares and provides
For the entirety of our beings.
Without God's provisions,
We would not survive one day.

Daily bread helps us focus
On the present,
Not dwell in the past
Or worry about the future.

Daily bread guards our hearts
Against greed and discontent,
Desiring only what we need,
Not for self-indulgent wants.

It represents trust in God
To provide for our needs today,
Recognizing our
     dependence on
Him alone.

"He humbled you, causing you to hunger and then feeding you with manna, which neither you nor your ancestors had known, to teach you that man does not live on bread alone but on every word that comes from the mouth of the LORD."

(Deuteronomy 8:3)

Darkness

"The people who walked in darkness have seen a great light; those who dwelt in a land of deep darkness, on them has light shone."

(Isaiah 9:2)

Darkness, the absence of light.
Light, a symbol of God's
Purity, wisdom, and glory.
Darkness is the opposite.
It is spiritual;
It is living apart from God.

Living in darkness
Is not having fellowship
With God through a
Relationship with Jesus Christ.
Until being reborn
Of God's Spirit,
We live in spiritual darkness;
We live in sin.
Sin darkens our understanding,
Destroys our spiritual sight,
Cloaks us in darkness.

Darkness is rebelling
    against God,
Against His will.
It is living with eyes shut tight.
Darkness is untruths,
It is lies.
It is evil.
Sinners prefer darkness over
    light,
Yet believers need not fear,
For God is our light.
He brings us out of our
    darkness,
Into His light.

"I am sending you to open their eyes, so that they may turn from darkness to light and from the power of Satan to God, that they may receive forgiveness of sins and a place among those who are sanctified by faith in me."

(Acts 26:17–18)

David

"Then Samuel took the horn of oil and anointed him in the midst of his brothers. And the Spirit of the LORD rushed upon David from that day forward."

(1 Samuel 16:13)

A man after God's own heart,
A shepherd boy,
Youngest son of Jesse.
Filled with courage and faith,
A killer of bears and lions.
Overcame the giant Goliath
With a sling and a stone.

Came into King Saul's service
As a young lad.
Soon an armor-bearer.
Rose in strength and fame,
Chosen by God,
Anointed king of Israel.

Described as a shepherd king,
A warrior poet,
Author of many psalms.
Life filled with a
Kaleidoscope of emotions.
Truly a man of contrasts:
Father of Solomon,
A great king of Israel.
Also fathered Absalom,
Who brought much
Bloodshed and grief.

David, courageous in battle,
Trusted God for protection.
Weak in many ways,
Especially with women—
Committed adultery
As well as murder.
Paid the consequences for this,
As did those dear to him.
Yet he recognized his sins,
Repented of all,
Turned to God for forgiveness.
When downcast and
    despondent,
David lifted his eyes to God,
Giving Him praise.

A covenant made,
A descendant to rule
On the throne forever.
This everlasting king—
This son of David,
Was Jesus, the Messiah.

"Truly my soul finds rest in God; my salvation comes from him. Truly he is my rock and my salvation; he is my fortress, I will never be shaken."

(Psalm 62:1–2)

Day of Atonement

"And the LORD spoke to Moses, saying, 'Now on the tenth day of this seventh month is the Day of Atonement. It shall be for you a time of holy convocation, and you shall afflict yourselves and present a food offering to the LORD.'"

(Leviticus 23:26–27)

Most solemn and the
    holiest day
Of all Israelite feasts, festivals.
Known as Yom Kippur to Jews.
Celebrated once a year,
Tenth day of the seventh
    month.
A day the high priest
Performs elaborate rituals
Atoning for the sins of the
    people.
Climax of the sacrificial system
In the Old Testament.
Displaying the holiness of God
The depth of humanity's sin.

A requirement of the
   Mosaic law,
Celebrated today by Jews,
Traditionally observing this
   holy day
With a twenty-five-hour fasting
   period,
As well as intensive prayer,
Usually in the synagogue.

The Day of Atonement,
A shadow of the coming work
Of Jesus Christ on Calvary.
His sacrifice on the cross
Appeased God's wrath
   against sin,
By taking that wrath upon
   Himself.
Jesus Christ, given to the world
By God, the Father,
So that whoever believes
   in Him
Should not perish but have
Everlasting life, cleansed from
   all sin.

Jesus completely, perfectly
   fulfilled
This Day of Atonement once
   for all.
Christ's atonement on the cross
Accepted by the Father.
Christ said, "It is finished,"

Then sat down at the right
   hand of God.
No further sacrifice was ever
   needed.

"But when Christ appeared as a high priest of the good things that have come, then through the greater and more perfect tent (not made with hands, that is, not of this creation) he entered once for all into the holy places, not by means of the blood of goats and calves but by means of his own blood, thus securing an eternal redemption."

(Hebrews 9:11–12)

Deacon

"Paul and Timothy, servants of Christ Jesus, To all the saints in Christ Jesus who are at Philippi, with the overseers and deacons: Grace to you and peace from God our Father and the Lord Jesus Christ."

(Philippians 1:1–2)

From the Greek, meaning
"One who ministers to
   another."

Commonly translated as
servant.
One with responsibilities
Within the church.
One who ministers to
The church's physical needs,
While the elder ministers
To spiritual needs.
Yet much overlaps these roles.

Depending on church needs,
Along with a deacon's gifts,
Responsibilities could entail
Administrative, organizational
tasks,
Ushering, maintenance,
treasury,
Assisting those in need—
And, at all times, serving.

Qualifications clearly outlined
In scripture:
Be dignified, sincere, faithful
to spouse,
Not addicted to wine, not
greedy,
Strong believers, proven
blameless,
Manage children and
household well.

Bible is not clear regarding
possibility
Of women serving as deacons.
Does include examples of
women,

Such as Phoebe, serving
faithfully.
Not much biblical support,
But neither does it clearly
disqualify them.
Regardless, serving must be in
submission
To church authority and
structure
And, ultimately, to Christ
Jesus.

"For those who serve well as deacons gain a good standing for themselves and also great confidence in the faith that is in Christ Jesus."

(1 Timothy 3:13)

Death (Physical)

"Therefore, just as sin entered the world through one man, and death through sin, and in this way death came to all people, because all sinned."

(Romans 5:12)

Simply defined as termination
of life.
Better defined as a separation.
Physical death is the separation
Of a soul from its body;

Spiritual death is the separation
Of a soul from God.

Physical death is the absence
Or withdrawal of breath,
Causing separation of body
    and soul
Where the body returns to
    dust,
And the soul returns to God.
As God gave life,
God gives death.

Death begins the
Moment we are born.
The human body is
    described as
A body of death.
Sometimes fast, in a moment;
Other times, a slow process.
But always the same result,
Without exception.
This inevitable physical death,
An enemy of humanity—
Inescapable, undeniable.
Entered into this world
With the fall of Adam,
For the wages of sin
Is death.

As different types of life,
Different types of death:
Physically alive, spiritually
    dead,
Spiritually alive, physically
    dead,

Alive in sin, dead in God,
Alive in God, dead in sin.

The Word of God tells us
Death was swallowed up in
The victory of Christ on the
    cross.
For those in Christ,
The sting of death will be
    removed.
Yes, this body will fall to dust,
But one day, a glorious
    resurrection
And glorified bodies wait
    for us,
Like that of Christ Jesus.

"For as in Adam all die, so in Christ all will be made alive."

(1 Corinthians 15:22)

Death (Second)

"But as for the cowardly, the faithless, the detestable, as for murderers, the sexually immoral, sorcerers, idolaters, and all liars, their portion will be in the lake that burns with fire and sulfur, which is the second death."

(Revelation 21:8)

More of a place, a location.
Exclusively for those who reject
Christ.
A place believers in Christ
Need not fear.

The second death: a lake of fire.
A final condition.
Banishment is permanent—
No going back.
A dwelling for eternity.
No escape.

This second death,
At times called eternal death,
An unending separation
Between God and
Those who reject His Son.
Begins at the final judgment
Never ends.

This subject of second death,
A theme throughout scripture;
Always in the background,
A dire warning to those
Who choose to remain
In opposition to God,
Choosing to live in sin.
A certain fearful expectation
Of judgment containing
Fiery indignation.

Opposition to God—
Not sudden, dramatic turns,
But smaller things:

False teachers, deception,
Cares of this life,
Enticements of this world.
Carelessness opening the
same lie
That Eve fell for,
Leading to the second death.

Warnings abound:
Repent and believe,
Live eternally with God.

"Whoever has ears, let them hear what the Spirit says to the churches. The one who is victorious will not be hurt at all by the second death."

(Revelation 2:11)

Death (Spiritual)

"For the wages of sin is death, but the free gift of God is eternal life in Christ Jesus our Lord."

(Romans 6:23)

Although not literally stated
In scripture, concept is explicit.
Separation of the soul
from God.
Not the annihilation of the
spirit,
Yet a deadly disunion.
A greater significance

Than physical death,
The separation of body and
  soul.

Man without Christ,
Spiritually dead indeed.
Alienated from God
  through sin,
The status of all humanity
In our fallen state.
Yet Christ makes us alive,
We who were dead in
Trespasses and sin,
Unable to save ourselves.
Christ quickened us;
Through His mercy,
We become reborn.

Not created this way—
But due to Adam's sin,
All humans died an immediate
Spiritual death:
Unable to please God,
Incapable of loving Him,
Powerless to come to Him.
Only through regeneration
Accomplished by the Holy
  Spirit
Are we made alive in Christ—
A second birth.

This death, while still bodily
  alive,
Results in following
The desires of the flesh.
Children of wrath,

Slaves of sin,
Hostile to God and His ways,
Born to a sinful nature,
Separated from God,
Spiritually dead.

"And you, who were dead in your trespasses God made alive together with him, having forgiven us all our trespasses."

(Colossians 2:13)

Debtors

"So then, brothers, we are debtors, not to the flesh, to live according to the flesh. For if you live according to the flesh you will die, but if by the Spirit you put to death the deeds of the body, you will live."

(Romans 8:12–13)

All the bills paid,
Owing nothing to the bank,
Even-Steven with the
  neighbors—
We are paid in full.

Yet debtors we will always be—
Debtors to God's grace and
  mercy,
For all He showers on us
Day and night.

At sunrise, we are in debt
    to Him
For the day. Each breath,
We are in debt to Him for
    the air.
At mealtimes, we are in debt
    to Him
For the food. At night,
We are in debt to Him for the
    rest.

But for our salvation, we have
    no debt.
Christ paid in full the debt of
    our sins.
Jesus stood in our stead,
Dying the death that we
    deserved.

Now God sees us not as guilty,
But as cloaked in Christ's
    righteousness.
He sees innocent children
When we bow before Him.

Yet our debts are not a debt
In dictionary definitions,
But debts of love.

Because He loved us first,
Now we are able
To love Him in return—
Through praise, worship, and
    prayer.

Oh yes, we are in debt,
But what a wonderful debt it is!

A debt we gladly pay
With heartfelt love every day.

"Give us this day our daily bread, and forgive us our debts, as we also have forgiven our debtors."

(Matthew 6:11–12)

Deserts

"The one who led you through this vast and terrifying desert of poisonous snakes and scorpions, of cracked ground with no water; the one who made water flow for you out of a hard rock."

(Deuteronomy 8:15 CEB)

Places ill-suited for people,
Extreme geographical
    features—
Lack of water, sparse
    vegetation,
Often fill with dangerous
    creatures.
Although physical locations
In this world of ours,
Deserts speak of our
    relationships
With our heavenly Father.

Filled with symbols,
Caution of life without God,

Signs of punishment for
  rebelling,
Result of neglectful leadership,
Warning signs of divine
  judgment.

A locale that invites
Deep spiritual reflections.
Stripping the lushness of
The material world,
The barrenness of the desert
Turns our hearts toward God,
Seeking to discover
What is truly important in life.

Even in this wilderness
God cares for us.
Look at Moses and the
  Israelites.
Quail, manna, water—
Gifts in the desert.
John the Baptist cries,
"Prepare the way of the Lord."
Jesus Himself enters the desert
For forty days to fast and pray,
Rejecting temptation by Satan.
It became a place of renewal.

Deserts are undoubtedly
  troubling—
Places of temptation and
  doubt—
But on occasion are also places
Of deep spiritual
  transformation.

"And so John the Baptist appeared in the desert, preaching a baptism of repentance for the forgiveness of sins."

(Mark 1:4 NIV)

(See also **Wilderness.**)

Deserving

"Rise up, O judge of the earth; repay to the proud what they deserve!"

(Psalm 94:2)

We suppose we deserve
  much—
Cars, toys, and material
  things—
But who decides?

Does a guilty person
Deserve to be beaten?
Or a murderer
Deserve to die?

Merit, justification, warrant—
How do we determine?
Overestimating ourselves,
  perhaps?
Judging is a dangerous game.

There is one thing we all
  deserve:
Since we are fallen beings,

Sinful in our hearts,
We deserve the wrath of God.

We try to earn our way,
Soon find this impossible.
The more we strain,
The further we fall.

The only way
To avoid eternal wrath:
Find Christ at the cross.

All are forgiven there,
Justice is paid in full.
The blood has cleansed
Our hearts of darkness.

So now we are deserving—
But not on our own accounts.
Christ's sacrifice was once
    for all.

A place in heaven,
As sons and daughters—
Our reward is great,
Earned at His cost.

Impossible to repay—
We can only give praise and
    thanks.
But is it deserved by us?
No, only by Christ alone.

"Then the officials and all the people said to the priests and the prophets, 'This man does not deserve the sentence of death, for he has spoken to us in the name of the LORD our God.'"

(Jeremiah 26:16)

Deuteronomy

"Be strong and courageous, for you shall go with this people into the land that the LORD has sworn to their fathers to give them, and you shall put them in possession of it. It is the LORD who goes before you. He will be with you; he will not leave you or forsake you. Do not fear or be dismayed."

(Deuteronomy 31:7–8)

Final book of the Pentateuch,
(The Old Testament's first five
    books,
Authored by Moses).
Moses urges the Israelites
Not to repeat past errors
When entering the Promised
    Land.
Canaan will fulfill God's
    promise,
But if idolatry rules, and they
Fail to keep the law,
Banishment will be their
    sentence.
Basically, a motivational
    sermon

Preached by Moses. A heartfelt
    appeal
From Almighty God for His
    children
To remain faithful to Him.

Deuteronomy offers a pause
In advancement of the story of
    redemption.
Begins and ends at the Jordan
    River.
Describes deliverance
From bondage in Egypt
To Canaan, where Israel could
    be free;
Deliverance from rootlessness
To security and rest
In the Promised Land—
Deliverance from a life of
    banishment
From the garden of Eden
To a life in the land where
God has pitched His tent.
Fulfillment of God's promise
To the patriarchs.

Moses calls the people
To renew their covenant
    with God
Not only before, but also after
Entering the Promised Land.
Although most of the book
Is occupied with laws,
All is surrounded by grace.

Truly a theological manifesto
Calling on Israel to respond
To God's grace
With unreserved loyalty and
    love.
Most quoted book by Jesus.

**"Jesus answered, 'The most
important is, "Hear, O Israel: The
Lord our God, the Lord is one.
And you shall love the Lord your
God with all your heart and with
all your soul and with all your
mind and with all your strength."
The second is this: "You shall love
your neighbor as yourself." There
is no other commandment greater
than these.'"**

(Mark 12:29–31)

Earth

**"In the beginning, God created
the heavens and the earth."**

(Genesis 1:1)

A creation of God
Where we presently stand.
Whether on the highest
    mountain
Or the lowest valley,
Earth is the planet where
    humans dwell.

A planet among many,
The home to humanity.
Although currently our abode,
Not permanent, a lodge of
    sorts—
For heaven is our true home.

Earth is in comparison to the
    heavens,
Which is everything else
Outside this planet.
All created by God—
A terrestrial globe with
Its aerial firmament.
Two opposites indicating a
    totality.
Some say it is old, others say
    young—
A matter of interpretation,
Both sides involving faith.

Earth had a beginning;
Earth will have an end.
The date unknown but sure to
    come.
It began without form,
    shapeless,
Destitute of all ornaments,
A chaos of waste, of void.
In this darkness of chaos
God's Spirit moved,
Giving form to the earth,
Filling it with life.
Establishing to us
Creator and creation.

Not originated by chance
But is the product of a
    creative God.
A place we are to care for
And not abuse.
Like any gift from God,
Something to always cherish
    and prize,
Reflecting His glory.

"Your kingdom come, your will be done, on earth as it is in heaven."

(Matthew 6:10)

Elder

"And when they had appointed elders for them in every church, with prayer and fasting they committed them to the Lord in whom they had believed."

(Acts 14:23)

A position not to take lightly—
One of responsibility within
    the church.
Pastors, overseers, and leaders
With wisdom, experience, and
    authority.
Ruling, teaching, praying,
Counseling, shepherding the
    church—

Responsible for spiritual
   leadership
And ministry to the church.

Qualifications are described in
   detail:
One must be above reproach,
The spouse of one only,
   sober-minded,
Self-controlled, respectable,
Hospitable, able to teach,
Not violent but gentle,
Not quarrelsome, not a lover of
   money,
Managing well his or her own
   household,
Not a recent convert,
Well regarded by outsiders.

Specific duties and obligations
   include
Settling disputes in the church,
Praying for the sick,
Leading in humility—
Not for personal gain—
Guarding the spiritual life of
   the church,
And spending time praying
   and teaching.
Simply put, peacemakers,
Prayer warriors, teachers,
Leaders by example,
And decision-makers.

Positions to be sought,
But never taken lightly.

For elders shall be judged
With greater strictness
By our Lord and Savior.

"So I exhort the elders among you, as a fellow elder and a witness of the sufferings of Christ, as well as a partaker in the glory that is going to be revealed: shepherd the flock of God that is among you, exercising oversight, not under compulsion, but willingly, as God would have you; not for shameful gain, but eagerly; not domineering over those in your charge, but being examples to the flock. And when the chief Shepherd appears, you will receive the unfading crown of glory."

(1 Peter 5:1–4)

Enemy

"Be alert and of sober mind. Your enemy the devil prowls around like a roaring lion looking for someone to devour."

(1 Peter 5:8 NIV)

Enemies all around,
But who are they?
Scripture identifies three:

The devil, the world, and the
    self.
All three are relentless;
All three are deadly.

This devil, a mighty opponent,
Angry at his defeat,
Cast from heaven,
Beaten by Christ at the cross.
He is the wicked one, a
    murderer,
The old serpent himself.
Does all in his power
To sow seeds of doubt.
Puts envy, discontent,
And malice in your heart.
Leads us away from God
In so many ways.
The devil is powerful, slick,
Crafty, wily, and subtle.
Known as Satan, Lucifer,
The father of lies.

The world, this cosmos,
This system we dwell in,
Leads us into sin,
To evil companions, to
    pleasures,
To fashions, opinions, and false
    aims.
The world wants us to walk
Hand in hand with its ways,
Ignoring the truth,
Grasping the pride of life.
This world is human society
With God left out.

Friendship of the world,
Enmity with God.
Friend of the world,
Enemy of God.

The flesh, faced daily,
The evil tendency of
Your inward self.
Your old nature,
With all its corruption,
As a traitor living within,
Striving for dominance,
Never conforming to
The will of God.
The flesh desires what is
Contrary to the Holy Spirit.
The two are constantly in
    conflict.

But victory is assured
For all who believe,
For those who accept
Christ as Lord and Savior.
Lean on Him
To defeat your enemies.
Walk in the Spirit.
Obey God's Word.

"As for you, you were dead in your transgressions and sins, in which you used to live when you followed the ways of this world and of the ruler of the kingdom of the air, the spirit who is now at work in those who are disobedient. All of

us also lived among them at one time, gratifying the cravings of our flesh and following its desires and thoughts."

(Ephesians 2:1–3)

Enmity

"I will put enmity between you and the woman, and between your offspring and her offspring; he shall bruise your head, and you shall bruise his heel."

(Genesis 3:15)

A positive, active, typically
    mutual
Hatred or ill will toward
    someone.
Being an enemy of another.
Having a hostile, unfriendly
Disposition toward another.
A deep and bitter hatred.

Due to the serpent's
    malevolence,
The spittle of a man and
The gall of the serpent
Are poison to each other.
Extending from the garden to
    today.
Satan versus man, man versus
    Satan.

Enmity not restricted
Between people and Satan.
Extends to fallen humanity
    and God.
Tragic condition of humankind
Is a natural enmity
    against God.
People clings to their sins,
Fighting the very one seeking
To save them.

"You adulterous people! Do you not know that friendship with the world is enmity with God? Therefore whoever wishes to be a friend of the world makes himself an enemy of God."

(James 4:4)

Epistle

"This is now the second letter that I am writing to you, beloved. In both of them I am stirring up your sincere mind by way of reminder."

(2 Peter 3:1)

A written communication.
Literal translation is "letter."
A term rarely used in
Familiar conversations and
    writings,
But chiefly in solemn,

Formal correspondence,
Particularly in referring
To letters of the apostles.

Epistles follow a familiar
    format:
Introduction with a name
Along with a greeting,
Sometimes with recipients
    named,
Followed by the main body
Possibly including
Exhortations, theological
    discussion,
Ethical admonitions;
Concluded with a general
    blessing,
Personal notes, and maybe a
    doxology.

Epistles in the New Testament
Number twenty-one in all—
Thirteen are penned by Paul,
Including his prison epistles
And pastoral epistles;
Eight others, called general
    epistles,
Were written by Peter,
    John, and
Family members of Jesus—
James and Jude.
Authorship of the letter to
    Hebrews
Not conclusively known.
All these were inspired by the
    Holy Spirit;

God-breathed, infallible,
    inerrant
Revelations of our Lord and
    Savior.

"I, Paul, write this greeting with my own hand. This is the sign of genuineness in every letter of mine; it is the way I write."

(2 Thessalonians 3:17)

Eternal Life

"For the wages of sin is death, but the free gift of God is eternal life in Christ Jesus our Lord."

(Romans 6:23)

The gift of gifts,
Contrasts to death
As a result of sin.
Eternal life is a gift to
    those who
Believe in Christ Jesus,
Who is Himself
The resurrection and the life.
Eternal, in that life never ends,
Continues for perpetuity,
In and outside of time.
A gift not deserved, not earned;
A gift of God's grace and favor.

Eternal life is in the present
As well as in the future.

It is not waiting for heaven.
Eternal life is knowing God.
It is having an intimate, close,
Personal relationship with God.

As such, eternal life is not
    simply
Life that never ends.
It is a fullness of life that is
    unending.
All will have life eternally,
It is the quality that separates
Believers from unbelievers.
For those who accept Christ
    Jesus,
That quality will be with God.
For those who reject Christ,
That eternity is described as
    death.

No, eternal life is not simply
Unending existence;
It is also the quality of one's
    life—
A life of acquaintance
With God in Christ.
Eternal life functions
Outside and beyond time
As well as within time.
It is the Christian
    experience now.
It is our current possession.
It is experiencing the blessings
Of Jesus Christ today and
    forever.

It is the contentment,
    satisfaction,
Freedom, confidence,
Comfort, and humility—
All that comes to all believers
Who accept Jesus Christ
As Lord and Savior.

Eternal life—
The free gift of God
To all who believe in Jesus
    Christ—
Begins when faith is placed in
    Christ,
Continues with God in
    eternity.
It relates not only to time
    eternal
But to a quality of life,
Experiencing the blessings
    of God,
Growing in the knowledge
    of God,
On a continual, unending
    basis,
Forever.

"And this is eternal life, that they know you, the only true God, and Jesus Christ whom you have sent."

(John 17:3)

Evil

"For from within, out of the heart of man, come evil thoughts, sexual immorality, theft, murder, adultery, coveting, wickedness, deceit, sensuality, envy, slander, pride, foolishness."

(Mark 7:21–22)

Any action, thought, even
    attitude,
Contrary to the character or
    will of God.
An opposition to all God is.
Evil is not the presence of
    something;
Evil is the absence of
    righteousness.
Evil cannot be created because
It does not exist as a created
    entity.
Evil is negative.
Evil is the absence of
    perfection,
The absence of holiness,
The absence of goodness.

Evil became a reality only
    when
Creatures chose to
    disobey God.
It came into existence initially
With Satan and the fall of
    angels

And was repeated in the fall of
    Adam.
How this came to be,
We do not know.

Evil is not God-made,
For everything God created
    was good.
God is light; in Him is no
    darkness at all.
He did not author evil,
Did not bring it into existence.
God is not culpable for it. It is
Impossible, for God is good;
    evil is not.
God is holy; evil is not.

Evil is not even a created thing.
It is not a substance.
It is no entity or being, no force
    or spirit.
Evil is a lack of moral
    perfection.
It is where sin exists.
Evil exists because God's
    creatures
Fall short of His standard of
    perfection.

God uses evil as part of His
    eternal plan.
It brings about the need for
    salvation.
It demonstrates His grace and
    mercy,
Forgiveness and salvation.

Evil is the thing that God
Will forever destroy upon
Completion of redemptive
    history,
When sorrow is no more,
No sadness, no sin, no death—
A final and eternal end
To all woes, all evil.
All these are reasons that
God decreed evil within His
    plan
Without creating it.

All God produces is good.
In scripture, evil is never
    assigned
To God. Ever.
Evil is always assigned
To creatures, never the Creator.
We do know evil exists—
If nowhere else, in us.
It brings great pain,
Great suffering into the world.
Yet it always and ever serves
The ultimate good interest
Of God Himself.

**"Love does not delight in evil but
rejoices with the truth."**

(1 Corinthians 13:6 NIV)

Exalt

**"Exalt the LORD our God and
worship at his footstool; he is
holy."**

(Psalm 99:5)

To lift up, to become higher,
To elevate in rank, honor,
    power,
Character, and quality.
To raise above something
Or someone.

May be applied to both God
    and people.
For humanity, God does the
    exalting.
For if we exalt ourselves,
God humbles us.
If we humble ourselves,
God exalts us.

We exalt God by
Recognizing He is already
Higher than all creation
In terms of glory, greatness.
In light of His exaltedness,
We proclaim His glory,
Proclaiming what is true
About Him.
We obey His commandments.
We love one another.
We exalt God by

Raising our voices to
    praise Him,
By lowering ourselves
    before Him
In worship.

The Father exalted the Son,
Raising Him to His right
    hand,
One in all glory and majesty.
Christ's exaltation means
Our eternity is secure,
For we shall be with Him
In glory.

"Whoever exalts himself will be humbled, and whoever humbles himself will be exalted."

(Matthew 23:12)

Exodus

"Come, I will send you to Pharaoh that you may bring my people, the children of Israel, out of Egypt."

(Exodus 3:10)

Generally, a mass departure of
    people,
Especially emigrants.
Specifically, the departure
Of Israelites from Egypt.
A great redemptive event,
A redemption from slavery.

It is the escape of God's people
From the land of oppression
Into the Promised Land.
It includes the judgment
    of God
Upon Egypt, giving of the law,
And the years of wilderness
    wanderings.

The reformation of the
    Israelites,
Forming them into a nation
Through the establishment
Of the Mosaic Covenant
Between God and Israel—
Where, if Israel is faithful,
God showers blessings and
    protection;
If Israel is unfaithful, then God
    punishes.

This Exodus theme can be
    applied
Throughout redemptive history
Up to the present time.
For we experience our exodus
    from
Sin and its slavery
Through the blood of Jesus
    Christ,
Our Lord and Savior.

Just as God heard the cries
Of the Israelites and rescued
    them,
He still hears our cries

And delivers us from death and
evil.
Exodus reveals a God
Who is faithful and caring,
A God who not only hears us,
But a God who saves us.

**"Then the LORD said to Moses,
'Rise up early in the morning
and present yourself to Pharaoh,
as he goes out to the water, and
say to him, "Thus says the LORD,
Let my people go, that they may
serve me."'"**

(Exodus 8:20)

Faith

**"Now faith is the assurance of
things hoped for, the conviction
of things not seen."**

(Hebrews 11:1)

Trusting in something
That you cannot explicitly
prove.
Faith—the sole instrument by
which
People lay hold of the
righteousness of God.

We acknowledge that a chair
Is made to sit in.

Faith is actually sitting in the
chair—
Elements of both intellectual
assent
And trust.

Composed of three elements:
Knowledge, belief, and trust.
Knowledge: recognition of
The truth claims of the gospel;
Belief: acknowledgment of the
Truthfulness of those claims;
Trust: Personal commitment to
The Lord, Jesus Christ.

Believing alone is not sufficient
for faith,
For even demons believe
in God,
Acknowledging who Jesus is.
Faith requires reliance on
Jesus's atoning sacrifice.
It is "sitting in the chair" of
salvation,
Trusting Jesus for one's
salvation.

Only with faith can we
please God.
Only with faith can we be
saved.
Only with faith can we lead
A Christian life.
Requires the personal reliance
On Christ's death as the one

All-encompassing sacrifice for
our sins.
Saving faith hears, believes,
and responds.
Consists of mental, emotional,
And volitional elements.
It involves both mind and will.

Salvation is by grace through
faith,
And this is not from ourselves;
It is the gift of God, not by our
works.

Faith—a firm, certain,
knowledge
Of God's compassion
toward us;
Founded upon promised
certainties
Given in Christ,
Revealed to our minds,
Sealed upon our hearts
Through the Holy Spirit.

Salvation belongs to the Lord!

**"For God so loved the world, that
he gave his only Son, that whoever
believes in him should not perish
but have eternal life."**

(John 3:16)

Faithfulness

**"But the fruit of the Spirit is love,
joy, peace, patience, kindness,
goodness, faithfulness, gentleness,
self-control; against such things
there is no law."**

(Galatians 5:22–23)

Resoluteness, constancy,
Steadfast adherence,
Undeviating allegiance,
Carefulness in keeping
What we are entrusted with.
God is faithful,
Doing all that He promises.
We are to imitate God
By being faithful to Jesus
Christ.

Faithfulness necessitates belief
In what the Bible says
about God:
His existence, His works, His
character.
It is trusting in God at all
times,
Despite the vagaries of life,
Knowing He will work His
will in us.

Faithfulness is a fruit of the
Holy Spirit
Who testifies to the truth,
Impels us to seek God,

Regardless of wars, famines,
disasters.
Our faithfulness toward God
Grants us great peace,
Assurance of a glorious future
Of blessings and eternal life in
heaven.

Faithfulness is not an option
we choose.
God expects us to be faithful
to Him—
His heart becomes our hearts,
His mind becomes our minds,
His will becomes our will.

Our supreme example of
faithfulness,
Is Jesus Christ,
Having one desire only: to do
God's will.

**"By steadfast love and faithfulness
iniquity is atoned for, and by the
fear of the LORD one turns away
from evil."**

(Proverbs 16:6)

The Fall

**"So when the woman saw that the
tree was good for food, and that it
was a delight to the eyes, and that
the tree was to be desired to make
one wise, she took of its fruit and
ate, and she also gave some to her
husband who was with her, and
he ate."**

(Genesis 3:6)

The fall was initiated
In a decision to disobey.
Caused Adam to fall
From original righteousness,
From communion with God,
To become dead in sin,
Wholly defiled in all
faculties and
All parts of soul and body.

But this fall
Was not restricted to Adam
alone.
This fall is the fall of humanity.
Adam's disobedience brought
a curse
Upon every person yet to be
born.
Now born to walk in a broken
state,
In a broken world—
Now a slave to sin.

This first man, Adam,
A representative of humanity
In federal headship.
As such, Adam stood
At the "head" of all people.
Adam was placed in the garden
To act not only for himself,

But for all his progeny.
Every person ever born
Was already "in Adam,"
Represented by him.

You and I did not eat literally
Of the forbidden fruit,
But, if we had been in the
    garden,
We surely would have savored
    its juices.
God has said that we have
Inherited Adam's sinful nature.
Without a doubt,
His sin imputed to us all.

Yes, Eve ate first,
Being deceived by the serpent.
But Adam, under God's strict
    orders
Not to eat of the fruit, took it
    and ate,
Thereby causing sin and death
To enter our world.

The effect of the fall
Is impossible to overestimate.
Death made its appearance,
Spread to all people.
Once humanity was good;
Now, all are born with a sin
    nature,
A sinful disposition of the
    heart.
Worst of all, the loving
    relationship

Between God and people
Was dramatically altered.
God is no longer
The Father to be loved,
But a judge to be feared.
Because of the fall, humanity
    became
Alienated from God,
Hostile to God,
Enemies of God—
Children of wrath and
    disobedience.
The fall affected all relations,
Everything of nature.

But we have hope,
Through God's Son, Jesus
    Christ.
For the gift of Jesus is greater
Than the trespass of Adam.
Death came through Adam;
Eternal life comes
Through faith in Jesus Christ.
Christ triumphed on the cross
Overcame sin and death.
Rather than being bound to
    the fall,
We can trust in Christ through
    faith,
Having hope to one day be
    raised
To life again with Him.

**"But the free gift is not like the
trespass. For if many died through**

one man's trespass, much more have the grace of God and the free gift by the grace of that one man Jesus Christ abounded for many. And the free gift is not like the result of that one man's sin. For the judgment following one trespass brought condemnation, but the free gift following many trespasses brought justification. For if, because of one man's trespass, death reigned through that one man, much more will those who receive the abundance of grace and the free gift of righteousness reign in life through the one man Jesus Christ."

(Romans 5:15–17)

Fasting

"She did not depart from the temple, worshiping with fasting and prayer night and day."

(Luke 2:37)

Not a commandment or
    requirement,
Yet an act that can be
Good, profitable, beneficial.
It is the act of taking one's eyes
Off the things of this world
To focus solely on God.
It is humbling ourselves

Before God as our true
Sustainer and salvation.

Fasting, voluntarily abstaining
    from
Food or other gifts from God
Performed for many reasons:
To seek God's guidance,
To express grief,
To overcome temptation,
To express repentance,
To minister to the needs of
    others,
To strengthen prayer,
To express love for God.

Fasting is never done alone;
Always to be accompanied by
    prayer.
Prayer is our sustenance
Throughout a fast.
It is imperative to begin a fast
With a contrite heart.

Fasting is not intended as
    punishment,
But to redirect attention
    to God.
The idea is not to lose weight,
But to gain deeper fellowship
    with God.
It is never intended to punish
    the flesh,
But to redirect the soul, spirit,
And mind to God.

It is taking our eyes off this
world
To focus on Christ.
It is never intended to get God
To do what we want;
Fasting changes us, not God.
It is always to be carried out
In a spirit of humility,
And with joy.

Fasting sets you in good
company;
Jesus fasted in the desert.
Moses fasted when receiving
The Ten Commandments.
Esther fasted on behalf of her
people.
Daniel fasted in
Nebuchadnezzar's court,
Paul fasted when choosing
New church leaders.

As you empty yourself
Physically and spiritually
Through fasting,
You open the door for God to
step in,
To do His miraculous work.
We become more sensitive
To the work of the Holy Spirit.
Fasting is a spiritual exercise
That God honors.

**"But when you fast, anoint your
head and wash your face, that
your fasting may not be seen by
others but by your Father who is
in secret. And your Father who
sees in secret will reward you."**

(Matthew 6:17–18)

Fear

**"For God gave us a spirit not of
fear but of power and love and
self-control."**

(2 Timothy 1:7)

Paul speaks here
Not of fear of the Lord,
But of fear of darkness,
Fear of what hides beneath
the bed.
Fear of the Lord is beneficial,
To be encouraged.
This other fear is a detriment
To be overcome.

This spirit of fear
At times is overwhelming.
Fear of the future envelops us.
Fear of being alone,
Fear of being too weak,
Fear of lacking necessities—
We live with a spirit of fear.

This spirit of fear ranges
From mild uneasiness to stark
terror.

It arises from our fallen world.
It preys on our minds,
A hindrance to our lives
And walks with God.

Often used as an excuse
For not moving forward.
Satan does all in his power
To encourage this spirit of fear,
Causing us to doubt
The love of God.
Believing the lies of fear
Becomes an obstacle to
    experiencing
And living out the freedom
Of God's perfect love.

Fears are a fact of life,
But one doesn't have to live in
    fear.
By seeking out the Lord,
He will find you, deliver you
From all such fears.
Confess your fears;
Take them to the Lord.
Trust Him; trust His love
    for us,
Experience His peace—
Not this world's fear.

"I sought the LORD, and he answered me and delivered me from all my fears."

(Psalm 24:4)

Fear of God

"And now, Israel, what does the LORD your God require of you, but to fear the LORD your God, to walk in all his ways, to love him, to serve the LORD your God with all your heart and with all your soul."

(Deuteronomy 10:12)

Luther described two types of
    fear:
Servile and filial.
Servile—the fear felt for a jailer
By his prisoner in a torture
    chamber.
A fear that a slave has at the
    hands
Of a malicious master with a
    whip.
It is a fear toward a malevolent
    owner.
But a filial fear is that which
A child has for his or her father,
A child with tremendous
    respect and love,
Who dearly wants to
    please him.
This fear is anxious not to
    offend
The one he or she loves;
Not afraid of punishment,
    but of

Displeasing the one who is
The source of all security and
love.

Difference depends on whether
one is
A believer or an unbeliever.
For the unbeliever,
Fear of judgment, eternal
death.
For the believer,
Something much different.
It is awe, reverence of God—
A veneration for His power and
glory
Extending to honor and
worship.
It includes respect for His
wrath and anger.
Fear of God is total
acknowledgment
Of all that God is.

Fearing the Lord brings
Untold blessings and benefits:
Teaches a person wisdom,
Enables one to avoid evil,
Brings wealth and honor,
Adds length to life.
God confides in those who
fear Him,
Makes His covenant known to
them,
Has compassion on them,
Delights in them,
And loves them.

Fearing the Lord
Is not a barrier to intimacy;
It opens doors to a closer
Relationship with Him.

**"By steadfast love and faithfulness
iniquity is atoned for, and by the
fear of the LORD one turns away
from evil."**

(Proverbs 16:6)

Feast of Tabernacles

**"You shall keep the Feast of
Booths seven days, when you
have gathered in the produce
from your threshing floor and
your winepress. You shall rejoice
in your feast ... because the LORD
your God will bless you in all
your produce and in all the work
of your hands, so that you will be
altogether joyful."**

(Deuteronomy 16:13–15)

This is the feast of feasts,
Taking place on the
fifteenth day
Of the Hebrew month Tishri,
Usually in late September to
mid-October.
It begins five days after Day of
Atonement;

75

A time of completion of fall
harvest.

An eight-day feast, beginning
And ending with a Sabbath
rest.
All male Jews commanded to
participate.
Mentioned many times in
scripture:
Feast of the Ingathering,
Feast to the Lord,
Feast of Booths—
Israelites were commanded to
dwell
In booths or huts during the
celebration.

Joyous celebration,
Remembrance of God's
deliverance
Of Israel out of Egypt.
Looking forward
To the coming Messiah, Jesus
Christ,
Who would deliver His people
Out of bondage to sin.

Symbolizes restoration,
Demonstrates God's desire
To tabernacle with humanity.

Foreshadows Christ's second
coming
As well as reflects on
His first coming.

For just as God provided for
And protected the Israelites
In the wilderness,
Christ provides for and protects
Christians as they sojourn
Through this world,
Anxiously awaiting arrival
In the Promised Land,
When Jesus returns
To tabernacle among us.

**"On the last day of the feast, the
great day, Jesus stood up and cried
out, 'If anyone thirsts, let him
come to me and drink. Whoever
believes in me, as the Scripture
has said, "Out of his heart will
flow rivers of living water."'"**

(John 7:37–38)

Fig Tree

**"From the fig tree learn its lesson:
as soon as its branch becomes
tender and puts out its leaves, you
know that summer is near."**

(Matthew 24:32)

A popular biblical tree
From Old Testament to New
Testament,
From blessings to curses—

An image of prosperity and
 judgment.
Scripture mentions it fifty plus
 times.

Important for nutritional
As well as economic reasons.
When every man is sitting
 under
His own fig tree—all is well;
Predicts judgment, just speak
Of fig trees being destroyed.

In the garden, Adam and Eve
Covered themselves with fig
 leaves.
Fig trees were among the
 blessed trees
In Canaan. On the road to
 Jerusalem,
Jesus cursed a fig tree.
He spoke of how figs do not
 grow
Upon thorn bushes, for this
 good fruit
Flows from the heart.

Unusual in that its fruit
Appears before its leaves.
Christ had a right to expect
 fruit
When He saw leaves on the
 tree
While traveling to Jerusalem.

A powerful symbol of purpose,
This tree represents so much.
As Christians, we are to
 produce fruit—
Fruit that glorifies God,
Fruit that generates good works
That are pleasing to Christ
 Jesus.

**"And Peter remembered and said
to him, 'Rabbi, look! The fig tree
that you cursed has withered.'
And Jesus answered them, 'Have
faith in God.'"**

(Mark 11:21–22)

Fire and Brimstone

**"On the wicked he will rain
fiery coals and burning sulfur; a
scorching wind will be their lot."**

(Psalm 11:6 NIV)

Idiomatic expression
 referring to
God's wrath, what one finds in
 hell.
Often referring to the fate
Of the unfaithful.
But not mere symbols—
Rather, a description reflecting
The awful truth. For God's
 wrath

Is truly horrific; it is never
    quenching
Fire and brimstone.

God is patient, long-suffering,
Merciful and gracious,
Just and righteous,
Yet He expresses His anger
In furious rebukes,
Devouring those set
    against Him.
On Sodom and Gomorrah
He rained fire and brimstone,
Those cities never to rise again,
In punishment for their grave
    sins.

Fire and brimstone,
All-consuming flames,
Burning rocks, most likely
    sulfur,
Evokes the arid odor of sulfur
    dioxide
Emitted by lightning strikes.
The result: Eternal destruction.

At times, used as an adjective
Referring to a preaching style
Using vivid descriptions of
Judgment, eternal
    damnation, and
A means to encourage
    repentance.

Also denotes the lake of fire
    where Satan,

Along with the ungodly, are
    cast.
A lake afire with brimstone,
A place of eternal punishment.
It is grave, apocalyptic,
    catastrophic.
It is hell.

This enduring metaphor
Demonstrates how seriously
God takes sin.
An emotionally potent picture
Of the deadly result of
    disobedience.
In addition to fire and
    brimstone,
Hell is described as a
    bottomless pit,
Darkness, everlasting torment,
Destruction, and
    punishment—
A place of wailing and
    gnashing of teeth.
A place worse than death,
Darker than darkness,
Deeper than any abyss,
Beyond what any single
    descriptor
Could ever portray.
Yet a powerful one for sure—
Fire and brimstone.

**"But the fearful, and unbelieving,
and the abominable, and
murderers, and whoremongers,**

and sorcerers, and idolaters, and all liars, shall have their part in the lake which burneth with fire and brimstone, which is the second death."

(Revelation 21:8 KJV)

Firmament

"Then God said, 'Let there be a firmament in the midst of the waters, and let it divide the waters from the waters.' Thus God made the firmament, and divided the waters which were under the firmament from the waters which were above the firmament; and it was so."

(Genesis 1:6–7 NKJV)

The vault, the arch of the sky,
Curves of the sky above,
The heavens are above the
earth.
Translation of the Hebrew
word
Simply means "expanse."
Denotes the space or expanse
Appearing immediately
above us.

In creation it formed the
division

Between waters above and
waters below.
On the fourth day of creation,
God set in the firmament the
sun and stars,
Lights to rule by day and night.

The firmament—
A vast expanse created by God,
The space over our heads.

"The heavens declare the glory of God, and the firmament sheweth his handywork."

(Psalm 19:1 KJV)

Firstfruits

"The best of the firstfruits of your ground you shall bring into the house of the LORD your God."

(Exodus 23:19)

Firstfruits are a religious
offering
Of the first produce of the
harvest and
The unblemished newborn of
animals.
Derived from God's work of
creation,
As God created everything that
exists,
All of creation belongs to Him.

Consequently, that which is
first
And best belongs to Him,
To be given to Him.
An instruction in the Old
Testament,
Though not directly applied
To Christians in the New.

Yet still valid as offerings or
tithes.
Christians are to give to the
Lord
Cheerfully and freely,
representing
The firstfruits of our labors
To honor the Lord with our
substance,
To show gratitude for His
blessings,
Acknowledging His sacrifice
On the cross
And glorious resurrection.

The firstfruits offering
Found its fulfillment in Jesus.
His resurrection paved the way
For our resurrections.
It illustrates giving to God
From a grateful heart,
Sets a pattern of giving back
to Him
The first and best
Of what He has given us.
Since Christians are no longer
Under the law,

We are to give from our hearts.
Generously and cheerfully.

**"Honor the LORD with your
wealth and with the first fruits of
all your produce."**

(Proverbs 3:9)

Flesh (Is Weak)

**"Watch and pray that you may not
enter into temptation. The spirit
indeed is willing, but the flesh is
weak."**

(Matthew 26:41)

We all have our flesh.
It does not magically vanish
When we become believers
And are justified by Christ.
Flesh is our old, carnal nature,
That weak-willed person
within.
The flesh has no character,
No resolve, no backbone,
And no self-control.

This flesh of ours—
A slave to impurity,
lustfulness—
Serves the law of sin,
Brings corruption,
Wages war against the soul,
Has nothing good in it.

It is the flesh that desires and
generates
All immorality, idolatry, and
anger.
It is the weak-willed person
Residing inside each of us.

This weakness of the flesh
Is true for us all. We are
So easily distracted
From prayer and worship.
The flesh shouts loudly
When it is wanting.
Its cries drown out
Desires of the spirit.
Even when the spirit is willing
To obey God,
The flesh remains weak.

The antidote to this weakness
Is to walk in the Spirit
Through prayer and staying
alert.
Pray in His name,
According to His will, not
yours,
And you will receive
All that is needed:
The strength to obey, to
worship,
To do what is right and true
According to God's will,
To conquer fleshly desires.

Stay alert at all times—
This is a weapon against

The weakness of the flesh.
God is faithful, supplying all
we need;
He always opens avenues for us
To avoid sins of the flesh.
Be alert for these avenues;
See the temptations coming.
Turn to the Holy Spirit
For strength and wisdom.

Walk in the Spirit,
For when we watch and pray,
Remaining spiritually alert,
Appealing to God for help,
Strength will be supplied
In our time of need
To fight weaknesses of the
flesh.

"For to set the mind on the flesh is death, but to set the mind on the Spirit is life and peace. For the mind that is set on the flesh is hostile to God, for it does not submit to God's law; indeed, it cannot."

(Romans 8:6–7)

Forbearance

"Or do you presume on the riches of his kindness and forbearance and patience, not knowing that

God's kindness is meant to lead you to repentance?"

(Romans 2:4)

A godly character trait,
A holding back, a refraining of
    wrath.
Not the condoning of evil,
But the willingness to restrain
Judgment for a time,
Giving opportunity for
    repentance.

An attribute of God who is
Slow to anger,
Being long-suffering toward
    His people.
Divine forbearance displays
A constant tension between
Present grace and future wrath.
Allows time for repentance
Before final judgment arrives.

Forbearance is not a tolerance
    of sin.
It is not passive. It is a holding
    back,
A restraining action,
Allowing time for righteousness
To emerge before final
    judgment
Is carried out.

God's forbearance pledges
    Christians
To a similar forbearance.

A fruit of the Holy Spirit,
Controlled by a love
That leads to repentance of sin.
A spiritual force originating
In divine glory,
Working itself out in joyful
    endurance.

As children of God,
Made in His image,
We are to imitate Him.
He gave us Christ as our
    example.
Our lives are to magnify His
    life.
We rejoice, always forbear,
Without anxiety,
Being long-suffering,
    patient, and
Dealing with difficult
    circumstances
With gentleness, calmness,
Demonstrating self-control.

"Put on therefore, as the elect of God, holy and beloved, bowels of mercies, kindness, humbleness of mind, meekness, long-suffering; forbearing one another, and forgiving one another, if any man have a quarrel against any; even as Christ forgave you, so also do ye."

(Colossians 3:12–13 KJV)

Foreknowledge

"This Jesus, delivered up according to the definite plan and foreknowledge of God."

(Acts 2:23)

God's knowledge is
    all-encompassing,
Perfect, and unerring.
As God is free from all limits
    of space,
His knowledge is linked
With His omnipresence.
As God is free from all limits
    of time,
His knowledge is linked with
    eternity.

Defined as knowing something
Before it exists or happens,
This foreknowledge infers a
    decree,
For God could not foreknow
The things to be,
Unless he had decreed that
    they should be.
God did not make His choices
Based on merely knowing the
    future;
The future is based solely on
The will of God for His own
    pleasure.
No dependence on people's
    desires

Or efforts;
Solely based on God's divine
    plan,
According to the purpose of
    His will.
All this from before
The foundation of the world.

The decrees of God relate
To all future things, without
    exception.
The decrees of God are free,
For He is sovereign.
The decrees of God are most
    wise,
Made from unerring wisdom.
The decrees of God are eternal,
Ordaining everything
    whatsoever
That comes to pass.
The decrees of God are
Absolute and unconditional.
He has not decreed anything
Because he foresaw it as future.

Foreknowledge is often
    associated
With predestination.
Some believe that because
God foreknew who would
    believe,
He predestined them.
Yet those who would believe,
Believe only through faith.
And the faith that God foresees
Is the faith He Himself creates.

His eternal foreknowledge of
     faith
Is preconditioned by His decree
To generate this faith
In those whom He foresees
As believing.

Foreknowledge describes
An intimate, personal
     relationship.
Before time began, God knew
His elect in a personal way,
Chose them to belong to Him,
Chose them not because
     one day
They would follow Him,
But to guarantee that
They would follow Him.
His knowing and choosing
     them
Is the sole reason they
     follow Him.

"To those who are elect exiles
of the Dispersion in Pontus,
Galatia, Cappadocia, Asia,
and Bithynia, according to the
foreknowledge of God the Father,
in the sanctification of the Spirit,
for obedience to Jesus Christ and
for sprinkling with his blood: May
grace and peace be multiplied
to you."

(1 Peter 1:1–2)

Forgiveness

"And you, who were dead in your
trespasses and the uncircumcision
of your flesh, God made alive
together with him, having forgiven
us all our trespasses, by canceling
the record of debt that stood
against us with its legal demands.
This he set aside, nailing it to the
cross."

(Colossians 2:13–14)

Conscious, deliberate decision
Releasing feelings of
     resentment
And vengeance, toward another
Who has done you wrong.
To wipe the slate clean,
To pardon, cancel a debt.

Integral component of
     justification
Whereby God, in forgiving sin,
Absolves the sinner from
Condemnation of the law,
Past, present, and future.
All on account of the suffering
And death of Jesus Christ.

God removes the guilt of sin,
A sinner's actual liability to
     eternal wrath.
We are freely forgiven by God

Through the offering of
 His Son.

God's forgiveness is forever—
No more guilt,
No more penalty.

Received at the beginning
Of Christian life;
As God offers His forgiveness,
He obliges us to forgive others.

All sin is an affront to God.
Forgiveness is the grace of God,
An act of love, mercy, grace.

Through forgiveness,
We pass from death to life.

"Put on then, as God's chosen ones, holy and beloved, compassionate hearts, kindness, humility, meekness, and patience, bearing with one another and, if one has a complaint against another, forgiving each other; as the Lord has forgiven you, so you also must forgive."

(Colossians 3:12–13)

Fornication

"Ye do the deeds of your father. Then said they to him, We be not born of fornication; we have one Father, even God."

(John 8:41 KJV)

Sexual immorality
Is both spiritually and
 typologically
Different from marital sex,
The one-flesh union of
 marriage.
Fornication is voluntary
Sexual intercourse between
Persons not married to each
 other.
It is different from adultery
But includes adultery.

Most often translated today
As "sexual immorality,"
Fornication includes
All illicit, unlawful sex:
Adultery, homosexuality,
Bestiality, incest, prostitution,
Harlotry, and whoremongering.

A sexual sin
Is forbidden by God.
Refers not only to sexual sin,
But also to idolatry,
Promiscuous behavior,
Indulging in unlawful lust
By either sex or
Engaging in unrighteous
 behaviors
Of anything other than God.

To prevent fornication,
One needs to be
Both proactive and active:
Be *proactive* in studying
    scripture,
Attending church, praying,
Socializing with believers, and
Being accountable to a mentor,
And *active* in being on guard
For situations of temptation,
Not being alone with a
    member
Of the opposite sex,
Avoiding pornography,
Suggestive entertainment, and
Anything that causes us
To think unholy thoughts.
We must fill our lives
With wholesome things
That will lead to a deeper
Relationship with Christ.

**"For this is the will of God, even
your sanctification, that ye should
abstain from fornication."**

(1 Thessalonians 4:3 KJV)

Fortress

**"I will say to the LORD, 'My refuge
and my fortress, my God, in whom
I trust.'"**

(Psalm 91:2)

In times past, separate from the
    city,
Walled off from all else,
Supplied with food,
Water, ammunition, and tools
For protection and defense.

Throughout the Psalms,
David refers to God as his
    fortress.
During his long life,
He faced spiritual battles and
Many physical battles.
Saw firsthand how God
Provides a strong fortress,
An ever-present help
In times of trouble,
Regardless of the attack.
This fortress brought peace to
    the soul
In the midst of chaos.

Building a fortress
Is not accomplished overnight.
Built day by day, brick by
    brick.
Knowing God is also a daily
    process.
We grow in His knowledge
By reading the scriptures,
Meditating on His Word,
Pursuing fellowship with
    others,
Serving His kingdom, and
Obeying His commands.

No moat, no drawbridge,
No wall, and no battlement
Could make us so secure
As when the attributes
Of the Lord of Hosts
Are our fortress,
Surrounding us with
His loving protection.

God, as our fortress,
Not only is our defense
Against worldly troubles,
Freeing us from every misery,
But He is also our offense,
Leading us into victory—
Victory that is assured
By the resurrection of Christ
    Jesus,
Our Lord and Savior.

"The LORD is my rock and my
fortress and my deliverer, my God,
my rock, in whom I take refuge,
my shield, and the horn of my
salvation, my stronghold."

(Psalm 18:2)

Free Will

"But thanks be to God that,
though you used to be slaves to
sin, you have come to obey from
your heart the pattern of teaching
that has now claimed your
allegiance. You have been set free
from sin and have become slaves
to righteousness.""

(Romans 6:17–18)

Two extremes exist:
People are completely free,
    libertinism;
People are merely puppets,
    determinism.
Neither is compatible with
    scripture,
For scripture's position is
One of compatibilism.
A person's freedom
Is compatible with his nature:
Sinful or regenerate, lost or
    saved.
Humanity chooses only in
    accordance with
What its nature allows it to
    choose.
Unbelievers are restricted to
    sinful choices.
Believer's choices will
    acknowledge
God as supreme.

God is sovereign, the Creator
    of all.
Sovereignty indicates control.
Yet within God's sovereignty,
We make real choices,
Choices with full responsibility.
Our free will always operates
Within the boundaries

Of God's sovereignty.
Our free will consists in our
	ability
To choose according to the
Disposition, inclination, bias,
Of our own hearts.

In our unregenerate state,
Our will is disposed toward self
	and sin,
Slaves to sin, ensnared by
	Satan.
Unregenerate people's free
	will—
Freedom to become ever
	greater
Slaves to sin, hence in reality
No free will exists for such
	people,
Who are forever hostile
	to God.

In the regenerated person
Who has accepted Christ
As Lord and Savior,
One's nature becomes
	Christ-focused,
Bringing freedom from love
	of sin.
Sin no longer holds dominion
Over the heart;
This person prefers the love
	of God,
Embracing Christ as
Supremely valuable.
This is the soul with free will,

For the truth has set him or her
	free.

Scripture affirms
God's total sovereignty,
Our responsibility.
Difficult to harmonize,
Impossible to fully understand.
God ordains not only the ends,
But the means as well.
Our free will, one of the means
Through which God
	accomplishes
His own will.

"The heart of man plans his way,
but the LORD establishes his steps."
(Proverbs 16:9)

Fruit of the Spirit

"But the fruit of the Spirit is love,
joy, peace, patience, kindness,
goodness, faithfulness, gentleness,
self-control; against such things
there is no law."
(Galatians 5:22–23)

Nine visible attributes
Of a true Christian life.
Not individual fruits
To pick and choose,
But a ninefold fruit
Characterizing all who

Truly walk in the Holy Spirit.
A physical manifestation
Of a transformed life
Into the image of God.

This fruit, a result
Of the Spirit's presence,
Works in the lives
Of all who accept Christ
As Lord and Savior,
Conforming us to His image,
Making us more like Him
As we mature in our faith.

Yet the fruit of the Spirit
Does not simply drift into
Spiritual maturity or
    excellence.
It demands a yielding of life
To the Spirit's leading
By means of scripture.
It demands an obedience to
God's commandments,
Cooperation with the Spirit
In His work in our lives.

This fruit of the Spirit
Can be described as
An active love for God
And one's neighbor,
Joy in all circumstances,
Maintaining peace and
    harmony
Among others,
Patience and long-suffering
Toward all persons,

Kindness toward all others,
Goodness that seeks to love
    others,
Faithfulness in one's
    relationships
With God and people,
Gentleness and meekness
In accepting God's will and
In dealing with others,
And the ability to keep oneself
Under control in all
    circumstances.

The fruit of the Spirit
Exhibits the reality of God's
    promise
Of a new nature and new
    identity
In Christ.

**"Thus you will recognize them by
their fruits."**

(Matthew 7:20)

Generosity

**"They are to do good, to be rich
in good works, to be generous and
ready to share, thus storing up
treasure for themselves as a good
foundation for the future, so that**

they may take hold of that which is truly life."

(1 Timothy 6:18–19)

An act of the heart,
An act of love.
Obeying the Lord by
Loving your neighbor.
Not only giving what you are
 able,
But giving beyond ability.

Not restricted to money, food,
 clothes;
Also includes giving of oneself.
Generosity is the quality of
 being
Kind, unselfish, and loving.
By giving your love to the
 Lord,
You give unto others.
God is generous;
We are to follow His example.

Scripture teaches the principle
That those who are generous
Will find favor.
God remembers and rewards
 generosity
In this life or the next.

Giving is manifested in many
 ways:
Time, resources,
Hospitality, and friendship.
We are to give to all,

Not just to friends, but
 strangers also—
Even to our enemies.
Repayment in kind is not to be
 expected;
Our rewards come from the
 Lord.

Truly being generous
Reflects an act of faith
In God's promise
To provide for our needs.
Remember the poor widow
 who gave
Her two small copper coins?
She put more into the treasury
Than the large sums of money,
For she put in her heart.

Generosity is a lifestyle—
Sharing all that we have,
All that we are, or will ever
 become.
It is a demonstration of God's
 love,
A response to God's grace.
It flows from the
 understanding
That all we have is not ours to
 possess;
What we possess has been
 given
For the advancement of the
 kingdom
For the glory of God.

Generosity embraces
    stewardship—
Where God is the owner of all,
All that we possess and are.
What we have has been given
    by God.
It is confessing that Jesus is
    Lord
Over all our money,
    possessions,
Talents—all that we have
    and are.
Give from your heart,
For God loves a cheerful giver.

"The point is this: whoever sows sparingly will also reap sparingly, and whoever sows bountifully will also reap bountifully. Each one must give as he has decided in his heart, not reluctantly or under compulsion, for God loves a cheerful giver. And God is able to make all grace abound to you, so that having all sufficiency in all things at all times, you may abound in every good work."

(2 Corinthians 9:6–8)

Genesis

"In the beginning, God created the heavens and the earth."

(Genesis 1:1)

The Greek title for the Bible's
    first book.
Root meaning: "to be,"
Or "begin to be."
The Hebrews titled it simply,
"In the beginning,"
The first words of this book.

Genesis unfolds the record
Of the beginning of the world,
Of human history,
Of family,
Of civilization, and
Of salvation.
It is the story of God's purpose
And plan for His creation.
It takes us from the creation of
    the world
And of human beings in
    paradise,
To their fall and on to the great
    flood,
On to the time of the
    patriarchs,
And on through the beginning
Of Israel's sojourn in Egypt.

Genesis sets the stage
For the entire Bible,

Revealing God's nature as
Creator, sustainer, judge, and
    redeemer.
Discloses the value and dignity
Of human beings,
The tragedy and consequences
    of sin,
And the promise and assurance
    of salvation.

Written by Moses, possibly in
    Midian
Or in the wilderness, around
    1400 BC,
Written as a great
    encouragement
To Israel, showing them
How great their God is—
The God who began with His
    people
Safe in Eden, and who now
    leads
His people to safety
In the Promised Land.
As such, a comfort to the
    church today.
For just as Israel was
    wandering,
So too the church is sojourning
As aliens in this present world,
Waiting for Christ to come
To usher us across the Jordan
    River
Into the greater Canaan.

"So God created man in his own
image, in the image of God he
created him; male and female he
created them."

(Genesis 1:27)

Gentleness

"Let your gentleness be evident to
all. The Lord is near."

(Philippians 4:5 TNIV)

This is a fruit of the Spirit,
One that is like waters of a
    stream,
Like wine flowing over one's
    lips.
Only as the result of the work
Of the Holy Spirit in our lives
May we possess such a
    powerful trait.

Never as a weakness,
For it takes strength to be
    gentle;
Requires humility and grace.
Stands in contrast to baseness,
Harshness, and wildness.

While closely related to
    meekness,
Gentleness does not mean
    docility.

Involves humility and
thankfulness
Toward God,
Polite, restrained behavior
Toward others.
Nothing is as strong as
gentleness;
Nothing is so gentle as true
strength.

This gentleness doesn't mean
acting
In a tender and soft way,
Or even controlling physical
strength
For the benefit of another.
Rather, it is to have a humble
heart and
Peaceful mind,
Submitting wholly to God.

Akin to wisdom and spiritual
growth,
An important ingredient for
repentance,
A gentle heart accepts God's
wisdom
And yields to His discernment.
It is more than just a
personality.
Gentleness shows who we are
From the Spirit's work
within us.

"But in your hearts honor Christ
the Lord as holy, always being
prepared to make a defense to
anyone who asks you for a reason
for the hope that is in you; yet do
it with gentleness and respect."

(1 Peter 3:15)

Glorification

"And those whom he predestined
he also called, and those whom
he called he also justified, and
those whom he justified he also
glorified."

(Romans 8:30)

Ultimate perfection of
believers.
Occurs at Christ's second
coming,
Accompanied by the
resurrection
Of believers,
And the day of judgment.
Its duration is eternal.
It is the work of God.

The final step of the Christian
process.
Justification: being made right
With God;
Sanctification: the ongoing
process

Of being made holy,
Being made in the image
Of Christ Jesus;
Glorification: the final removal
of sin.

Glorification is the
completeness
Of our sanctification as
believers,
Of our moral perfection,
In which we are
Made holy and blameless.

The body is a participant
In glorification
As it becomes immortal,
imperishable,
Powerful, and spiritual.
A day of great victory—
For then our last enemy,
Death itself, will be destroyed.
Glorification is the future and
final
Work of God on Christians,
In which our mortal bodies
Are transformed to eternal
bodies
Wherein we will dwell forever.

"And we all, with unveiled face, beholding the glory of the Lord, are being transformed into the same image from one degree of glory to another. For this comes from the Lord who is the Spirit."

(2 Corinthians 3:18)

Glory

"So, whether you eat or drink, or whatever you do, do all to the glory of God."

(1 Corinthians 10:31)

Beauty, majesty, splendor.
Often focusing on size, rarity,
beauty,
Adornment, wealth, power—
External characteristics
That attract attention,
Such as the temple Solomon
builds:
"A house of fame and of glory."
Or a reference to heavenly
bodies
Or to ornateness of expensive
clothing.

Most significant is the glory
of God.
Chiefly His possession,
His characteristic,
His distinctive quality,
His glory is the external
Manifestation of His being,
The manifestation of His
holiness.

94

It appears, is revealed, and can
be seen,
Yet is more than solely external.
God's glory existed
Before the world was created
For God is glory.
It is His quality of perfection
That cannot be improved upon
Or imitated or surpassed.
It determines all that He is.
This glory is the infinite
beauty and
Greatness of all His
perfections.

As a verb,
Glorify reflects "giving
weight to,
Honor and praise,"
Recognizing God's essential
nature,
And recognizing His
righteousness
And justice.

Glory to God in the highest!

"By this my Father is glorified, that you bear much fruit and so prove to be my disciples."

(John 15:8)

God

"God said to Moses, 'I AM WHO I AM.'"

(Exodus 3:14)

A self-existent being,
The first cause of everything
else.
God is necessary;
His nonexistence is impossible.
All other things are contingent
beings,
They exist only because
of God.
God is a personal, purposeful
being
With a will; He creates and
direct events
To suit Him.
A triune being, one but three.
Mystery of mysteries:
Father, Son, and Holy Spirit.
God is a loving being,
For He is love itself.

Only God is able to say,
"I AM WHO I AM."
He is pure existence,
Infinite in being and
perfection,
Self-existent, without origin,
Source of everything
That possesses existence.
God is unchangeable, eternal.

God is holy,
Complete and infinite
    perfection.

Comprehending fully
What or who God is—
A task too great
For our limited minds.
God is unique, without
    comparison.
Words fall short of capturing
God's full identity, for words
Can never describe God
    adequately.
Yet God reveals Himself
Sufficiently for His people
In scripture, in creation.

The Westminster Shorter
    Catechism says:
"God is a Spirit,
Infinite, eternal, and
    unchangeable
In his being, wisdom, power,
Holiness, justice, goodness,
    and truth."
We are created in His likeness;
Therefore, God is all we will
    ever need.

**"This is the message we have heard
from him and proclaim to you,
that God is light, and in him is no
darkness at all."**

(1 John 1:5)

Godhead

**"For in him dwelleth all the
fulness of the Godhead bodily."**

(Colossians 2:9 KJV)

A Greek term signifying
    "divinity"
Or "deity," A reference to
    God's
Divine nature, His divine
    essence,
His limitless power and
    wisdom.

A term revealing that the
Divine essence is shared by
Three distinct personalities:
Father, Son, and Holy Spirit.
The three functioning
In absolute divine unity,
Each sharing the identical
Divine nature.
Three in one, one in three.
One God, the Godhead.

The trinity leads to the
    Godhead;
The Godhead leads to the
    trinity.
Three persons, one essence.
Divine essence subsisting
Wholly and indivisibly,
Simultaneously, eternally,

In the three members of one
Godhead.
Foundational to the Christian
faith.

The Godhead—
The Father, the Son, and the
Holy Spirit—
One God, the same in
substance,
Equal in power and glory,
Divine.

**"For the invisible things of him
from the creation of the world are
clearly seen, being understood by
the things that are made, even his
eternal power and Godhead; so
that they are without excuse."**

(Romans 1:20 KJV)

(See also **Trinity.**)

Golden Rule

**"So whatever you wish that
others would do to you, do also to
them, for this is the Law and the
Prophets."**

(Matthew 7:12)

Term not explicitly found in
scripture,

Yet refers to direct words of
Jesus.
Addresses interpersonal
relationships,
Yet its message is essentially
theological.
In this rule, God's very
character
Prescribes how we should relate
To one another.
This golden rule encompasses
The empathic essence of
morality.

A simple-yet-powerful means
Of saying that we should
recognize
The respective dignity
Of our fellow humans,
Never forgetting that we all are
capable
Of inflicting immoral actions.
Vital in following the
Commandments of God,
Creating a more virtuous
world.

When Jesus spoke this golden
rule,
He knew the human heart,
Its selfishness.
This rule gives us a standard
By which naturally selfish
people
Can evaluate their actions,
And actively treat others

The way they themselves
Desire to be treated.

Obeying this golden rule,
This Christian imperative
To love others—
To treat others as we
Would like to be treated—
Is a mark of a true Christian.
Impossible to love God
If we do not love one another.
For if anyone says he or she
    loves God
But hates his or her brother,
That person is a liar.

Simple words we like to hear
But difficult to put into action.
We all too often fail,
No matter how hard we try—
Fail to treat others in the way
We ourselves wish to be
    treated.
By our own selfishness,
We fail to see the needs of
    others.
We think only of our own
    needs,
Not the needs of those
    around us.
We desire to do what is good
But cannot carry it out.
Our sins have made us weak,
Unable to do what is right.
For that reason, we need
    Christ and

The strength and wisdom
That come only from Him.

We can then, and only then,
Obey this golden rule,
Treating others as we ourselves
Wish to be treated.

"You shall not take vengeance or bear a grudge against the sons of your own people, but you shall love your neighbor as yourself: I am the LORD."

(Leviticus 19:18)

Goodness

"Surely goodness and mercy shall follow me all the days of my life, and I shall dwell in the house of the LORD forever."

(Psalm 23:6)

A wonderful word,
One that loves company.
For it is never by itself,
But surrounded by close
    friends.
Love, joy, peace, patience,
Kindness, faithfulness,
    gentleness—
Oh, it does love a crowd!

Goodness carries a great
weight,
Shouldering much
responsibility.
This trait is no passive quality
But a deliberate preference of
Right over wrong. Goodness is
virtue,
Holiness in action.

The Greek definition of
goodness:
Uprightness of heart and life.
Expressions of goodness
include
Giving to the poor, visiting the
sick,
Praying for another, loving the
unloved,
As well as confronting a sinner.

One does not possess goodness;
Goodness possesses one's heart.
Yes, it is a beautiful gift
from God.
May its light engulf you.

"For this very reason, make every effort to add to your faith goodness; and to goodness, knowledge; and to knowledge, self-control; and to self-control, perseverance; and to perseverance, godliness; and to godliness, mutual affection; and to mutual affection, love."

(2 Peter 1:5–7)

Gospel

"For I delivered to you as of first importance what I also received: that Christ died for our sins in accordance with the Scriptures, that he was buried, that he was raised on the third day in accordance with the Scriptures."

(1 Corinthians 15:3–4)

Literally, "glad tidings, good
news."
Broadly speaking: the whole of
scripture.
Narrowly: the good news
concerning
Christ and the way of salvation.
The gospel is a divine message,
Not a man-made invention.

The gospel is of first
importance.
It proclaims the crucifixion
And resurrection of Christ.
It is accompanied by proofs:
Christ died; He rose from the
dead.
All that the gospel contains is
According to scripture.

The Bible's theme is the
salvation
Of humanity through Christ.
The Bible is the gospel.

The gospel is the good news
That God loves the world
enough
To give His only Son to die for
our sins.

The gospel is good news
When we grasp the fact
That we cannot earn our
salvation,
And that all work was
accomplished
On the cross.

The gospel is good news
That we, once enemies of God,
Have been reconciled
By the blood of Christ.

The gospel is good news
That there is now
No condemnation for those
Who are in Christ Jesus.

The gospel is good news
That Christ offers salvation
As a free gift
Received by faith alone.

The gospel is true, gracious,
and glorious.
It evokes hope

In the people of God.

God created humans for His
glory.
All people should live for God's
glory.
Yet we have sinned,
Fallen short of God's glory,
Deserving of eternal
punishment.
God sent His only Son, Jesus
Christ,
That whoever believes in Him
Should not perish but have
eternal life.
Eternal life is a free gift to
all who
Trust Christ as Lord and
Savior.

"For God so loved the world, that he gave his only begotten Son, that whosoever believeth in him should not perish, but have everlasting life."

(John 3:16)

Great Commission

"Go therefore and make disciples of all nations, baptizing them in the name of the Father and of the Son and of the Holy Spirit, teaching them to observe all that

I have commanded you. And behold, I am with you always, to the end of the age."

(Matthew 28:19–20)

Command given by Jesus
Shortly before He ascended
     into heaven,
Describes what He expects
To be done in His absence
By the apostles and all who
     follow Him.
Last recorded instruction
Given by Jesus to His disciples.

The command: Make disciples.
How? By going into the world,
By baptizing them, and
By teaching them
All that Jesus commanded.
Making disciples is the main
     focus.
Going, baptizing, and
     teaching,
Are the means to fulfill the
     command
To make disciples.

This great commission
Is a Christian obligation.
It inspires missionary activities
In many Christian
     denominations.
Not an option to be considered
But a command to be obeyed
By all Christians.

Jesus gives Christians
The assured comfort
That in faith, He will
     accompany and
Support us to the end of
     the age.
This commission is a personal
     calling,
Urging every Christian to
     step out
In faith to spread the gospel.
It is faith in action.
It is life changing.

"But you will receive power when the Holy Spirit has come upon you, and you will be my witnesses in Jerusalem and in all Judea and Samaria, and to the end of the earth."

(Acts 1:8)

Green Pastures

"He makes me lie down in green pastures. He leads me beside still waters."

(Psalm 23:2)

A place for us to rest
Under the shepherd's
     watchful eye.
A place where He offers

His peace and contentment
To those who seek it.
A place secure from all dangers,
Safely under His watch.
A place for breathing deeply,
Surrounded by calmness.

Still waters, almost motionless,
A place to refresh
Amid confusion.
Water, pure, clean, and
    refreshing,
Satisfying our thirst.

The Lord brings us on His path
For His name's sake,
For His glory.
We are blessed through His
    grace,
Which supplies our daily
    needs,
Offers us peace and rest,
And restores our souls.

Freshness of the meadow,
Coolness of the stream—
Images of total contentment.
Consolations of God and
Joys of the Holy Spirit.
Green pastures, still waters—
Both are within reach
Of all who seek the Lord.

"For the Lamb in the midst of the throne will be their shepherd, and he will guide them to springs of living water, and God will wipe away every tear from their eyes."

(Revelation 7:17)

Hallowed

"Pray then like this: 'Our Father in heaven, hallowed be your name.'"

(Matthew 6:9)

As an adjective: "holy,
    sanctified";
As a verb: "to consecrate,
To sanctify, to make holy."
A point to note in the Lord's
    prayer:
A petition or request, not a
    declaration.
A request to God that His
    name
Be hallowed. To hallow God's
    name
Is to sanctify God,
To treat Him as holy.

To hallow God is to
    believe Him,
Trust His promises and His
    Word.
It is to revere God to such a
    high degree
That losing Him is worse
Than losing anything else.

Harmony

It is obeying His
    commandments,
Not profaning His orders.
It is glorifying His name
In all we say and do.

To hallow is to separate,
To raise above all else,
To make distinct from earthly
Purposes and employments.
We hallow God with our lips,
In our thoughts, in our lives,
In our families, in our callings.
It is impossible to hallow God
In one area but not another.

By hallowing God,
We recognize His nature
As distinct and holy from us.
Hallowing God leads us
Into a closer walk with Him,
Our Creator.
Hallowing God develops
Holiness in ourselves,
Mirroring the nature
Of the God we worship.

"And you shall not profane my holy name, that I may be sanctified among the people of Israel. I am the LORD who sanctifies you."

    (Leviticus 22:32)

"And above all these put on love, which binds everything together in perfect harmony."

    (Colossians 3:14)

Apart from God's
    empowerment,
Christian harmony is
    impossible.
It represents the attitude of
Loving others as yourself.

Harmony involves being
Of the same mind with others,
Having our minds geared
    together
Toward Christian love,
Seeking the highest good
In one another.

Harmony involves
Having the same love,
A love that yields
For the sake of others.

Harmony involves
Unity in spirit.
It is not outward, but of the
    heart.
It is being one with others
Who truly know Christ.

Harmony involves
Intent on one purpose,
Being single-minded on one
    thing:
The faith of the gospel,
The exaltation of Jesus,
Honoring His Word of truth.

Harmony is the reflection
Of the holy trinity,
Of the unity and diversity
Characterizing God's very
    existence.
It is imaging fully
The truth of our Lord.
It is giving all glory to God.

"May the God of endurance and encouragement grant you to live in such harmony with one another, in accord with Christ Jesus."

(Romans 15:5)

Heal

"He himself bore our sins in his body on the tree, that we might die to sin and live to righteousness. By his wounds you have been healed."

(1 Peter 2:24)

To make whole, well.
The restoration to physical
    health

But also (and especially)
    spiritual health,
Restoration of the soul.
Yes, healing may refer to
Sickness and disease,
But what concerns us
Is sin and righteousness,
Forgiveness and salvation—
The healing that comes only
Through faith in Christ Jesus.

Ultimately, full physical
    healing
Awaits us in heaven, where
There will be no more
Pain, sickness, or disease,
And no more suffering or
    death.
But we are to be less concerned
With pain, sickness, and
    suffering,
And be more concerned
With our spiritual health,
Our condemnation due to sin,
Our relationship with
Our Lord and Savior.
Only through Him can we be
    truly
Healed for eternity.

He alone will
Wipe away every tear.
He alone will end
Death, mourning, crying.
Sin is a disease,
A natural, hereditary one,

An epidemic infecting all
people.
It reaches all our faculties,
Touches our very souls.
It is nauseous, loathsome;
It is mortal,
Yet it is curable.
Not by people, and not by
medicine,
But only by Christ.
He is the only physician;
His blood is the balm,
The sovereign medicine
That heals us from sin,
For the forgiveness
Of our iniquities.

Our faith is the means of
restoration.
As Jesus repeated,
"Your faith has made you well."
Yet this faith is ultimately a gift
from God.
Healing is contingent upon
one's faith,
But more so upon the healer,
The one who prescribes the
cure:
Belief and repentance.

**"Heal me, O LORD, and I shall
be healed; save me, and I shall be
saved, for you are my praise."**

(Jeremiah 17:14)

Heart of Flesh

**"And I will give them one heart,
and a new spirit I will put within
them. I will remove the heart of
stone from their flesh and give
them a heart of flesh."**

(Ezekiel 11:19)

That part of the body that
Controls the will and emotions,
The inner person, one's soul.
The heart, created to mirror
God's own heart, to love Him
And love righteousness,
To walk in harmony with Him,
Seeking Him in all things.

Yet at the fall in Eden,
Humanity's heart hardened,
Turned to stone,
Refused to follow God—
No repenting, no seeking
of God.
This heart of stone is
Deceitful above all things
And beyond self-cure.

God's desire is for people
To be the image of His Son.
Impossible with a heart of
stone;
Possible only with a heart of
flesh,

Which the power of the Holy
    Spirit
Gives us upon salvation,
    justification.
Changing our hearts
From sin-focused to
    God-focused—
Hearts of flesh, not of stone.

Only by receiving Jesus Christ
As Lord and Savior
Do we have access to the power
Of God, a power that
    transforms
Our hearts from stone to flesh.
From hearts hardened by sin,
Destitute of spiritual life,
Stubborn, inflexible,
    impenitent,
To hearts submissive to God's
    will,
Sensible of sin, penitent,
Overflowing with spiritual
    life—
A heart walking in God's
    statutes.

A person's heart is not only
The center of spiritual activity,
But also the seat of the
    conscience.
What is in the heart flows out
To the whole life and character.
The knowledge of good and
    evil
Captured the heart of humans,

For not only do we know
Good and evil,
We love them both.

We must pray humbly,
Calling upon our Creator,
Not just for forgiveness of our
    sins
But also for renewed hearts,
For hearts of flesh
That only He can give.

"And Peter said to them, 'Repent and be baptized every one of you in the name of Jesus Christ for the forgiveness of your sins, and you will receive the gift of the Holy Spirit.'"

(Acts 2:38)

Heaven

"I tell you, many will come from east and west and recline at table with Abraham, Isaac, and Jacob in the kingdom of heaven."

(Matthew 8:11)

When combined with earth,
"heaven and earth"
Signifies the whole universe.
When used in the plural,
"The heavens"

Refers to the firmament in
     which
The sun, moon, and stars are
     fixed.
But when we use the term
As God's abode,
Indicates eternal paradise.

In heaven, God makes all
     things right
In relation to Himself.
It is where God is truly God,
Where Christ's work on the
     cross
Is forever celebrated,
Where our lives will be
     intoxicated
With divinely intended joys,
Where death and evil are never
     threats,
Where we shall live in the
     joys of
Love, justice, and peace.

Heaven exists for us because
Christ was raised from the
     dead
And now sits at God's right
     hand;
Because God is a faithful God
Who promised us a heaven,
With his covenant to Abraham.
Because God is a just God,
There is both a heaven and a
     hell;
The Bible says they both exist.

Physical heaven is this paradise
Where His name is revered,
His kingdom reigns, and His
     will is done.
To our human minds,
Heaven is everywhere God is.
Presently a nonphysical,
     unobservable,
Existing outside our time and
     space.
But at the second coming of
     Christ,
This heavenly realm will
     transition
Into a final state that includes
A new heaven, a new earth,
And a new heavenly city
Where God and His faithful
     ones
Will dwell forevermore.

**"But according to his promise we
are waiting for new heavens and a
new earth in which righteousness
dwells."**

(2 Peter 3:13)

Heir

**"But in these last days he has
spoken to us by his Son, whom he
appointed the heir of all things,**

through whom also he created the world."

(Hebrews 1:2)

As Christ is the "firstborn"
He holds the birthright
As heir of all the Father has,
All of creation, including
    believers
Who are coheirs with Him.

Historically, an heir was
The firstborn of a father,
Receiving a larger portion
Than his brothers.
Detailed in Mosaic law,
A matter of right, not favor.
Notable exceptions during
    history include
Jacob and Esau, and
Reuben and Joseph.

Believers who have received
The Spirit of adoption as
    children
Cry out, "Abba, Father."
As His children, we become
    His heirs,
Coheirs with Christ,
Sharing an inheritance so great
It makes all present suffering
Not worthy to be compared
    with
The glory to be revealed to us.
An inheritance where no tears,
No pain, and no death exist;

All is made new, dwelling
    with God
For eternity.

This inheritance can never
Perish, spoil, or fade.
Our gift in Christ is not
    subject
To corruption or decay.
This inheritance is free from
Deform, defect, and flaw.
It is holy, blameless, and pure.
It endures for eternity,
Never diminishing.
And it is being kept in heaven
    for us.
Our crowns of glory have
Our names on them,
Guarded by the Almighty
    Himself.
For we are His heirs.

"According to his great mercy, he has caused us to be born again to a living hope through the resurrection of Jesus Christ from the dead, to an inheritance that is imperishable, undefiled, and unfading."

(1 Peter 1:3–4)

Hell

"They will suffer the punishment of eternal destruction, away from the presence of the Lord and from the glory of his might."

(2 Thessalonians 1:9)

The imagination of the worst
    of all
Possible suffering here and now
Is no comparison to the
    dreadful
Reality of hell.
Make no mistake, hell is real.
No human experience in this
    world
Is comparable to eternal hell.

Biblical descriptions of hell
    include:
A place of outer darkness, a
    lake of fire,
A place of weeping and
    gnashing of teeth,
A prison, a place of torment,
Eternal punishment, and
The blackness of darkness
    forever.

A repugnant idea to our
    sensitive minds,
Try as we might to minimize it,
Teachings about hell come
From the lips of Jesus.

It is the doctrine of hell that
    can strain
A Christian's loyalty
To the teachings of Jesus.

Common definition of hell:
"Eternal separation from God."
But in hell, there is no
    separation;
God will be present in the
    fullness
Of His divine wrath,
Exercising His just punishment
Of the damned for eternity—
An eternity before the
    righteous,
Ever-burning wrath of God.

The most terrifying aspect of
    this torment:
The eternity of it. Jesus
    describes it as
Everlasting punishment,
Everlasting fire,
Fire that will never be
    quenched,
The worm that never dies—
Torment day and night,
    forever.

Hell is the vindication of God's
    justice.
It is the tragedy of human
    rebellion.
Hell represents the danger of

Living life for self instead of for
  Christ.
In scripture, hell is seen
As something human beings
  choose—
Choosing self over Christ.
Just as heaven is the natural
Consequence of
  God-centeredness,
Hell is the natural consequence
Of self-centeredness.

Hell is important to
  understand
Because Jesus taught about it.
This doctrine tests our reliance
  on God,
Because it shows the dangers
Of living for self;
It also shows how much Jesus
  loved us and
What He did for us.
Because of the reality of hell,
Jesus's proclamations of grace
  and love
Are ever so astounding.

**"And do not fear those who kill
the body but cannot kill the soul.
Rather fear him who can destroy
both soul and body in hell."**

(Matthew 10:28)

Holy Spirit

**"But the Helper, the Holy Spirit,
whom the Father will send in my
name, he will teach you all things
and bring to your remembrance
all that I have said to you."**

(John 14:26)

The Father, Son, and Holy
  Spirit.
Who is this Holy Spirit?
Member of the triune God for
  sure.
But not the Father or the Son.
Unseen, yet everywhere—
Outside us, inside us.

In the Bible's original
  languages,
Spirit is "breath" or "wind"—
Unseen life-giving force.
Unite "Holy" to it, it becomes
  divine.
It is a heavenly breath.

Not a mystical force or
  impersonal power,
But God Himself.
The Holy Spirit is a divine
  person,
With a mind, emotions, and a
  will.
Ananias lied to the Holy
  Spirit, was

Convicted of lying to God.

Introduced to us in Genesis,
A participant in creation.
In the vision of the valley,
Breathed life into dry bones.
In the book of Revelation,
It is a breath of life.

The Holy Spirit holds many
    titles:
Author of scripture,
Comforter, counselor,
Advocate, convicter of sin,
Intercessor, Spirit of truth and
    life,
Witness, indweller of believers,
Guide, teacher—
All denoting His loving power,
All aspects of His ministry.

Jesus witnessed to the Spirit,
Referred to as the *Paraclete*—
Signifying "counselor,
    comforter,"
Promising the Spirit of God
Would dwell within believers,
Enabling them to carry on
Without Christ's physical
    presence
On earth.

Only the Holy Spirit enables us
To be reborn in faith,
To confess the lordship of
    Christ,

Have victory over sin,
Gain spiritual wisdom,
And be glorified at our
    resurrections.

God pours out His Spirit on
    believers.
Our bodies are to be temples
Where the Spirit resides.
Causes us to seek our heavenly
    Father,
Meditating, believing, obeying,
And thirsting for Him.

He opens our spiritually blind
    eyes
To see the truth,
Opens our deaf ears
To hear God's voice,
Softens our hearts of stone
To receive the gospel,
Activates our dead wills
To believe God's message,
Overcomes all resistance,
Triumphs in the hearts of the
    elect,
And enables us to apply the
    will
And purposes of God.

The fruit of the Spirit is so
    delicious:
Love, joy, peace, patience,
Kindness, goodness,
    faithfulness,
Gentleness, and self-control.

Against these, no law exists.
Live life through the Holy
    Spirit.

**"May the God of hope fill you with
all joy and peace in believing, so
that by the power of the Holy
Spirit you may abound in hope."**

(Romans 15:13)

Hope

**"For I know the plans I have for
you, declares the LORD, plans for
welfare and not for evil, to give
you a future and a hope."**

(Jeremiah 29:11)

What the world lives upon—
Invisible, yet sustaining all.
Without hope, we have despair.
With hope, a glorious future.

Unable to grasp our hope,
Yet always straining to
    obtain it,
Knowing it must be there—
For hope to flourish,
We must have faith.

Character produces hope.
Hope springs from confidence;
Expectation gives it life,
Conviction waters it.

Not merely a desire.
Unseen but real.
The plowman plows in hope,
Mothers birth children in
    hope.

Our hope, promised by the
    Father
Before the ages began—
Hope through His grace,
A living hope through His Son.

Our faith is assurance of things
    hoped for,
Conviction of things unseen;
Our hope is laid up for us in
    heaven.

Rejoice in hope, live in hope—
For a Christian's hope
Is assured hope.

**"But those who hope in the LORD
will renew their strength. They
will soar on wings like eagles; they
will run and not grow weary, they
will walk and not be faint."**

(Isaiah 40:31 NIV)

Humility

**"But he gives more grace.
Therefore it says, 'God opposes**

the proud, but gives grace to the humble.'"

(James 4:6)

Humility, grounded in the
Character of God.
The Father stoops down
To help the poor and the
needy.
The Son exhibits humility
From the manger to the cross.

Proverbs sums up humility's
meaning:
Trust in the Lord with all your
heart,
Deceive not yourself with
vanity or lust.
It is trusting God
To show us the righteous path,
Through prayer, meditation,
and fasting.
It requires us to open our
hearts and
Withdraw the arrogance of our
egos.

Humility is the fear of the
Lord,
Recognizing the magnificent
Power of God.
It is doing nothing out of
Vain pursuit or selfish
ambition.
It is valuing others above
yourself,

Looking to their interests,
Not your own.
Humility is the opposite
Of arrogance, boastfulness,
and vanity.

By humility we acknowledge
That God created us for His
purposes,
Not for our own
self-glorification.
By humility, we acknowledge
The dignity of God's people.
By humility, we turn
Enemies into friends.

Jesus was not ashamed
To humble Himself as a
servant,
Even to death on the cross.
In His humility,
He was obedient to the Father.
As such, the Christian should
Be willing to put aside
All selfishness,
And submit in obedience
To God and His Word.
True humility produces
Godliness, contentment, and
security.

The humble person submits to
God's will.
The person repents of his or her
sins,

Refuses to speak evil of
neighbors,
Declines to boast of
achievements.
The humble person recognizes
That his or her every failure to
do good
Is a sin against God.

We must confess,
Put away all pride.
If we exalt ourselves,
We place ourselves
In opposition to God,
Where God, in His grace,
Will humble us.
If we humble ourselves,
God will exalt us.

"Put on then, as God's chosen ones, holy and beloved, compassionate hearts, kindness, humility, meekness, and patience."

(Colossians 3:12)

Hunger for Righteousness

"Blessed are those who hunger and thirst for righteousness, for they will be filled."

(Matthew 5:6)

An expression of vehement
desire,
A search for relief from sin
Occurs when a sinner turns
To Christ by faith.
Continues as a longing
Perpetuated in the heart
Of every saved sinner
Until his or her dying day.

It is to possess an active
Spiritual longing for God.
Never passive, but
A fervent hunger,
Always seeking for
righteousness.

A panting after God
In the renewed heart. A
yearning
For a closer walk with Him.
A longing for a more perfect
Conformity to the image of
Christ.

When God creates such a
hunger
In our souls, it is so that
He may satisfy it.
One who hungers for
righteousness
Will be filled with the Spirit,
With the peace of God
That passes all understanding.

"But seek first his kingdom and his righteousness, and all these things will be given to you as well."

(Matthew 6:33)

Idolatry

"You shall have no other gods before me. You shall not make for yourself an idol in the form of anything in heaven above or on the earth beneath or in the waters below."

(Exodus 20:3–4 NIV)

Worship or excessive devotion
To some person or thing.
In Christianity, an idol is
    anything
That replaces our one
    true God.
It is divine honor paid to
Any created object
Instead of the Creator.

Scripture links idolatry
With covetousness.
When wanting something so
    much
That we covet it, it becomes an
    idol.
We seek it rather than God.

It controls our desires and our
    time;
It becomes life's purpose.

Historically, idols consisted of
Carved images and statutes
Made of mere wood or stone.
These stirred up God's wrath.
Continues today in our fallen
    state,
But now we have expanded
The types of idols in our daily
    lives.

Pride, money, popularity,
Body images, hobbies,
    materialism—
Their common cores:
    self-idolatry.
People no longer bow down
To graven images;
Instead, they worship at the
    altar
Of the god of selfishness.
An insatiable appetite
For more, more, more.

Three lusts can be found
At the core of self-idolatry:
Lust of the flesh,
Lust of the eyes, and
Lust of pride.
All three turn people away
From the one true God.

Most effective way to defeat
   idolatry:
Accept Christ into your heart;
Trust in Him for all things.
Never stop looking to God
Through study, prayer, and
   devotion.
Identify your idols,
Then guard yourself against
   them
And flee when tempted.

"The acts of the flesh are obvious: sexual immorality, impurity and debauchery; idolatry and witchcraft; hatred, discord, jealousy, fits of rage, selfish ambition, dissensions, factions and envy; drunkenness, orgies, and the like. I warn you, as I did before, that those who live like this will not inherit the kingdom of God."

(Galatians 5:19–21)

Incarnation

"And the Word became flesh and dwelt among us, and we have seen his glory, glory as of the only Son from the Father, full of grace and truth."

(John 1:14)

The taking on of human flesh
By our Lord and Savior, Jesus
   Christ.
Defined as the act of being
   made flesh.
It is not His coming into
   existence,
For Christ always existed
As the second person of the
   triune God.
Yet being incarnated,
He slept, ate, perspired,
Bled, expressed emotion, and
   cried—
Experienced all human needs.

Wholly man and
   wholly God—
A biblical fact, difficult for the
Finite mine to comprehend.
Imperative that Jesus become
   human
While maintaining His divine
   nature.
As He was born a human
Under the law of God,
Only He could keep the law—
Perfectly fulfill it—
Thereby redeeming us sinful
   people
From our transgressions.
Jesus accomplished our
   redemption
On the cross, exchanging
   our sin
For His perfect righteousness.

The incarnation shows Jesus's
humility.
He did not come to be served;
Jesus came to serve.
He humbled Himself
By becoming obedient
To the point of death—
Death on the cross.

The incarnation fulfills
prophecy.
No accidental or random act;
Predicted in the Old Testament
In accordance with God's
eternal plan.
"To us a child is born,
To us a son is given"—
Predicted almost seven
centuries
Before His incarnation.

Our trying to understand this
Is a fruitless exercise.
The incarnation is a great
mystery,
Yet is confirmed in
scripture and
Recognized in two natures,
Without confusion, without
change,
Without division, without
separation.
Two distinct natures, both
preserved,
Forming one person and
subsistence.

The incarnation displays
The greatness of our God—
Our eternal God, born in a
stable,
Who walked among us.
Our humble, generous God,
With a purpose and plan.
Our God, who redeemed us
By His blood.
Our God is great indeed!

"For to us a child is born, to us a son is given; and the government shall be upon his shoulder, and his name shall be called Wonderful Counselor, Mighty God, Everlasting Father, Prince of Peace."

(Isaiah 9:6)

In Christ

"For in Christ Jesus you are all sons of God, through faith."

(Galatians 3:26)

In Christ—this is one way of
describing
What it means to be a
Christian.
Those in Christ
Are spiritually united to Him
And identified with Him

Such that all blessings and
    benefits
Obtained by Christ belong to
    them.

We are not born in Christ;
Scripture tells us we are born
In a state of separation
    from God,
Alienation from Him.
Our union with Christ
Is realized only by the grace
    of God
When we repent of our sins
And place full faith in Jesus
    Christ.

In Christ, we are adopted
Into God's family.
We are made children of God.
In Christ, we are accepted
    by God.
In Christ, we experience the
Eternal, unbreakable love
    of God.
In Christ, we are being
Progressively transformed
Into His image and likeness.
In Christ, we experience
The peace of God.

Being in Christ is who we are,
What we are;
It is our identification.
It is what we live for.
Yes, we are Christians,

But more importantly,
We are in Christ.
We are alive to God
By being in Christ.

"So then, just as you received
Christ Jesus as Lord, continue to
live your lives in him, rooted and
built up in him, strengthened in
the faith as you were taught, and
overflowing with thankfulness."

(Colossians 2:6–7)

Infallible

"All Scripture is breathed out by
God and profitable for teaching,
for reproof, for correction, and
for training in righteousness that
the man of God may be complete,
equipped for every good work."

(2 Timothy 3:16–17)

Incapable of error, never
    wrong,
Absolutely trustworthy.
To confess that the Bible
Is infallible is to confess
That the scriptures are
    incapable
Of teaching any error.
A reflection of the
Perfection of scripture.

Infallible—a stronger
Word than *inerrant*.
Inerrant means that
There are no errors;
Infallible means that
There can be no errors.

As the Bible in totality
Has been inspired by God
Through the Holy Spirit,
All of it is totally
Infallible and inerrant,
Since both the Father and the
    Spirit
Are totally perfect in all
Their attributes.

God breathed out the
    scriptures;
This ensures the Bible's
    infallibility,
For God cannot breathe out
    error.
If God is infallible,
Then so is His Word.

The real question is not where
The Bible is capable of erring;
The real question is this:
Is God capable of erring?
As the Bible is a reflection
Of its author, and its author
Is perfect, the Bible is perfect.
It is infallible.

"The words of the LORD are pure words, like silver refined in a furnace on the ground, purified seven times."

(Psalm 12:6)

Inherit the Earth

"Blessed are the meek, for they shall inherit the earth."

(Matthew 5:5)

Jesus is using
Old Testament language
To express New Covenant
    truth—
A promise having both
Literal and spiritual meaning.

Inheritance implies being given
Something as a right
Because of a relationship.
An inheritance cannot be
    earned.
Since Jesus is the one giving,
This establishes that the earth
And all things on it belong
    to Him.
As heirs, Christians are those
Who submit to His lordship
By believing in Him, and thus
Are adopted into His family,
Becoming His children.

And as children, we have the
right
To inherit what God owns—
We have the right to inherit
This earth and its fullness,
And the new earth to come.

The meek who inherit are those
Having the greatest enjoyment
Of good things in this present
life.
They are content with such
things
As they have, all given by
Christ—
Including contentment of
mind.

For the meek who inherit the
earth,
Their meekness is not
weakness,
But strength brought under
control.
They channel their strengths
Into the service of God.
As their inheritance is also
spiritual,
They are heirs in the kingdom
of God,
Citizens in that kingdom
Available now on this earth,
And having an eternal
inheritance
In the new heavens and earth.

"But the meek shall inherit the land and delight themselves in abundant peace."

(Psalm 27:11)

Inspired (Divinely)

"All scripture is given by inspiration of God, and is profitable for doctrine, for reproof, for correction, for instruction in righteousness, that the man of God may be perfect, thoroughly furnished unto all good works."

(2 Timothy 3:16–17 KJV)

God-breathed, divine
influence.
Scripture is known as the Word
of God.
The inspiration extends
From Genesis through
Revelation,
From the greatest religious
doctrines
To the smallest words.

Different writers from different
ages,
Of various personalities,
Penned the words.
But God divinely inspired
The very words they wrote.
Every word, every term,

Influenced by God—
Literally, "God-breathed."

Since the Bible is divinely
    inspired,
All its words are inerrant, and
All its words are authoritative.
As such, it is to be valued
For exactly what it is:
God's Word to humanity.
As the prophetic messages
Of God's chosen spokesmen
Were spoken revelations,
The Bible is God's written
    revelation—
God revealing Himself to us.

The words of the Bible
Were not self-initiated by the
    writers.
The divine inspiration of
    scripture
Starts with the God of the
    Bible.
God guided scripture's human
    authors
In all they wrote.
The Holy Spirit guaranteed
The accuracy of all that was
    written.
Yes, inspired—divinely
    inspired.
God-breathed—God's Words.

"Sanctify them in the truth; your word is truth."

(John 17:17)

Israel

"I bring near my righteousness; it is not far off, and my salvation will not delay; I will put salvation in Zion, for Israel my glory."

(Isaiah 46:13)

Hebrew name meaning
"God contends" or
"One who struggles with God."
Name given to Jacob,
Abraham's grandson,
Following a night spent
Wrestling with God.
Later, it was given to the nation
Jacob's sons eventually
    formed—
Israel.

Israel is much more than an
Extended family's nation.
Israel is unique in that God
Used this nation to further
His plan of redemption for
    humanity.
God called Israel
To be a covenant
    community—
To live out and exhibit

The kingdom life
Before all nations of the world.

A land that spans from the
Mediterranean Sea in the west
To the Jordan River in the east,
From Acre in the north
To Ashkelon in the south,
Included both Galilee and the
    Golan.
Referred to as the Holy Land.

A long and rich history
Beginning before 1000 BC,
Filled with blessings, curses,
Wars, and kings.
Has the two most renowned
    kings:
David and Solomon.
Throughout the millennia,
Ruled by Babylonians,
    Persians,
Greeks, and Romans, among
    others.
United, divided, and
    conquered,
It was reestablished in 1948.

All of Israel's ancient history
Was moving toward
The coming of Jesus.
The law and prophets spoke
    of Him;
Jesus came to fulfill the
    prophecies
Written in the Old Testament,

Produced in Israel.

Today, there is much debate
    about
What Israel is.
Regardless, the name refers
    back
To God and His purposes.
Whether distinct or united
With the church today,
Israel points toward the
New humanity created in
    Christ,
Citizens of the kingdom
    of God.

**"But it is not as though the word
of God has failed. For not all who
are descended from Israel belong
to Israel."**

(Romans 9:6)

Jehovah

**"That men may know that thou,
whose name alone is Jehovah, art
the most high over all the earth."**

(Psalm 83:18 KJV)

The unchanging, eternal,
Self-existent God.
The I AM THAT I AM—
Not an appellative title such as
    Lord;

A name given to the Most
High.

Jehovah Nissi: The Lord my
banner.
Jehovah-Raah: The Lord my
shepherd.
Jehovah Rapha: The Lord that
heals.
Jehovah Shammah: The Lord is
there.
Jehovah Tsidkenu:
The Lord of righteousness.
Jehovah Mekoddishkem:
The Lord who sanctifies you.

A Latinization of Hebrew,
Of the unpronounceable name:
YHVH—
The name of the God of Israel
In the Hebrew Bible.
One of seven names of God in
Judaism.
Now popular in English,
especially
In the King James Version
Bible.

An approximation of the
Holiest name of God in
Hebrew—
A name so sacred, it was never
spoken.
A name meaning "I Am that I
Am," or
"I Am the One Who Is."

**"Behold, God is my salvation; I
will trust, and not be afraid, for
the Lord Jehovah is my strength
and my song; he also is become my
salvation."**

(Isaiah 12:2 KJV)

Jesus

**"She will bear a son, and you shall
call his name Jesus, for he will save
his people from their sins."**

(Matthew 1:21)

The one who saves—
This name literally means
"Savior."
This is His special role,
Saving His people from
The guilt of sin
By cleansing them
In His own atoning blood.

He saves them from
Sin's domineering power
By giving their hearts
The sanctifying Holy Spirit.
He saves them from
The presence of sin
When removing them
From this world
To rest with Him.
He will save them from
All the consequences of sin

When He shall give them
A glorious body
At the last day.
Jesus truly saves!

This name, *Jesus*,
Significant for whom it
    represents.
God came to earth as a human
To die in our place
To become our Savior.
This name reminds us
Of the amazing humility
Of the Son of God,
When He came as a man
To die for us.
A name of unmatched
    humility,
Yet it is a name of infinite
    exaltation.
For His name is glorified far
    above
Every other name.
Jesus, the one who saves.

"Therefore God has highly exalted him and bestowed on him the name that is above every name, so that at the name of Jesus every knee should bow, in heaven and on earth and under the earth, and every tongue confess that Jesus Christ is Lord, to the glory of God the Father."

(Philippians 2:9–11)

(See also **Christ.**)

Jesus Christ or Christ Jesus

"To those who have been called, who are loved in God the Father and kept for Jesus Christ."

(Jude 1)

Any difference is slight
    indeed—
Jesus Christ and *Christ Jesus*
Essentially mean the same
    thing.
Jesus, the human name
Chosen by God,
A personal name.
Christ, a title meaning
"Messiah, Anointed One."
Having *Christ* next to
Jesus ascribes honor to Him,
Whether placed first or second.

In scripture, the two names
Basically interchangeable
    regarding order.
Any difference subtle in nature,
Most likely insignificant.
Both are used many times in
    scripture:
Jesus Christ, more than seventy
    times;

Christ Jesus, more than ninety
times.
Placing Christ first emphasizes
His deity.
Placing Jesus first emphasizes
Our Lord's humanity.

Examples abound:
Paul uses both in Roman 1.
Referring to the birth
And resurrection, Paul
calls Him
Jesus Christ (Romans 1:4),
Emphasizing His humanity.
In reminding us that Jesus
Is bondservant, Paul uses
Christ Jesus,
Emphasizing His divinity.

Regardless of how you
order it—
Jesus Christ or Christ Jesus—
Jesus is Christ, the Messiah,
The Son of God.

"Grace, mercy and peace from God the Father and Christ Jesus our Lord."

(2 Timothy 1:2)

Jew

"But if you call yourself a Jew and rely on the law and boast in God

and know his will and approve what is excellent, because you are instructed from the law; ... you then who teach others, do you not teach yourself?"

(Romans 2:17–21)

A name initially given to those
Belonging to the tribe of
Judah,
One of the twelve tribes of
Israel,
Bearing the name of Jacob's
fourth son.
After the fifth century BC,
The term came to refer to all
Israelites,
Regardless of their tribal
ancestries.
A shortening of the word
Judah.

Abraham is commonly called
the first Jew,
A Hebrew, one of the chosen
people,
Although he lived prior to tribe
of Judah.

The term *Jew* is used to refer
To all physical and spiritual
Descendants of Abraham.
Technically, a Jew is anyone
Born of a Jewish mother
Or having undergone proper
conversion.

Not simply a private matter;
A choice one makes on his or
her own.
Has nothing to do with what is
believed.
Judaism is more a nationality
than religion,
More akin to holding
citizenship.

A physical pedigree is not equal
To holding onto true faith.
Salvation is a work of the Spirit
In the heart.
Being of Jewish descent
Is no guarantee of heaven being
home.
Only through the grace
of God,
Through faith in Christ,
Is salvation received.

An all-important difference
Between Christianity and
Judaism:
The person of Jesus Christ,
Who is the fulfillment of
Old Testament prophecies.
Not solely a good teacher
And perhaps a prophet,
As the Jews believe.
Jews strongly deny that Jesus
is God,
Refuting His atoning sacrifice,
Relying rather on their good
works.

Christians live on the belief
that
God became man,
Laid down His life to pay
The price for our sins;
No works of people involved,
Only faith in Christ through
grace,
The sole means of salvation.

**"For no one is a Jew who is merely
one outwardly, nor is circumcision
outward and physical. But a Jew is
one inwardly, and circumcision is
a matter of the heart, by the Spirit,
not by the letter. His praise is not
from man but from God."**

(Romans 2:28–29)

John

**"One of his disciples, whom Jesus
loved, was reclining at table close
to Jesus."**

(John 13:23)

The beloved disciple,
Among the first to be called by
Jesus.
Previously a fisherman,
Along with James, Peter, and
Andrew.
Author of five books:

The gospel of John;
Three epistles: 1, 2, and 3 John;
And the book of Revelation.
Brother of the apostle James;
These two are known as sons of
thunder,
Characterized by zeal, passion,
ambition.

The gospel of John was written
So all may believe in Jesus as
The Son of God, who gives life
eternal.
This gospel speaks of the love
of Christ,
The authority of Christ,
The security found in
Christ, and
The divinity of Christ.
It includes seven great "I am's."

Jesus was God,
Eternal Word made flesh,
He was born of and rejected by
humans—
But to all who believe,
Authority is given to call
themselves
Children of God.
John's gospel focuses more
On the spiritual than on the
historical.
Includes lessons and
instructions
On how to live according to
God's will.

Three letters—1, 2, and 3
John—
Encourage followers of Jesus
To remain faithful to the truth.
All are addressed to Christians,
Supporting believers,
While warning about
opponents.
Each includes a prayer and
thanks.

John was exiled by Rome's
emperor
To the island of Patmos,
where he
Continued his writings.
Released, he moved to Ephesus.
Theories abound about his
death;
Most likely, he died peacefully
As an old man of ninety-two.

**"I have no greater joy than to hear
that my children are walking in
the truth."**

(3 John 4)

(See also **Revelation, Book of.**)

John the Baptist

**"John appeared, baptizing in
the wilderness and proclaiming**

a baptism of repentance for the forgiveness of sins."

(Mark 1:4)

A man filled with faith,
A role model to those who wish
To share their faith in Jesus
　　Christ.
His coming was foretold by
　　Isaiah
Seven hundred years earlier.
A miraculous birth.
Selected by God as His
　　ambassador
Proclaiming the coming of
　　Jesus Christ,
The Son of God.

A pivotal figure in salvation
　　history,
His public ministry ended
Four hundred years of
　　prophetic silence.
His voice, crying in the
　　wilderness,
Prepare the way for Messiah's
　　coming.
A transitional figure, the link
　　between
The Old and New Testaments.

His theme: "Repent, for the
　　kingdom
Of heaven is near."
Called "the Baptist" because he

He baptized those who
　　responded
To his message, those who
Repented of their sins.

Not a crowd pleaser, he
　　angered many,
Including King Herod.
A fiery prophet,
He died a martyr's death.

"A voice cries: 'In the wilderness prepare the way of the LORD; make straight in the desert a highway for our God.'"

(Isaiah 40:3)

Joy

"You make known to me the path of life; in your presence there is fullness of joy; at your right hand are pleasures forevermore."

(Psalm 16:11)

More than an emotion,
A combination of happiness
With a state of blessedness.
A characteristic gift of the
　　Spirit
From whom all joy flows.

Yes, joy is a good feeling,
But true joy of the soul

Is produced only by the Spirit,
As He opens our eyes to the
    beauty
Of Christ in the Word and the
    world.
In His Word, yes, but also in
    His gifts
To the world: people, nature,
    food,
Love, health, family—in
    everything
Our Lord bestows on us.

A choice on our part whether
    to value
God's presence, His gifts,
And His work in our lives.
When we yield to the Spirit,
He gives us eyes to see
The beauties of Jesus,
Which fill our hearts with joy.

A revelation of God's grace
    around us
That cannot be found
In this fallen world.
A grace that fills us with
    His joy,
An eternal joy,
Giving us true happiness and
Cheerful hearts and minds.

One can have joy and be
    happy,
But true lasting happiness
Cannot be experienced without

The joy found in fellowship
    with God,
Making it complete,
    everlasting,
And full.

**"Clap your hands, all peoples!
Shout to God with loud songs
of joy!"**

(Psalm 47:1)

Judges

**"Then the Lord raised up judges,
who saved them out of the hand of
those who plundered them."**

(Judges 2:16)

Leaders in Israel during a
    certain time,
And a book of the Bible about
    them,
These judges ruled Israel
Before the time of kings.
Began after the death of
    Joshua,
Continued until Saul
Anointed a king of Israel.
A time of great apostasy.
A clear pattern emerges: People
    rebel
Through idolatry and disbelief,
God brings judgment, and

God raises up a new judge,
People repent,
People turn back to God—
Then they return to sin;
The cycle starts anew.

Filled with many heroes of
     faith—
Including Gideon, Samson,
     and Deborah.
The stories are graphic, filled
With violence and disturbing
     scenes—
Some in the name of
     righteousness,
Others in the name of evil.

The author of Judges is
     unknown;
Possibly is the prophet Samuel.
An account of lost faith,
An account of deliverance—
A story of the downward spiral
Of Israel into chaos
And rebellion against God.
Demonstrates the consequences
Of unfaithfulness to the
One true king.

One message is abundantly
     clear:
God is not willing to let sin
Go unpunished.
The exodus had established
     Israel

As God's people; He was their
     king.
In Judges, He disciplines them
For following other gods,
Disobeying His laws,
Engaging in immorality, and
Even descending into anarchy
     at times.
Yet He hears their cries
And shows mercy on them
Time and time again.

In the end,
Israel demands a king,
Despite abundant warnings.
The people refused to listen.
A king is what they wanted;
A king is what they got.
The first one was Saul.

**"Then all the elders of Israel
gathered together and came to
Samuel at Ramah and said to him,
'Behold, you are old and your sons
do not walk in your ways. Now
appoint for us a king to judge us
like all the nations.'"**

(1 Samuel 8:4–5)

Judgment

**"Do not judge, or you too will be
judged. For in the same way you
judge others, you will be judged,**

and with the measure you use, it will be measured to you."

(Matthew 7:1–2)

No absolute prohibition
From judging others,
But from rash, harsh,
Uncharitable judgments.
Truth exists;
We are to distinguish
Between truths and falsehoods.

Judgment—the act of
    determining
That which conforms to law
    and justice.
It is to declare an opinion,
To discriminate between
Perceived right and wrong.
It is to uphold truth.

Many types of sinful
    judgments exist:
Superficial judgment based
Solely on appearance;
Hypocritical judgments while
We ourselves commit the
    same sin;
Harsh judgments
Without showing mercy;
Self-righteous judgments
Without humility; and
False judgments bearing false
    witness.

Judgments opposing sin are not
    wrong.
There is "right" judgment. It is
    to be
A discerning judgment,
Through the counsel of God.
It is to be given gently, done in
    love,
Spoken in truth.

Scripture is clear on this fact:
We have one supreme judge:
The Lord God.
He alone has authority
To determine right from
    wrong.
He is a just judge.
He judges the world in
    righteousness.

We are to judge ourselves first,
Before judging others.
First we must remove the plank
From our own eyes,
Then, with discernment,
    we can
Remove the speck from
Our brother's eye.
If we are not personally
Repenting of our own sins,
We are in no position
To judge others in their sins.

Scripture tells us to judge,
Instructing us not to associate
With sexually immoral people.

This requires judgment.
But we are to judge actions,
Not motives. Only God knows
What is in the heart.
We are to judge only
When we can objectively
Discern people's actions.
With sex before marriage,
Stealing from others,
Adultery, untruths—
No doubt is involved.

True judgment seeks to restore,
Not to condemn, not to
    destroy—
Always with the intent to help,
Never to elevate ourselves.
Always in humbleness,
Always in love.

"Brothers, if anyone is caught in any transgression, you who are spiritual should restore him in a spirit of gentleness. Keep watch on yourself, lest you too be tempted."

(Galatians 6:1)

Justice

"Righteousness and justice are the foundation of your throne; steadfast love and faithfulness go before you."

(Psalm 89:14)

What is right, as it should be;
Also, to render a verdict,
Pronounce a sentence.
Justice is an attribute of God.
Flows out of His
Holiness and righteousness.

Sin is lawlessness, iniquity.
Sin sets itself in opposition
To God's holiness.
The wages of sin is death.
God's holiness requires
Justice to be carried out.

The greatest demonstration
Of God's justice to the world:
Sending His Son, Jesus Christ,
To earth to satisfy this justice.
Through the death of
Christ on the cross,
Christ paid the penalty that
Justice demanded for sin;
He made salvation available
To all who believe in Him.

To ignore sin,
To turn a blind eye to it,
To sweep it under the rug—
This cannot be justice.
God did none of this.
For all the sins of His people
He poured out His wrath,

Poured out His justice
Upon Christ as He carried
    them
On His shoulders to the cross.

Just as Jesus underwent
The punishment we deserve,
God can show us
His mercy without
    compromising
His goodness, His
    holiness, and
His justice.
God has done this
So that He would be
Just and justifier
Of the one who has faith
In Christ Jesus.

To the believer,
This is wonderful news.
God's justice frees us
To trust His character.
God acts according to His
    character.
This means standards will be
    upheld.
God upholds justice through
    Christ.

We are to uphold standards
Of right and wrong.
God's justice destroys evil.
It vanquished death on the
    cross.

Soon, this justice will overcome
    all sin,
And all pain, tears, and sorrow
Will be gone forever.
All believers will be made
    whole again.

**"For the wages of sin is death, but
the free gift of God is eternal life
in Christ Jesus our Lord."**

(Romans 6:23)

Justification

**"It will be counted to us who
believe in him who raised from
the dead Jesus our Lord, who was
delivered up for our trespasses and
raised for our justification."**

(Romans 4:24–25)

An act of God
Taking place the moment a
    sinner
Places trust in Jesus Christ
As Lord and Savior.
A declaration of God
Declaring a person just or
    righteous
In His sight.

For the repentant sinner
With faith in Christ,
God pronounces the sentence:

"Not guilty!"
Now righteous in His sight,
Forever at peace with each
    other.
The great exchange is this:
Sinners' guilt for Christ's
    righteousness.

All sins and guilt were
    transferred
To the Lord, Jesus, on the
    cross,
Who took the full brunt
Of God's holy wrath,
Cloaking the sinner
In Christ's holy righteousness
Now and forevermore.

Justification is a gracious act
    of God,
A free gift, not dependent on
    baptism,
Or on the works of man.
It is only available through
    grace alone,
Through faith alone,
In Christ alone.

Justification is the blessed
    answer
To people's greatest questions.
How can a sinner be forgiven?
By what means is it
    accomplished?
God answers through His Son
Nailed upon the cross.

The judgment of God declared:
All sins are forgiven.

We are justified by God,
By grace alone,
On the basis of Christ's blood
And righteousness;
Through the means of faith;
For the glory of God alone;
As taught in scripture.

Faith accepts the saving work
    of Christ
And by grace we are justified.

"The righteousness of God through faith in Jesus Christ for all who believe. For there is no distinction: for fall have sinned and fall short of the glory of God, and are justified by his grace as a gift, through the redemption that is in Christ Jesus."

(Romans 3:22–24)

Kindness

"Or do you presume on the riches of his kindness and forbearance and patience, not knowing that God's kindness is meant to lead you to repentance?"

(Romans 2:4)

An attribute of God,
Bestowed upon us
As a gift of the Holy Spirit.
A word overlapping with many
    others:
Goodness, mercy, love,
Favor, compassion, gentleness.
It is constant and unchanging.

As a fruit of the Spirit,
Kindness is the resulting
    character
For one who allows the Spirit
To develop maturity in his or
    her life.
In Greek it is gentleness,
Tender concern, uprightness.
It is of the heart,
Reflected in one's actions.

A much bigger word than most
    think.
It is the characteristic that
    led God
To provide salvation for us
    sinners.
It leads God to give us
Green pastures, quiet waters,
And restoration of our weary
    souls.
It makes Him want to
    gather us
Under his wings, protect us,
And keep us near.

Kindness is manifested
In common grace.
For God is kind to everyone
    He created,
Even those who scorn Him.
Intended to lead all to
    repentance.
What is true of God is
    attributed
To Christ, who is gentle,
Making salvation possible.

When we exhibit God's
    kindness,
We are tender and benevolent
    to others,
Friend and foe alike.
Kindness is to be the center
Of Christian living.
As with other attributes,
It is not only an inner
    disposition,
But an attitude expressed
    through deeds.

A proper definition of kindness
Is voiced in two words: love's
    actions.
For that is how true love
    behaves:
Good deeds springing from
    love.
As with love, kindness is gentle,
Never harsh.
It is love's conduct, how love
    behaves.

"Be kind to one another, tenderhearted, forgiving each other, just as God in Christ also has forgiven you."

(Ephesians 4:32)

King

"For at just the right time Christ will be revealed from heaven by the blessed and only almighty God, the King of all kings and Lord of all lords."

(1 Timothy 6:15 NLT)

Speaking of Christ,
Who alone reigns supreme
As king and Lord of all the
    earth.
No power, no king, no lord
    exists
Who can oppose Him
    and win—
Christ, whose everlasting
    dominion
Is over all people, nations,
    languages.
The radiance of the glory
    of God,
The exact imprint of His
    nature,
Upholds the universe
By the word of His power.
Absolute king over all creation.

Jesus is King of kings;
No higher authority exists.
His reign is absolute and
    inviolable.
Raised from the dead,
Placed over all things,
Far above all rule and
Authority, power,
    dominion, and
Above every name that is
    named
In this age and the one to
    come;
All things are put under his
    feet.
Christ alone reigns supreme.

King is defined as one invested
With authority over a nation.
Many kings are named in
    scripture,
But only one as Christ the
    king,
The king over all others.
Earthly kings wore royal robes;
Christ dressed in holy
    righteousness.
Earthly kings carried royal
    scepters;
Christ carries a scepter of
    justice.
He is the king before whom,
    one day,
Every knee will bow. He is
Seated at the right hand
    of God.

"Lift up your heads, O gates! And be lifted up, O ancient doors, that the King of glory may come in. Who is this King of glory? The LORD, strong and mighty, the LORD, mighty in battle! Lift up your heads, O gates! And lift them up, O ancient doors, that the King of glory may come in."

(Psalm 24:7–9)

Kingdom of God

"The LORD has established his throne in the heavens, and his kingdom rules over all."

(Psalm 103:19)

This kingdom of God,
It is a reign—God's reign,
His sovereign governance,
His kingly rule over all
    creation.
He holds over it the scepter of
    justice.
The years of His reign will
    never end.

A mystery of the kingdom:
It is here now but also yet to
    come.
Part of our present spiritual
    life and
Of righteousness, peace,

And joy in the Holy Spirit.
Its fullness will manifest itself
In the future when we inherit
The kingdom in all its glory,
Taking our place at the feast
With Abraham, Isaac, and
    Jacob.
The kingdom exists here
    and now
In lives and hearts,
And in perfection and fullness
In the future.

On a human level, the
    kingdom of God
Is a spiritual rule over the
    hearts and lives
Of those accepting Christ
As Lord and Savior.
To receive this heavenly rule,
Repentance of sin is a necessity.
Salvation occurs through faith
    alone,
By grace alone.

But what does it mean
To be in this kingdom of God?
How are we then to live?
Seek the things of God—
This is our priority:
Live in obedience to God,
Share the gospel of Christ,
Love God, love our neighbors.
Enter this kingdom by doing
    the will
Of our Father in heaven.

The Kingdom of God is
    within you,
It is in your midst
In the person of Christ Jesus.

"Being asked by the Pharisees when the kingdom of God would come, he answered them, 'The kingdom of God is not coming with signs to be observed, nor will they say, "Look, here it is!" or "There!" for behold, the kingdom of God is in the midst of you."'

(Luke 17:20–21)

Kingdom of Heaven

"And Jesus said to his disciples, 'Truly, I say to you, only with difficulty will a rich person enter the kingdom of heaven. Again I tell you, it is easier for a camel to go through the eye of a needle than for a rich person to enter the kingdom of God.'"

(Matthew 22:12–14)

Kingdom of heaven,
Kingdom of God—
These are used interchangeably.
Jesus makes no distinction
Between the two;

He considers them
    synonymous.
Matthew might use
"Kingdom of heaven,"
While Mark or Luke uses
"Kingdom of God,"
In parallel accounts of a
    parable.
The two phases are simply
Two different ways
To indicate the same reign.

All power and authority to rule
Has been given to Jesus Christ
By the Father
Who is enthroned in heaven,
Where Christ is seated
At His right hand.

"The LORD has established his throne in the heavens, and his kingdom rules over all."

(Psalm 103:19)

(See also **Kingdom of God.**)

Know God

"Thus says the LORD: 'Let not the wise man boast in his wisdom, let not the mighty man boast in his might, let not the rich man boast in his riches, but let him who boasts boast in this, that he understands

and knows me, that I am the
LORD who practices steadfast
love, justice, and righteousness
in the earth. For in these things I
delight, declares the LORD.'"
(Jeremiah 9:23–24)

To know God is
The reason for our existence,
The goal for our lives.
A complex undertaking
Commencing with faith.

Step one: Know Jesus Christ.
Accept Him as Lord and
    Savior.
Only through knowing the Son
Can we know the Father.
Acknowledge His claim,
Trust in His promises,
Answer His call.

Knowing God
More than knowing about
    Him is
A matter of interacting
    with Him—
A personal involvement of
Mind, will, feeling.

Taste His friendship
As a beautiful meal.
We know it is real and
    delicious
Only after we have tasted it.
Commit to His company;

Identify with His concerns.
Be emotional as well as
    intellectual.
Savor His Word.

Knowing God is
A matter of grace.
We do not make friends
    with God;
God makes friends with us.
He brings us to know Him
Through His love, His Son,
    and His Spirit.
It is God's personal affection,
Redeeming action,
Covenant of faithfulness,
Providential watchfulness,
And salvation, now and forever.

Live out the faith,
Obey His Word.
Be the salt and the light,
Bring God's flavor to the
    world,
The light amid darkness.
Love God with your heart,
    mind, and soul.
Love your neighbors.
Only then can you know God.

To know God is to
Accept Christ, read His Word,
And be filled with His Spirit.
Seek Him through prayer and
    fellowship.
Live life with the saints.

Bask in His glory.

"But now that you have come to know God, or rather to be known by God, how can you turn back again to the weak and worthless elementary principles of the world, whose slaves you want to be once more?"

(Galatians 4:9)

Last Days

"And this is the will of him who sent me, that I should lose nothing of all that he has given me, but raise it up on the last day."

(John 6:39)

That day—the day of the
Lord—
The future time when God's
will
And purpose for His world and
humanity
Will be fulfilled.

We live within the day
Of the old and the new.
Last days are now, but not yet.
We live in that tension of
Expectation and realization.

This will be the time
surrounding
The second coming of Jesus.
The present course of history
will end
When Jesus returns.
The certainty of the first
coming
Guarantees the certainty
Of the second coming.

God knows the timing;
We do not. Not even the angels
know.
Yet we are in the last days.
Exactly where on the
continuum—
That is unknown.

It began at Pentecost;
It will be consummated
By the successful preaching
Of the gospel to all nations.

We are called to wait
For these last days,
Faithfully seeking
Answers to our questions
In the context of redemption.
We are not to quarrel over the
Sequence, details, or imagery,
But to wait patiently, eagerly.
A holy waiting, which is active:
Living the gospel,
Teaching the gospel,
Proclaiming the gospel.

"Each day is a sacred gift
Of the life at the nexus
Of time and eternity.
We are called to receive
The gift of *this day*,
Not in futile speculation,
But in bowed doxological
Humility" (C. S. Lewis).

And so we pray:
"Come, Lord Jesus."

"Long ago, at many times and in many ways, God spoke to our fathers by the prophets, but in these last days he has spoken to us by his Son, whom he appointed the heir of all things, through whom also he created the world."

(Hebrews 1:1–2)

Law

"For by works of the law no human being will be justified in his sight, since through the law comes knowledge of sin."

(Romans 3:20)

Instituted by God Himself.
Instruction might be a better word.

God's way of shaping His relationship
With His people.

Different types of law are laid down—
Judicial, ceremonial, moral law.
Each has its place and purpose.
Some laws relevant to purposes and times,
Others are everlasting.

Judicial law was God's way of shaping
Hebrew society but is not binding today.
Ritual laws were sacrifices, festivals,
Portraying lessons on sin and atonement
Superseded by the work of Christ.

Ceremonial laws were for regaining
Right standing with God.
Old Testament describes this law
In detail: circumcision, sacrifices,
Offerings, purifications, holy days,
And sanctuary services.
Many of these point
To the coming Messiah.
All were nailed to the cross;

They are not in force for the
Christian.

Moral laws, an eternal
manifestation
Of the mind and will of God
Are based on God's holy
nature,
Declaring what is good, what
is evil,
What we are to do,
What we are not to do, and
What duties we owe to God
And to our neighbors.

This moral law discovers sin.
Without law, there is no
knowledge
Of wickedness,
No discernment of right from
wrong.
Revealed in the Ten
Commandments, it is
Relevant today unto the people
of God.

The law is the life-directing
power,
Showing faults and weaknesses.
Opens a window to our hearts
And minds.
It has the power to direct and
instruct,
Not just to condemn or justify.

A condition of justification

Is perfect and perpetual
obedience.
Fallen humanity is unable to
abide this law,
With all its requirements and
duties;
People try, but forever fail.

Only Christ perfectly kept
the law.
Yet, all its penalties for sinful
people
Were poured out on Him.
Christ has redeemed us from
its curse,
Being made a curse for us.

The law is now no longer
The path to righteousness;
Christ alone is that path.
The ultimate goal of the law
Is not for law-keeping
But for making our eyes
Stay on Christ.

**"What then? Are we to sin because
we are not under law but under
grace? By no means! Do you not
know that if you present yourselves
to anyone as obedient slaves, you
are slaves of the one whom you
obey, either of sin, which leads
to death, or of obedience, which
leads to righteousness?"**

(Romans 6:15–16)

Leviticus

**"You shall be holy to me, for I the
LORD am holy and have separated
you from the peoples, that you
should be mine."**

(Leviticus 20:26)

Third book of the Old
Testament,
Part of the Pentateuch
(The Old Testament's first five
books,
Authored by Moses).
Written to guide the Israelites
In the ways of holiness,
Setting them apart from the
world
To receive blessings, not
judgments,
In living near the special
presence
Of their holy God.

Reports the words of God
To Moses and Aaron, his
brother.
Leviticus translates as "about
Levites,"
Who had responsibility
For maintaining worship.
Not addressed solely to them,
But to all Israelites,
Instructing them how to be
pure,

How to offer sacrifices,
Sharing requirements for
entering
The presence of God in
worship.
Basically, how to coexist
with an
All-powerful, holy God.

Although filled with
ceremonies
And rites
That challenge the modern
reader,
These ideas are fundamental
For New Testament theology
Of sin, sacrifice, atonement,
And interpreting the death of
Jesus Christ.

Part of the Mosaic covenant
Given at Sinai, it includes
God's sovereign grace
In choosing Israel,
And requirements of loyalty.
Prominent themes include
God's presence with His
people.
Because God is holy,
His people must be holy.
Atonement for sins
Through the offering of
sacrifices
Of paramount importance—
All pointing to Christ.

"He has no need, like those high priests, to offer sacrifices daily, first for his own sins and then for those of the people, since he did this once for all when he offered up himself."

(Hebrews 7:27)

Lily of the Valley

"I am a rose of Sharon, a lily of the valleys."

(Song of Solomon 2:1)

Suggestions include
Wild-growing anemone,
Hyacinth, tulip, iris,
And maybe gladiolus.
In any case,
A beautiful, fragrant plant.

A flower conspicuous on the
Shores of the Lake of
    Gennesaret,
Flourishes in the deep
Valleys of Palestine,
Even living among thorny
    shrubs
And pastures of the desert.
Remarkable for rapid,
Luxuriant growth.
Brilliant in color and was
Compared with the gorgeous
Robes of Solomon.

Opposite of thorns—which
    were
Ugly, uninviting, and
    unattractive.
Lilies—oh, so lovely!

A metaphor for the church?
A lesson on husbandry?
In marriage, each spouse is
    to see
The other's beauty in
This world so fallen.
Yes, it may be a cultivated
    flower
With colors that will shine
    bright,
But a lily among the thorns?
Now that is true beauty.

The lily as the bride of Jesus—
This is another thought.
This bride is defined as the
    church.
One more beautiful analogy
Demonstrating the church's
Grace, loveliness, and beauty
Received from Christ.
Also intimating her exposure
To this world's dangers,
    enemies, and
Her need of His protection and
    love.

Others say this lily
Represents Christ Himself,
A picture expressing

His presence in this world,
The ease of access to Him,
And the beauty and sweetness
To be found in Him,
Teaching us to adorn ourselves
With Him.

So many choices.
Whatever the meaning,
Remember the lily as
God created it to be:
Sweet and fragrant,
Pure, beautiful, seeds of gold,
Fruitful in many ways,
Tall yet with humility,
And soothing.

"And why do you worry about clothes? See how the flowers of the field grow. They do not labor or spin. Yet I tell you that not even Solomon in all his splendor was dressed like one of these."

(Matthew 6:28–29)

Lord's Prayer

"This, then, is how you should pray: 'Our Father in heaven, hallowed be your name.'"

(Matthew 6:9)

The prayer of prayers,
Taught by Jesus Himself

Directly to the apostles
And to you and me.
So full, yet so simple.
The germ of everything:
Every saint can desire.
This prayer is
To God, from God, and
for God.

Ten short phrases,
In each, we are taught
To say, "we" and "our,"
Never forgetting others
As well as ourselves.

First sentence declares who
We are to pray to—
"Our Father in heaven."

Second: a petition respecting
God's name—
"May your name be kept holy."

Third: a petition concerning
God's kingdom—
"May your kingdom come."

Fourth: a petition concerning
God's will—
"May your will be done
On earth as in heaven."

Fifth: a petition respecting
Our own daily needs—
"Give us this day our daily
bread."

Sixth: a petition respecting
Our sins—
"Forgive us our debts."

Seventh: a petition respecting
Our feelings toward others—
"as we also forgive our debtors."

Eighth: a petition respecting
Our weaknesses—
"Bring us not into temptation."

Ninth: a petition respecting
Our dangers—
"Deliver us from the evil one."

Ending, the tenth:
An ascription of praise—
"For yours is the kingdom,
The power, and the glory."

We are truly blessed
To call God our Father
Through Jesus Christ, our
    Savior;
Therefore, saying a heartfelt
    amen
To all the Lord's Prayer
    contains.

"For thine is the kingdom, and the power, and the glory forever. Amen."

(Matthew 6:13 KJV)

Lord's Supper

"For as often as you eat this bread and drink the cup, you proclaim the Lord's death until he comes."

(1 Corinthians 11:26)

During the age-old celebration
Of the Passover,
On the eve of His death,
    this was
A new fellowship meal.
An integral part of Christian
    worship,
A remembrance of Jesus's
    death,
Of His Resurrection, and
Of His glorious future return.
This supper consists of bread,
Representing His broken body;
And wine, symbolizing the
    blood
He shed on our behalf.
In this supper we proclaim
Faith in all that Jesus did
For us in the past,
Is doing for us in the present,
And will do for us in the
    future.

Contains a threefold meaning:
Past, present, and future.
Past, in that partaking of this
    meal,

146

We look back to the death of
Christ
On the cross, which showed
The depth of God's love for us.
Present, by continually sharing
In Christ's crucifixion and
resurrection,
His death and life.
It helps us to look heavenward,
Mindful that true life comes
only
In Christ and with Christ.
Future, by remembering His
words
Of celebrating the meal until
He comes again—
A remembrance of His promise
To return to us.

Comes with a sober warning
Concerning the manner in
which one
Approaches and participates
In this sacrament.
Partaking in an unworthy
manner
Brings God's judgment.
One must examine his or her
heart,
Confess, and repent of sin,
Resolve conflicts with
others, and
Prepare his or her mind and
heart
Through reflection and prayer.

Participating in the Lord's
Supper
Is proclaiming the gospel.
We proclaim it to ourselves
To sustain faith;
We proclaim it to unbelievers
To awaken faith.
It is a savoring of the new
covenant,
Whereby Jesus promises
To forgive our sins,
And to write God's law on our
hearts,
That all covenant people
Shall know God, and
That He will be our God
And we, His people.

A sacrament to partake of
With reverence and love,
With a deep sense of gratitude
For the sacrifice of our Lord
On the cross,
His constant presence in our
lives,
And His promise to return in
the future.

**For I received from the Lord what
I also passed on to you: that the
Lord Jesus, on the night He was
betrayed, took bread, and when
He had given thanks, He broke it
and said, "This is My body, which
is for you; do this in remembrance**

of Me." In the same way, after supper He took the cup, saying, "This cup is the new covenant in My blood; do this, as often as you drink it, in remembrance of Me." For as often as you eat this bread and drink this cup, you proclaim the Lord's death until He comes.

(1 Corinthians 11:23–26)

Love the Lord

"Jesus replied: And he said to him, 'You shall love the Lord your God with all your heart and with all your soul and with all your mind. This is the great and first commandment.'"

(Matthew 22:37–38)

With all your heart, soul, and
    mind—
A love so profound that it
    overflows
Into all aspects of your being.
This threefold command
Leaves no room for divided
    affections
Or allegiance.
A love that stands supremely
    powerful,
Supremely valuable.

Loving with all the powers and
    faculties
Of one's affections, will, and
Understanding—in the most
    sincere,
Upright, and perfect manner,
Without any disguise or
    hypocrisy.
Placing this love above all else.

Starts with the heart,
From where the springs of life
    flow,
Filling it to abundancy,
Flows to the soul, so rich and
    deep
That no part is untouched.
Then flows to the mind,
Loving God in the riches
Of knowledge, insight, and
    wisdom.

Fallen people are unable to
    achieve
A love so monumental,
Yet this is the most important
Commandment from God.
Our failure demonstrates
Our utter spiritual
    bankruptcy and
Our need for a Savior.
It drives us to Jesus Christ,
Who gives us the strength
To grow in our love for Him,
Desiring to love Him
More completely as we witness

His compassion, mercy, grace,
And love for us.

When in heaven,
Glorified with Christ,
We will then fully and truly
Love the Lord our God
With all our hearts,
With all our souls,
And with all our minds.

"We love because he first loved us."

(1 John 4:19)

Love Your Neighbor

"Jesus replied: 'Love the Lord your God with all your heart and with all your soul and with all your mind. This is the first and greatest commandment. And the second is like it: Love your neighbor as yourself. All the Law and the Prophets hang on these two commandments.'"

(Matthew 22:37–40)

A version of the golden rule,
But much more is sandwiched
Between two powerful
    statements:
Love the Lord, your God;
All the law and the prophets

Hang on these two
    commandments.

All begins with loving God.
Loving God makes
Loving your neighbors possible.
Loving your neighbors is a
Visible expression of
    loving God.

The importance of these laws,
Of loving God and loving
    neighbors,
Impossible to overstate.
For on these commandments
Everything else in the Bible
    depends—
The law and the prophets.
It is the visible goal
Of the whole Word of God.
All depends on loving God
And loving your neighbors.

Leviticus contains specific
    descriptions
On how to love one's
    neighbors:
Live generously toward
The poor and the outsiders,
Do not steal from anyone,
Do not be deceptive in your
    dealings,
Do not swear in God's name,
Do not curse the deaf or put
A stumbling block before the
    blind,

Do not be partial to the poor,
Judge honestly,
Do not commit financial fraud,
Do not hate your brothers and
    sisters,
Do not seek revenge or hold a
    grudge,
But extend forgiveness.
Add to these by
Praying for your neighbors,
Rejoice and mourn with your
    neighbors,
Share the gospel with your
    neighbors.

We do not need to worry
About whom to love or not to
    love;
We are to love indiscriminately.
Love those we meet in
Everyday activities, regardless
Of race or religion or country.
Love all without prejudice.

And we shall love ourselves,
Longing for joy, hope, love,
Security, fulfillment, and
    significance.
The source of all this?
Only God Himself.
Only God gives us true
Joy and contentment,
Satisfying our hearts, souls,
    and minds.
What scripture tells us

Is that the love for our
    neighbors
Is the measure and content
Of our love for ourselves.
Let our neighbors receive
    from us
The love we have received
    from God.

"Finally, all of you, be like-minded, be sympathetic, love one another, be compassionate and humble."

(1 Peter 3:8)

Love

"Love is patient and kind; love does not envy or boast; it is not arrogant or rude. It does not insist on its own way; it is not irritable or resentful; it does not rejoice at wrongdoing, but rejoices with the truth."

(1 Corinthians 13:4–6)

How to define this finicky
    word?
Some say it's infatuation—
Others call it intense attraction,
Or maybe strong affection,
Or even deep tenderness.
Or possibly amorousness?

Yet, how can something so
  true,
So eternal, be a mere emotion?
God is defined as love,
Yet He is no emotion.
A warm fuzzy feeling?
I think not.

But being love,
God does not merely love;
He *is* love itself.
And God loves because
That is His nature,
The expression of His being.

Love is not based on feelings;
It is a determined act of will,
The joyful resolve to place
Another's good above
  your own.
It is not natural.
It must come from its source.

The fullest expression of love
Is manifested in the Son
  of God.
God created us, sustains
  us, and
Revealed Himself to us
  through Jesus.
God's love led to the cross,
Unmerited love for those He
  loves.

True love is unconditional,
Always giving, never taking.

The response of the receiver
Is immaterial to the giver.
Selfless and enduring—
Two qualities that shine forth.

Impossible to love God
Without loving one another.
Inconsistent to love God
Without obedience to
His commandments.
Yet God gave his Spirit
To dwell within us,
Empowering us to love as He
  loves.

Love that extends beyond
  emotions,
Demonstrating itself in actions.
All that one does
Is to be done in love,
Reflecting God's light,
Motivating every move.

**"So now faith, hope, and love
abide, these three; but the greatest
of these is love."**

(1 Corinthians 13:13)

Luke

**"Judge not, and you will not be
judged; condemn not, and you**

151

will not be condemned; forgive, and you will be forgiven."

(Luke 6:37)

Physician, Gentile,
Writer of the gospel of Luke
And the book of Acts.
Both were written with
    accurate detail
About the person and work of
    Jesus.
A close friend of Paul,
Who called Luke a beloved
    physician
And his fellow laborer.
Luke, well-educated,
Was an observant, careful
    writer.

Luke was an evangelist,
    historian,
Physician, pastor, missionary,
Apostolic companion, and
A brother theologian.
His goal and purpose
For writing his gospel:
To put on paper the
Exact truth concerning Jesus,
And the plan of salvation—
An infallible history and
    theology
Inspired by the Holy Spirit.

The gospel of Luke,
Is a meticulous history,
An orderly account,

Full of unique details.

The book of Acts provides
A history of the early church,
The fulfillment of
The Great Commission.
Sheds light on the gift
Of the Holy Spirit.

Luke lived long,
Settled in Greece, and
Died in his eighties—
Peacefully or martyred,
History does not reveal.

"But you will receive power when the Holy Spirit has come upon you, and you will be my witnesses in Jerusalem and in all Judea and Samaria, and to the end of the earth."

(Acts 1:8)

Lust

"But I say to you that everyone who looks at a woman with lustful intent has already committed adultery with her in his heart."

(Matthew 5:28)

Lust has as its focus
The pleasing of oneself.

Often leads to unwholesome
actions
Regardless of the consequences.
Lust is about possession, about
greed.
It has to do with
Strong cravings or desires,
Quite often of a sexual nature.
In scripture, it is almost always
relating to
Strong cravings for sexual
immorality
Or idolatrous worship.
The word is used for a strong
yearning
That is negative and forbidden.

Lust is something we willfully
choose,
Is not forced upon us.
It is a desire that arises
From the heart and the mind.
Lust is not always physical;
It can be found in the heart,
In dreams, and in the eyes.
Our lusts come not from God,
But from the world.
They are a direct violation of
God's perfect will.

Necessary not only to
overcome lust,
But to avoid it altogether.
We must admit our
weaknesses,

Knowing we are not exempt
from sin.
We must put on the armor
of God
To protect ourselves from the
enemy.
We must remember the Word
of God,
Which is our only defensive
weapon.
And we must establish
boundaries
To guard against lust.
Always be alert in the pursuit
To avoid sin, guarding against
The lusts of this world.

Lust is the opposite of
Holiness and honor.
Our desires, made by God
From the beginning,
Have their proper place.
They are to be governed
By honor toward another
person
And holiness toward God.
Lust is the corruption of a good
thing
By the absence of honor
And the absence of the utmost
Regard for God.

**"For lust is a shameful sin, a crime
that should be punished. It is a**

devastating fire that destroys to hell."

(Job 31:11–12 NLT)

Majesty

"He is the radiance of the glory of God and the exact imprint of his nature, and he upholds the universe by the word of his power. After making purification for sins, he sat down at the right hand of the Majesty on high."

(Hebrews 1:3)

We speak of the majesty
    of God,
Of our maker and our Lord,
Declaring His greatness and
Accepting His invitation to
    worship.
Defined as "greatness, dignity,"
Majesty belongs to God, the
    Father,
To whom all greatness belongs,
And who is clothed with it.

God, the Son, shares this
    greatness,
This majesty, with God, the
    Father.
Majesty denotes the glorious
    exaltation
Of Christ in human nature,

His suffering, death, and
    resurrection.
He now enjoys honor and
    glory, and
Sits at the right hand of God,
    the Father,
In the highest heavens.

As the Father and Son
Glory in majesty,
The Holy Spirit is majestic
In manifesting God in the
    world,
In the church, and in our very
    hearts.

God is majestic in His
    omniscience,
In His omnipresence,
And in His omnipotence.
His majesty is unlimited
In His wisdom, presence, and
    power.
Difficult for human minds
To reconcile this majesty,
This limitless greatness.
Our need is to wait upon the
    Lord
In meditations on His majesty.

God is robed in majesty;
His understanding is infinite.
He made the earth by His
    power,
Established the world by His
    wisdom,

Stretched out the heavens
By His understanding,
Calling forth honor and
    demanding praise.
His majesty has a glorious
    splendor
In His wondrous works.
Great is our Lord!

"For we did not follow cleverly
devised myths when we made
known to you the power and
coming of our Lord Jesus Christ,
but we were eyewitnesses of his
majesty."

(2 Peter 1:16)

Man

"Then the LORD God formed a
man from the dust of the ground
and breathed into his nostrils the
breath of life, and the man became
a living being."

(Genesis 2:7)

Created by God
On the sixth day,
In His own image,
Having the reflection of
The Lord's own holy character.
Raised from the dust,
Life breathed in our nostrils.

A unique creature,
Having both body and soul,
Man is a created being,
Dependent, finite, and derived.
Moreover, man is accountable
To God.

This image of God,
Imago dei,
Refers to the spiritual aspect
Of humanity, not the physical;
For God is a spirit, without a
    body.
His image sets man apart from
    animals,
Fits them for dominion over
    the earth,
Enables them to commune
    with
Their maker. It is a likeness,
Mentally, morally, socially.

Mentally, in that man was
    created as
A rational, volitional agent,
With the ability to reason and
    choose.
Morally, in that man created in
Righteousness and perfect
    innocence,
Reflecting God's holiness.
Socially, in that man was
    created for
Fellowship,
Reflecting God's triune nature
And His love.

155

Man was created with a
     purpose:
To be fruitful and multiply,
Filling the earth, and
Subduing it.
Ruling over fish of the sea,
Birds in the sky,
And every living creature.
But more than this,
Man's purpose is to know God,
Have a relationship with
     Him, and
Glorify Him in all things.

Man was created as gendered
     creatures,
For God created male and
     female—
Created equally in the image
     of God,
Not one to rule over the other,
But with harmonizing roles,
Giving glory to their maker.

This image of God was
     distorted
By the fall in the garden,
Passing this damaged likeness
To all of Adam's descendants.
Today, we still bear God's
     image,
But we also bear
The scars of sin.

This distorted image is to be
     fully

Restored to the original
Image of God
Through the redemption
     available
By God's grace through faith
In Jesus Christ as Savior.
Through Christ, we are made
New creations
In the likeness of God.

"So God created mankind in his own image, in the image of God he created them; male and female he created them."

(Genesis 1:27)

Manna

"When the people of Israel saw it, they said to one another, 'What is it?' For they did not know what it was. And Moses said to them, 'It is the bread that the LORD has given you to eat.'"

(Exodus 16:15)

One of God's miracles—
Bread from heaven.
Appeared each morning,
Except on the Sabbath.
Manna is translated from
     Hebrew
As "What is it?"—

A question the Israelites asked.

No recipe exists.
Described as coriander seed,
White, and having the taste of
    wafers
With honey.
Also called the bread of angels.
Appeared in the wilderness
During the forty years of
    wandering.
Ceased upon Israel's entering
The Promised Land.

Manna was also a
    foreshadowing of Jesus,
Who called Himself the bread
    of life.
Just as God provided manna
To the Israelites
To save them from starving,
He has provided Jesus Christ
For the salvation of our souls,
To save us from eternal
    damnation.

The physical manna saved
The Israelites from physical
    death.
The spiritual manna saves us
From eternal death.

"Your fathers ate the manna in the wilderness, and they died. This is the bread that comes down from heaven, so that one may eat of it and not die. I am the living bread that came down from heaven."

(John 6:49–51)

Mark

"She who is at Babylon, who is likewise chosen, sends you greetings, and so does Mark, my son."

(1 Peter 5:13)

Mark, the evangelist,
Author of the gospel of Mark—
Was not one of the twelve
    apostles
But perhaps among the
    seventy-two
Sent out by Jesus,
And may have met Jesus face
    to face.
Possibly the young man who
Fled naked from the Mount of
    Olives
At Jesus's arrest.
Also referred to as John Mark,
Companion of the apostle Paul,
Founder of the
Church of Alexandria.

Became close to the apostle
    Peter,
Who called Mark his son.
Wrote down Peter's

Teachings and sermons,
Preserved them in accuracy,
Approved by Peter,
Read in Rome, and carried to
    Egypt.

This short gospel, rich in facts,
Is saturated in detail, written
    to show
That Jesus is the Messiah,
The Son of God,
Who was sent to suffer, to
    serve,
To rescue, and to restore
    mankind.
A story of action,
A powerful witness to His life,
His death, and His
    resurrection.
It is full of miracles, full of
    parables,
Focusing more on the deeds of
    Jesus
Than on His teachings.
It reveals the humanity of
    Christ,
Christ, the suffering servant.

Mark, friend of the apostles,
Shared their commitment
To proclaiming the gospel.
Martyred in Alexandria while
Preaching the gospel of Christ.

"Therefore I tell you, whatever you ask in prayer, believe that you have received it, and it will be yours."

(Mark 11:24)

Marriage

"Therefore a man shall leave his father and his mother and hold fast to his wife, and they shall become one flesh."

(Genesis 2:24)

Marriage is defined as the
Union between a man and a
    woman,
To the glory of God.
Ordained by the Creator,
Intimate and complementary
In all aspects of life.

Marriage is intended to last a
    lifetime.
Literally as "one flesh," with
No separation—together
    forever.
No escape clause with the
    words
"Till death do us part."

One flesh, a powerful symbol.
No longer two entities; now a
    single unit.

Takes precedence over
All previous and future
    relationships—
Emotionally, spiritually,
    intellectually,
Financially as one.
A physical union for joy,
    procreation,
Serving God together as one.

Marriage reflects Christ's
    relationship
With His church.
The church is sacrificially loved
By Christ
As husbands should love their
    wives.
A husband's responsibility is
    leadership,
As Christ is the head of the
    church.

The nature of marriage
Is complementarian.
The wife, as a helper,
Complements her husband,
As the husband complements
    his wife.
Together in marriage,
They are a single entity.
No inferiority is implied,
Only distinct complementary
    roles.

Wives are told to submit to
    husbands

As they submit to the Lord,
As all Christians are to submit
To the Lord. Yet, even when
    this
Mandate applied to wives, the
Bulk of responsibility remains
On the husband to love his
    wife
As Christ loves the church.

This submission is to husbands
    only,
Not society. A loving response
To a loving leadership,
Not a reflection of inferiority
Or lesser worth.
Each retains dignity,
    self-respect.
Christ submitted Himself to
    the Father,
Yet retained full worth as
    the Son.

The husband's role of leading
Is no permission for selfishness
Or dominance. Husbands are
    commanded,
"Love your wife." Selfless,
Sacrificial, unconditional love,
Desiring, working continuously
For what is best for his wife.

In marriage, one does not ask,
"What is best for me?"
Rather, "What is best for my
    spouse?"

Always thinking of the other.
Ask what you can put into the
 marriage,
Not what you can get out of it.

Togetherness and desire
To benefit each other
Is not automatic, not natural.
A man is to cleave to his wife,
A woman to submit to her
 husband.
Not with selfish ambition or
 vain conceit—
Only love for the glory of God.

"The heart of her husband trusts in her, and he will have no lack of gain. She does him good, and not harm, all the days of her life."

(Proverbs 31:11–12)

Mary Magdalene

"Soon afterward he went on through cities and villages, proclaiming and bringing the good news of the kingdom of God. And the twelve were with him, and also some women who had been healed of evil spirits and infirmities: Mary, called Magdalene, from whom seven demons had gone out, and Joanna, the wife of Chuza, Herod's household manager, and Susanna, and many others, who provided for them out of their means."

(Luke 8:1–3)

Oh, the stories told, the myths
 invented.
Said to be once a prostitute—
Yet nowhere in scripture is this
 suggested.
The label, penned by Pope
 Gregory I—
Defies evidence to the contrary
In the gospels.
Said to be the wife of Jesus—
Though hardly a fact.
She was many things:
A close associate,
A dedicated servant,
A financial supporter.
But a lover or wife—never.

Mary Magdalene—
From a life oppressed by seven
 demons
To a life radically changed
By Jesus Christ.
She was from the town of
 Magdala
On the coast of Galilee,
A woman of Jewish descent.
On the day of her Lord's
 resurrection,
She was there first at His empty
 tomb.

Shamed by demon possession,
Either physical or
    psychological.
Beauty and wealth did not
Spare her this disgrace.
Looked upon by Jesus—
    only He
Could see who she really was,
Regardless of her demonized
    state.
He issued forth the command
For all seven spirits to depart
    from her.
This freedom led Mary to
    dedicate her life
To Jesus and His ministry.

She was present at the mock
    trial
Of Jesus. She heard Pontius
    Pilate
Pronounce the death sentence.
She saw Jesus beaten and
Humiliated by the crowd.
She was one of the women
Who stood near Jesus
At the foot of the cross.
The earliest witness to the
Resurrection of Jesus,
She was sent by Jesus
To tell the others.
Although not mentioned in
    Acts 2,
She was likely present with the
    apostles
To await the promised

Coming of the Holy Spirit.

Mary, a woman living apart
    from God
Until she encountered Jesus.
She went from a life
Oppressed by seven demons,
To participating in Jesus's
    ministry,
Witnessing the greatest miracle
Of all time.

"Now when he rose early on the first day of the week, he appeared first to Mary Magdalene, from whom he had cast out seven demons."

(Mark 16:9)

Matthew

"As Jesus passed on from there, he saw a man called Matthew sitting at the tax booth, and he said to him, 'Follow me.' And he rose and followed him."

(Matthew 9:9)

An apostle of Christ,
Former tax collector (publican),
In the town of Capernaum.
His name means "gift of God."
Also called Levi and was

Inspired to write the gospel of
Matthew.

Well to do, like most publicans,
Who enriched themselves
through
Tax collections from their own
people.
Hosted a large banquet for
Jesus, with
A large crowd, including tax
collectors,
Who were seen by many
As sinners to be avoided.
Yet they were saved by Jesus.

His gospel,
The first book in the New
Testament,
Tells the good news
Of the long-awaited arrival
Of the Messiah, who had come
to save
Both Jew and Gentile.

The gospel of Matthew,
Largest of the four gospels,
Covers much ground:
Lineage, birth, and early life of
Jesus,
His ministry, many of His
teachings
(Including the Sermon on the
Mount),
The mission and purpose
Of the disciples,

A collection of parables, and
The arrest, torture, and
execution of Jesus.
This gospel ends with the
resurrection
And the Great Commission.
An excellent introduction
To the core teachings of
Christianity.

His death is a mystery—
Probably in Ethiopia.
Conflicting reports.
Earliest accounts say he died
naturally;
Others say he was martyred,
Burned, stoned, stabbed,
And possibly beheaded.
Regardless of his manner of
death,
He was a true saint of saints.

**"In the same way, let your light
shine before others, so that they
may see your good works and give
glory to your Father who is in
heaven."**

(Matthew 5:16)

Meek

"Blessed are the meek, for they shall inherit the earth."

(Matthew 5:5)

Many definitions:
Patience, unselfishness,
    gentleness,
Bearing afflictions quietly.
Yet one stands out: humility—
Humility toward God and
    others.
It is being patient,
Bearing with one another in
    love.

The meek are those whom God
    promises
To counsel and instruct.
He guides them in judgment
And teaches them His way.

Christ, the meekest of all—
He was "meek and lowly in
    heart."
He took the nature of a
    servant,
Being born in human likeness,
Becoming obedient to death on
    the cross—
Yet fully God.

Christians are to model
The attitude of Christ,

Sharing the gospel in
Gentleness and meekness.
Live in humility,
Forego personal rights
For the benefit of others.

The path to blessedness
Is not supremacy and high
    stature,
But through meekness of heart
    and mind.
Imitate Christ as a true servant;
Be true, be meek.

"Therefore put away all filthiness and rampant wickedness and receive with meekness the implanted word, which is able to save your souls."

(James 1:21)

Melchizedek

"And Melchizedek king of Salem brought out bread and wine. (He was priest of God Most High.) And he blessed him and said, 'Blessed be Abram by God Most High, Possessor of heaven and earth; and blessed be God Most High, who has delivered your enemies into your hand!'"

(Genesis 14:18–20)

A mysterious figure—
Scripture tells little about him.
A contemporary of Abraham,
Yet no recorded family.
A priest of God Most High
And the king of Salem.
His name means
"King of righteousness."
The order of Melchizedek is
Royal and everlasting,
A king greater than Abraham
    or Levi.
Introduced in Genesis 14
During the story of Abraham,
Mentioned again in Psalm 110,
    then
Discussed more fully in
    Hebrews.

This man is possibly a
    theophany—
An apparition of Jesus
Before His birth in the flesh,
A preincarnate appearance of
    Christ.
Both are high priests and
    kings,
With kingdoms eternal,
Kings of righteousness and
    peace.
No mere mortal ever was
A man of righteousness—
Only Christ our Savior.
Both are greater than
    Abraham,
Both are greater than Levi.

A stronger argument comes
In the book of Hebrews:
Melchizedek is like Jesus, but
Jesus is not like Melchizedek.
Jesus is not like this figure
Who existed hundreds of years
Before He came into this
    world,
But Melchizedek is like Jesus,
Who existed eons before
    Melchizedek.
Melchizedek is the
    foreshadowing
Of Christ the king and priest.

A case can be made either way.
Melchizedek is a type of
    Christ,
Prefiguring the Lord's
    ministry;
Or it is possible that Abraham
Met and gave honor to
The Lord Jesus Himself?

**"In the same way, Christ did
not take on himself the glory of
becoming a high priest. But God
said to him, 'You are my Son;
today I have become your Father.'
And he says in another place, 'You
are a priest forever, in the order of
Melchizedek.'"**

(Hebrews 5:5–6)

Mercy

"Have mercy on me, O God, according to your steadfast love; according to your abundant mercy blot out my transgressions."

(Psalm 51:1)

God's tenderhearted and loving
Compassion for His people.
Caring treatment of those in
distress,
As in forgiving sins or wrongs,
Healing, and comfort in times
of suffering.

Integrally related to grace.
Mercy and grace are two sides
Of the same coin.
For when a person is saved by
Christ,
God extends both mercy and
grace.
Mercy is forgiving the sinner,
Withholding the punishment
Justly deserved.
Grace is heaping underserved
blessings
Upon the poor sinner.
God does not bestow one
Without the other.
In Christ, the believer
experiences
Both mercy and grace.

Synonyms abound:
Lovingkindness, compassion,
Pity, sympathy.
Mercy is a quality intrinsic
To the nature of God.
God's mercy is inexhaustible.
As children of God,
We can confidently cry out
For mercy in times of need.

Demonstrating mercy to our
neighbors
Is a characteristic of life in
Christ.
Showing mercy is a mark
Of righteousness.
It is a response of God's people
To His covenant.
It is the essence of spiritual
living.

"Be merciful, even as your Father is merciful."

(Luke 6:36)

Messiah

"He first found his own brother Simon and said to him, 'We have found the Messiah.'"

(John 1:41)

The anointed one, Christ,
Predicted in the Old
    Testament,
Revealed in the New—
Jesus of Nazareth.

Called a deliverer by the Jews,
Chosen by God to redeem His
    people
From sin and damnation.

Jesus Christ means
Jesus, the Messiah,
Jesus, the anointed one,
Consecrated by God.

Messiah has many
    requirements:
First, a Hebrew man,
Born in Bethlehem of a virgin,
A prophet akin to Moses,
A priest in the order of
    Melchizedek,
A king, a descendant of David,
One who suffered before
    entering
His glory.
All conditions are fully met in
    Jesus.

King of kings,
Lord of lords,
Who came to rescue sinners—
Will return to establish
His kingdom on earth.

Jesus Christ,
Jesus, the anointed one.

"Simon Peter answered, 'You are the Messiah, the Son of the living God.'"

(Matthew 16:16)

Minor Prophets

"And afterward, I will pour out my Spirit on all people. Your sons and daughters will prophesy, your old men will dream dreams, your young men will see visions."

(Joel 2:28)

At times referred to as "the
    Twelve."
"Minor" is not because their
    message
Is less inspired than what is
    given
Through the major prophets.
Rather, God simply chose to
    reveal
More content through the
    major prophets
Than through these other
    twelve.
The difference is in length,
    volume.

These twelve prophets—
Hosea, Joel, Amos,
Obadiah, Jonah, Micah,
Nahum, Habakkuk,
    Zephaniah,
Haggai, Zechariah, and
    Malachi—
Each with a message
Revealing God's holiness,
Wrath, grace, and mercy.
All pointed to Christ,
Even to His return.
All are worthy of our attention,
All are worthy of our study.

The major prophets were
Isaiah, Jeremiah, Lamentations,
Ezekiel, and Daniel.
As with the minor prophets,
All had the privilege of sharing
Amazing news of redemption
And restoration.
Their calls of repentance
Often fell on deaf ears,
Unteachable hearts.

The minor prophets touch on
Many subjects:
God's love, judgment, hope,
Relationship with God, pride,
Repentance, mercy, wrath,
Encouragement, and
    covenants.
All these prophets have
    important roles
In the history of Israel.

They are all-important for
    studying.

**"The Lord is good, a stronghold
in the day of trouble; he knows
those who take refuge in him."**

(Nahum 1:7)

Money-Changers

**"In the temple he found those who
were selling oxen and sheep and
pigeons, and the money-changers
sitting there."**

(John 2:14)

Similar to tax collectors,
Money-changers extorted
    money
From their own people.
They sought to profit
    financially
From the worship of God.

A half-shekel tax was required
To offer temple sacrifices.
Foreign coins were not
    accepted,
Hence, the need for an.
    exchange—
Usually at exorbitant profits
    gained
By exploiting people's religious
    zeal

Taking advantage of the poor
And foreigners.

Additionally,
Many sold sacrificial animals,
Overcharging those who
Had not brought their own.
For those who did bring
  their own,
An examination was performed
  on them,
Usually declaring them
  "unapproved,"
Requiring the worshiper to
  purchase
Replacement sacrifices at
  inflated prices.

All this took place within the
  temple walls,
Making it a "den of thieves,"
As Jesus called it.
He could not tolerate mockery
Of the spirit of true worship;
He made a whip of cords,
Drove out the money-changers,
Upsetting the tables,
Spilling coins to the ground,
Scattering the animals.
His righteous anger was toward
The dishonoring of God's
  holiness.
He drove them out of
His Father's house.

"And in their greed they will exploit you with false words. Their condemnation from long ago is not idle, and their destruction is not asleep."

(2 Peter 2:3)

Mourn

"Blessed are those who mourn, for they shall be comforted."

(Matthew 5:4)

Lament, grieve, feel guilt—
An expression of the heart.
Many reasons to mourn:
Loss, death, mistakes—
  especially sins.
In this beatitude, it refers to the
Destitution of our spiritual
  states
Over sins that separated us
  from God.
It is that sorrow over rebellion
Against God,
Hostility to His will.

Example of true mourning:
The publican (tax collector)
Crying out over his iniquities,
Conscious of his corruption
  within:
"God, be merciful to me a
  sinner."

So many reasons to mourn:
Strife between brothers,
Weakness of faith,
Living to the flesh,
Disobeying commandments,
Propensity to wander from
　　Christ.
What wretched people we are!

Mourning is recognizing
Our fallen nature,
Our inclination to sin.
Heartfelt sorrow for our
　　condition,
Realizing we are helpless
Without the love of God,
Without Christ's sacrifice on
　　the cross,
Without the Spirit's constant
　　reassurance.
Let us mourn, let us be
　　comforted
In Christ Jesus.

"He will wipe away every tear from their eyes, and death shall be no more, neither shall there be mourning, nor crying, nor pain anymore, for the former things have passed away."

(Revelation 21:4)

Names of God

"I bow down toward your holy temple and give thanks to your name for your steadfast love and your faithfulness, for you have exalted above all things your name and your word."

(Psalm 138:2)

God is known not only by
His perfections and works,
But also by His names.
The names of God
Are miniature portraits and
　　promises
Of who God is.
People did not choose the
　　names for God;
God chose His own names.

In many instances,
Where no name of God is
　　employed,
Simply the term *name* is used
In reference to God. Abraham
　　called
On the name of the Lord.
Prayer is to be made in His
　　name.
His name embodies the entire
Person of God.

Some names of God
　　proclaimed

169

In scripture include these:

El, Eloah—God mighty, strong, prominent (Nehemiah 9:17);

Elohim—God as Creator, mighty and strong (Genesis 1:1);

El Shaddai—God almighty, mighty One of Jacob (Psalm 84:8);

Yahweh (YHWH)—the LORD (Exodus 15:26);

Yahweh-Jireh—the LORD will provide (Genesis 22:14);

Yahweh-Rapha—the LORD who heals (Exodus 15:26);

Yahweh-Nissi—the LORD our banner (Exodus17:15);

Yahweh-M'kaddesh—the LORD who sanctifies, makes holy (Leviticus 20:8);

Yahweh-Shalom—The LORD our peace (Judges 6:24);

Yahweh-Elohim—the LORD God (Genesis 2:4);

Yahweh-Tsidkenu—the LORD our righteousness (Jeremiah 33:16);

Yahweh-Rohi—the LORD our shepherd (Psalm 23:1);

El Elyon—God Most High (Deuteronomy 26:19);

El-Olam—everlasting God (Psalm 90:1–3);

Adonai—master, owner (Isaiah 10:16).

In our Bibles, these names have been
Translated for our understanding.

YHWH or *Yahweh* or the LORD—
As close to a personal name
As God has revealed to us.
This name, revealed to Moses,
Was unknown before his time.

To glorify God requires
A knowledge of God.
It is knowing who God is,
What God does. To know God
Is to know His names.
His many names in scripture
Constitute the revelation of
God's character, His
    works, and
His relationship to us.
We know what God is like
Not only by His perfections
And by His works,
But also by His names.

"God also said to Moses, 'Say this to the people of Israel: "The LORD [YHWH], the God of your fathers, the God of Abraham, the God

of Isaac, and the God of Jacob, has sent me to you." This is my name forever, and thus I am to be remembered throughout all generations.'"

(Exodus 3:15)

Narrow Gate

"Enter by the narrow gate. For the gate is wide and the way is easy that leads to destruction, and those who enter by it are many. For the gate is narrow and the way is hard that leads to life, and those who find it are few."

(Matthew 7:13–14)

A gate, a door, symbolizing one
thing:
Christ Jesus Himself.
The way to eternal life is one
gate only—
Only one way, for Jesus is
The way, the truth, and the life.
One factor alone permits us
To pass through this gate:
Accepting Jesus Christ
As Lord and Savior.
A person follows Christ
Wholeheartedly or not at all.
There is no lukewarm
commitment
To Jesus. If we are not on

The narrow road of discipleship
We are on the wide road
To eternal damnation.

Jesus has made Himself the
gate
Through which every person
Must enter for eternal life.
To enter this gate is not easy.
It is filled with difficulties:
Enduring the opposition
Of human pride,
Our natural love of sin, and
The opposition of Satan—
No, the way is not easy.

Many choose instead the wide
gate.
For that gate is easy:
Rejection of Christ's teachings,
Putting oneself before God.
Without exception, this wide
gate
Leads to destruction,
Yet is traveled by many.

Jesus has made Himself the
narrow gate
To save sinners like you
and me.
He has provided the path
For eternal life.
The exhortation to strive to
enter
Is a command to repent of our
sins,

To reject worldly ways.
All people are welcome,
Yet few take His path
Through this gate of all gates,
This narrow gate.

"Strive to enter through the narrow door. For many, I tell you, will seek to enter and will not be able."

(Luke 13:24)

Nature of God

"'For my thoughts are not your thoughts, neither are your ways my ways,' declares the LORD. 'As the heavens are higher than the earth, so are my ways higher than your ways and my thoughts than your thoughts.'"

(Isaiah 55:8–9)

We know certain things
  of God,
For God chose to reveal them
  to us—
Through His Word,
Through His creation,
Through His love.

God is spirit, intangible by
  nature.
God is one, yet exists in three:

God, the Father,
God, the Son,
God, the Holy Spirit.
God is infinite,
God is incomparable,
God is unchanging,
God is perfect,
God is sovereign,
God is faithful.
God exists everywhere.
God know everything.
God has all power and
  authority.
His nature is self-existent.

God's nature can be defined
But never fully
  comprehended—
Can never be called our own.
His nature is what makes
  Him God.
Distinguishing features that
He alone possesses. His
  nature is
The cause for our worship,
  praise, trust.
All glory to God!

"Have you not known? Have you not heard? The LORD is the everlasting God, the Creator of the ends of the earth. He does not faint or grow weary; his understanding is unsearchable."

(Isaiah 40:28)

Neighbor

"You shall not take vengeance or bear a grudge against the sons of your own people, but you shall love your neighbor as yourself: I am the LORD."

(Leviticus 19:18)

More, much more
Than the person living next
   door.
More than those similar to us,
More than those who can
Love us in return.
Broadly, a neighbor is
Anyone placed in our path
   by God.

The Samaritan found a
   neighbor
On the side of the road, in dire
   condition.
We find neighbors in
   whomever we meet,
Whomever we see today.
These neighbors are ones we
   can help,
Offering our time, talents, and
   treasures.

If someone is hurting: treat
   them.
If someone is hungry: feed
   them.

If someone is spiritually lost:
Share the saving message
Of salvation.
All are neighbors—
Each is our fellow person,
Who is deserving of our love.

The relationship of a neighbor
Is not restricted to the physical
   distance,
But extends to the moral.
It is based on the opportunity
   and capacity
For mutual love and help.
This is not so much a rigid fact,
But the idea that all
Are created in the image
   of God.
Our love for our neighbors
Is to imitate divine love,
Being impartial,
Having all people for its object.

Too often, we ask, "Who is my
   neighbor?"
The better question may be:
"Who am I?"

"If you really fulfill the royal law according to the scripture, 'You shall love your neighbor as yourself,' you are doing well."

(James 2:8)

Nephilim

"The Nephilim were on the earth in those days—and also afterward—when the sons of God went to the daughters of humans and had children by them. They were the heroes of old, men of renown."

(Genesis 6:4)

Possibly giants,
Possibly fallen angels.
There is much debate by
scholars.
Offspring of the sons of God
And the daughters of men.
Scripture is not clear on exactly
Who these Nephilim were.
The larger question is:
Who were their fathers,
These "sons of God"?

Many theories are discussed.
Were they first fallen angels?
Scriptural support for this
In Job 1:6 and 38:7, and
Jude 6–7.
Yet uncertainties remain.
Second, they could be
descendants of Seth,
Identified as the righteous line
of Seth
Who disobeyed God by
marrying

Ungodly women from Cain's
line,
Thus rejecting God.
Additional theories include
Human men possessed by
fallen angels.
Or maybe, just fallen men.

Regardless, these Nephilim
Were around before the flood
As well as afterward,
Which suggests perhaps that
These ungodly descendants
Who rejected God,
Who fell far into wickedness,
Were merely the offspring
of men
Who took ungodly wives
Against the commands of God.

"The land, through which we have gone to spy it out, is a land that devours its inhabitants, and all the people that we saw in it are of great height. And there we saw the Nephilim (the sons of Anak, who come from the Nephilim), and we seemed to ourselves like grasshoppers, and so we seemed to them."

(Numbers 13:32–33)

New Jerusalem

"Then I saw a new heaven and a new earth, for the first heaven and the first earth had passed away, and the sea was no more. And I saw the holy city, new Jerusalem, coming down out of heaven from God, prepared as a bride adorned for her husband."

(Revelation 21:1–2)

The fulfillment of God,
Exemplifying His goodness—
New Jerusalem will be a city
    of God,
A celestial city, holy city,
A tabernacle of God.
It has many names but is one
    place.
Literally, it will be heaven on
    earth.
Described as a precious jewel
    like jasper,
Clear as crystal. A huge city,
Lit by the glory of God.

It is often referred to as the
    eternal state,
Where righteousness dwells.
It is the place where God will
Dwell with His people forever,
Where all tears are wiped away;
No more death, grief, or pain.

A place of unimagined
    blessings.
The river of water and of life
    flowing,
The tree of life producing
Fruit every month.

All the ages will have come and
    gone;
Christ will have gathered His
    church;
The tribulation will have
    passed,
As will have Armageddon;
Satan will have received his just
    punishment;
And people will have been
    judged.

The Lamb will sit on the
    throne.
Angels will be at the gates,
The city will be filled with
    God's redeemed,
Those who accept Jesus,
The Son of God,
As Lord and Savior.

Real or allegorical?
There are many interpretations.
The truth is that our final
    home
Will be beautiful, immense,
And glorious.
At the consummation, we will
    dwell

In the brightest light
   imaginable,
The light of God's glory.
When Jesus returns to
Bring in this final state,
He will be our lamp.
We shall gaze on His
   countenance,
Rejoicing in His radiance
Forever and ever and ever
In the New Jerusalem.

"No longer will there be anything accursed, but the throne of God and of the Lamb will be in it, and his servants will worship him."

(Revelation 22:3)

New Testament

"My dear children, I write this to you so that you will not sin. But if anybody does sin, we have an advocate with the Father—Jesus Christ, the Righteous One."

(1 John 2:1)

The fulfillment of the Old
   Testament—
The Old and New are
   inseparable,
Just as God, the Father, is
   inseparable

From God, the Son, and
From God, the Holy Spirit.

Contains sacred books unique
To Christianity, twenty-seven
   in total.
Usually divided into five
   sections:
The Gospels—four books:
   Matthew,
   Mark, Luke, and John.
Historical—one book: Acts.
Pauline epistles—thirteen
   books:
   Romans, 1 and 2
   Corinthians, Galatians,
   Ephesians, Philippians,
   Colossians,
   1 and 2 Thessalonians, 1
   and 2 Timothy,
   Titus, Philemon.
General epistles—eight books:
   Hebrews, James, 1 and 2
   Peter,
   1, 2 and 3 John, Jude.
Prophetic—one book:
   Revelation.

The New Testament gives us
   accounts
Of the birth, life, ministry,
And the death and resurrection
Of Jesus Christ.
The gospels demonstrate how
Jesus was the Messiah promised

In the Old Testament. The gospels
Lay the foundation for the teaching
In the rest of the New Testament.
This includes a record of the deeds
Of Jesus's apostles, the beginning
Of the church and its rapid growth,
As well as letters to specific churches
And individuals, teaching
Christian doctrine and its application.
The New Testament concludes
With prophecies of events
That will occur in the end times.

The New Testament
Tells us of Jesus's death on the cross
On our behalf
And what our response should be.
It focuses on giving solid
Christian teachings along with
Applications to our lives.

The New and Old Testaments,
Despite their diversity
And separation of time,
Are united in proclaiming

The one true God,
And that our God loves His people
And seeks the salvation of all men
Through His Son Jesus Christ.

"All Scripture is breathed out by God and profitable for teaching, for reproof, for correction, and for training in righteousness."

(2 Timothy 3:16)

Numbers

"The LORD bless you and keep you; the LORD make his face to shine upon you and be gracious to you; the LORD lift up his countenance upon you and give you peace."

(Numbers 6:24–26)

Fourth book of the Old Testament
Part of the Pentateuch
(Old Testament's first five books,
Authored by Moses),
Revolves around Israel's journey
To the Promised Land.
Its Hebrew name means "in the desert."

Called *Numbers* for the two
censuses
Taken during Israel's journey.

Describes the justice and love
Of God toward His people.
Illuminates the sovereign
power
Of God to accomplish His
purposes,
Requiring Israel's responsibility
To be faithful to their
holy God.
Concisely:
The goodness and severity
of God—
Severe in the death of
The rebellious generation,
Those who never entered
The Promised Land.
Goodness in the new
generation,
Those protected, preserved,
And provided for by God,
Until their glorious entrance.

Christ is seen throughout this
book:
In the holy war that Christ
will win,
In the call to follow Christ's
holiness,
Bringing life out of death.
Christ as the greatest king
of all,
Christ as living among men.

God's demand for holiness in
His people
Is completely and finally
satisfied
In Jesus Christ, the Lamb
of God
Without spot or blemish,
Who was sacrificed for our
sins.
Sin, unbelief, rebellion will
reap
The judgment of God.

"Today, if you hear his voice, do not harden your hearts as in the rebellion, on the day of testing in the wilderness, where your fathers put me to the test and saw my works for forty years."

(Hebrews 3:7–9)

Old Testament

"Then he said to them, 'These are my words that I spoke to you while I was still with you, that everything written about me in the Law of Moses and the Prophets and the Psalms must be fulfilled.'"

(Luke 24:44)

The first part of our Bible,
The inspired Word of God

Includes thirty-nine books
Written over a thousand-year
    period.
Contains the history of God's
    people,
But more importantly,
The prophecies of the coming
Of Jesus, the Messiah.

Often sectioned into four parts:
Pentateuch—five books:
    Genesis, Exodus,
    Leviticus, Numbers,
    Deuteronomy.
Historical—twelve books:
    Joshua, Judges,
    Ruth, 1 and 2 Samuel, 1
    and 2 Kings,
    1 and 2 Chronicles, Ezra,
    Nehemiah,
    Esther.
Poetic—five books: Job,
    Psalms, Proverbs,
    Ecclesiastes, Song of
    Solomon.
Prophetic—seventeen books:
Major prophets—Isaiah,
    Jeremiah,
    Lamentations, Ezekiel,
    Daniel.
Minor prophets—Hosea, Joel,
    Amos,
    Obadiah, Jonah, Micah,
    Nahum,
    Habakkuk, Zephaniah,

Haggai,
Zechariah, Malachi.
In the Old Testament, God is
    revealed
Not only as the Creator who is
Forgiving, patient, and slow to
    anger,
But also as holy, just, and
    righteous.
This testament contains
    graphic stories
Of sin, evil, and death,
Within the overarching grand
    story
Of love, redemption, and grace.
This God of the Old Testament
Is the same God in the New
    Testament.

The Old Testament leads us
From the creation of the
    heavens and earth
And of all living things
    (including people),
To humanity's fall in the
    garden,
The flood and Noah,
To the tower of Babel,
And on through the lives of
Abraham, Isaac, Jacob, and
    Joseph,
Then on to Moses and the
    exodus,
The giving of the Ten
    Commandments,

And the crossing of the Jordan
River
Into the land of milk and
honey,
On to the reigns of David and
Solomon,
And then the divided kingdom,
The destruction of Israel and
Judah,
Their exile and return from
captivity.
Then comes a four-hundred-
year period
Between the Old and New
Testaments—
Until the birth of Jesus Christ.

God's Word is perfect and true.
The story it tells weaves its way
Through imperfect people.
From the Old Testament's
beginning
To the New Testament's
ending,
God is telling one story—the
true account
Of a sovereign, righteous God
Redeeming fallen humanity
For His glory.

**"All your words are true; all your
righteous laws are eternal."**

(Psalm 119:160)

Omnipotent

**"And God said, 'Let there be light,'
and there was light."**

(Genesis 1:3)

All-powerful. Synonyms
include:
Almighty, authority,
sovereignty.
Refers to God alone as having
All power over all things,
At all times,
In all ways.

The greatest example of this
attribute
Is seen in creation.
God stated, "Let there be ..."
And it was so.
People need tools and
materials;
God simply speaks.
By the power of His Word,
All was created from nothing.

His omnipotence extends
To the preservation of His
creation.
Everything would cease to exist
Without His continual
provision.

Being omnipotent,

God can do anything,
everything.
What He does not do,
He chooses not to do.
For example, He never lies,
Because He chooses not to lie,
In accord with His own
Moral perfection.

As God incarnate,
Jesus is omnipotent.
His power is seen in His
miracles:
Healing many, feeding
thousands,
Calming the storm,
Raising Lazarus from the dead,
Showing His control
Over life and death.

It is God's omnipotence
That continues to hold us
In a state of grace despite
our sin.
By His power we are kept
From forever falling.

"He said to me, 'My grace is sufficient for you, for my power is made perfect in weakness.' Therefore I will boast all the more gladly of my weaknesses, so that the power of Christ may rest upon me."

(1 Corinthians 12:9)

Omnipresent

"The eyes of the Lord are in every place, keeping watch on the evil and the good."

(Proverbs 15:3)

All present, everywhere.
Closely related to God's
Omnipotence and omniscience.
Omnipresence is God's
attribute
Of being present in all ranges
Of both time and space.
He is not limited to the here
and now,
But is present everywhere
And in every now.

Since God is eternal,
Time cannot restrict Him,
As God is indivisible.
Space cannot restrict Him.
He is wholly present in
Every space at every time.
Through His Spirit,
God's reach extends
To every corner of the universe
As well as into
The hearts of mankind.

God's omnipresence is the
guarantee
Of the nearness of God;
Real communion with Him

May be enjoyed everywhere,
Under all circumstances.
It assures the believer
That God is at hand
To save and protect us
From any danger or foe.
God's omnipresence
Informs us of His greatness,
Highlights the love
He has for each of us.
A true source of comfort
For all believers.

"Where shall I go from your Spirit? Or where shall I flee from your presence? If I ascend to heaven, you are there! If I make my bed in Sheol, you are there! If I take the wings of the morning and dwell in the uttermost parts of the sea, even there your hand shall lead me, and your right hand shall hold me."

(Psalm 139:7–10)

Omniscient

"By this we shall know that we are of the truth and reassure our heart before him; for whenever our heart condemns us, God is greater than our heart, and he knows everything."

(1 John 3:19–20)

The state of having total knowledge,
The quality of knowing everything.
This attribute is not restricted
To any one person in the Godhead;
Father, Son, and Holy Spirit
Are all omniscient by nature.

Not only does God know
Everything that will occur
Until the end of history and beyond,
He knows our very thoughts
Even before we speak them.
He knows our hearts;
He knows every hair on our heads.

As God is omnipresent,
He knows everything at every time,
Past, present, future.
He knows everything in every place.
There is nothing He does not know.
This knowledge extends
From the smallest detail to the largest.

This knowledge is not attained
By reasoning, but as simply
    knowing,
For God is sovereign
And self-sufficient.

For the Christian,
God's omniscience lends
    support
And comfort in our suffering.
It acts as a deterrent
When we are tempted to sin,
Especially secret sins.
And it furnishes the source
From which people's desire
For self-knowledge
Can obtain satisfaction.
God's omniscience gives
    comfort,
For He knew everything
About us before we were born.
He knew all our mistakes and
    sins,
Yet he still chose us
To be part of His family for
    eternity.
He knows exactly what we
    need
To grow the peaceful fruit
Of righteousness and to be the
Christians He created us to be.

"Jesus, knowing their thoughts, said, 'Why do you think evil in your hearts?'"

(Matthew 9:4)

Original Sin

"Behold, I was brought forth in iniquity, and in sin did my mother conceive me."

(Psalm 51:5)

The moral corruption we
    own as a consequence of
    Adam's sin.
It is the sinful disposition
All people possess. As a result,
We not only own a sinful
    nature,
But also incur guilt
    before God,
For which we deserve
    punishment.
Original sin is not the first sin;
Original sin defines the
Consequences to all people
From that first sin.

Our sinful nature marks the
    human heart
As deceitful above all things,
Beyond our cure.
We are unable to please God.

Our "good deeds" are like dirty
    rags.
We are not sinners because
    we sin;
We sin because we are sinners.
Our natural tendency is to
    commit sin.

This sounds bad, and it is bad.
It is a radical corruption—
A corruption that permeates
To the core of our beings,
Even to our hearts.

The solution is to be made new
    again,
To be quickened (made alive)
By the power of the Holy
    Spirit.
We must have Christ;
We must be born again.
Only Christ removes the
    penalty
Of Adam's sin, the guilt of our
Corrupted human nature,
All the sins we commit.

This sinful nature is not
Instantaneously removed
When we first repent and
    believe.
The struggle between the Spirit
    and flesh
Is the struggle of the regenerate
    person.
But victory is assured

In Christ.

**"Therefore, just as sin entered
the world through one man, and
death through sin, and in this way
death came to all people, because
all sinned."**

(Romans 5:12)

Parables

**"This was to fulfill what was
spoken by the prophet: 'I will
open my mouth in parables; I will
utter what has been hidden since
the foundation of the world.'"**

(Matthew 13:35)

Illustrative stories
In which a familiar idea is cast
    beside
An unfamiliar idea in such
    a way
To help us better grasp and
    understand
The unfamiliar idea.
Earthly stories with heavenly
    meanings.
Stories containing meanings,
    messages,
Over and above the
    straightforward,
The literal—

Often with an element of
metaphor.

Three types of parables.
True parables offer daily life
illustrations
Within reach of anyone who
hears.
They are self-evident truths
Portraying nature or human
life.

Story parables usually refer to
An actual event,
Such as one person's
experience.
Reliability of the stories is not
at stake,
But the truth conveyed is
significant.

Illustrative parables exhibit
examples
Either to be imitated or
avoided.
They focus directly on the
character
And conduct of an individual.

All three types are true to life,
Usually teaching one basic
truth.

The parables of Jesus
Hold a twofold purpose:
To reveal the truth to those
Wanting to know it,

And to conceal the truth from
those
Who are indifferent.

A parable's most important
part
Is usually the ending—
The last person, deed, or
saying.
Do not drown in a parable's
details;
Focus on the main point.
Interpret parables according
To the simple principles
They're meant to teach.

These short stories
Teach moral and spiritual
lessons.
It is the lesson that is of
importance,
Not the story.
At times, this is difficult,
But it is always fruitful.

**"With many such parables he
spoke the word to them, as they
were able to hear it. He did not
speak to them without a parable,
but privately to his own disciples
he explained everything."**

(Mark 4:33–34)

Passion of Christ

"But God shows his love for us in that while we were still sinners, Christ died for us."

(Romans 5:8)

From the Latin word, meaning
"To endure, to suffer."
Refers to the period from
Jesus's prayer in the
Garden of Gethsemane
To His death on the cross—
The time of His greatest
    suffering.
Told to us in the four gospels:
Matthew, Mark, Luke, and
    John.

It is important to know that
Christ's suffering, His passion,
    was real.
He shed tears in the garden,
Was betrayed by Judas Iscariot,
Beaten by soldiers,
Abandoned by His disciples,
And nailed to the cross.
He suffered unto death.
He died on that cross—
Died the death that we
    deserved.
Foretold in Isiah 53:
"Surely he took up our pain
And bore our suffering."

Passion today has the sense
Of strong emotion. But the
    passion
Of Christ was no mere
    emotion.
It was suffering. Jesus came to
    earth
For the purpose of laying down
    His life
For us. He never wavered from
    this.
His passion (suffering)
Was not due to passion
    (emotion),
But to a settled purpose.

It is through the passion of
    Christ
That we are made right
    with God.
Only through Christ's
    suffering,
His death on the cross,
Can our sins be forgiven.
Jesus took our place;
He took our curse, in order
To clothe us in His
    righteousness,
To open to us the heavenly
    sanctuary
In which we can draw near
With a true heart
In full assurance of faith.
Be passionate about His
    passion.

"When Jesus had received the sour wine, he said, 'It is finished,' and he bowed his head and gave up his spirit."

(John 19:30)

Passover

"And when your children say to you, 'What do you mean by this service?' you shall say, 'It is the sacrifice of the LORD's Passover, for he passed over the houses of the people of Israel in Egypt, when he struck the Egyptians but spared our houses.'"

(Exodus 12:26–27)

For more than three thousand
        years,
A Jewish festival
        commemorating
The exodus from Egypt,
A remembrance of the Lord's
Deliverance of Israel from
        bondage,
The sparing of their firstborns
When the destroying angel
        smote
All the firstborns of the
        Egyptians.
This was deemed the starting
        point
Of the Hebrew nation—

No longer slaves, but now a
        free people
Owing allegiance to no one
        but God.

The actual Passover took place
During the final plague
Inflicted upon Egypt.
The Jews were instructed
To kill an unblemished lamb
        and to
Smear its blood onto their
        doorposts.
For God was to pass through
        Egypt
Striking all the firstborns. But
        when
He saw the blood on the
        doorposts,
He would pass over—no death
Would befall those inside.

The Jews were told that
        this day
Should be a memorial day.
They were to keep it as a feast
To the Lord for all generations,
A statute forever.
Celebrated during the Jewish
        month
Of Nisan (during our March or
        April),
From the fourteenth day to the
        twenty-first.
It is chief of the three great
        annual festivals

Of the Jews.

The principal ritual unique to
    this festival
Is the Seder, a meal eaten on
The first night of Passover, and
Known for its distinctive ritual
    foods—
Unleavened bread, bitter herbs,
    wine—
As well as accompanying
    prayers.
Also known as the
Festival of Unleavened Bread.

While primarily a
    commemoration,
Reminding Israel of their
Deliverance from Egypt,
It is also a type of the great
    deliverance
Accomplished by the Messiah
For all His people—deliverance
From sin's wages of death,
And from bondage to sin itself.

"This day shall be for you a
memorial day, and you shall
keep it as a feast to the LORD;
throughout your generations, as
a statute forever, you shall keep it
as a feast."

(Exodus 12:14)

Patience

"And we desire each one of you
to show the same earnestness to
have the full assurance of hope
until the end, so that you may not
be sluggish, but imitators of those
who through faith and patience
inherit the promises."

(Hebrews 6:11–12)

A characteristic of God,
To be imitated by Christians
Confronted with human
    failings
And uncertain circumstances.
Patience is a fruit of the Spirit.

Scripture has two meanings
For this blessed word. First,
Steadfastness in difficult
    circumstances—
Literally, a "remaining
    under" and
A resoluteness to embrace peace
Regardless of what we
    confront.

The second meaning is "long
    tempered."
Synonym: long-suffering. It is
The ability to hold one's
    temper,
Being slow to anger
Regardless of what one faces.

Scripture demonstrates God's
    patience.
He is patient with sinners,
Leading to our repentance.
His patience prevents Him
From destroying objects of His
    wrath.
He has patience with evil
    people.

Patience is a virtue,
The ability to endure
    discomfort,
Requiring additional virtues to
    join in:
Self-control, humility, and
    generosity.
Patience is a complex of various
    virtues.

Patience is a challenge for
    people.
To wait upon God requires
    faith.
To exercise faith requires
Surrender of control.
It is much easier to desire
    self-control.
But Christ gives the example,
And the Spirit gives the
    strength.

It is equally difficult to exercise
Patience with other people—
Less from selfishness, and

More due to egocentric
    predicaments,
When our natural tendencies
    are to
Be aware only of our own
Thoughts and feelings,
Ignoring those of others.

Patience is to be developed.
All misfortunes are designed
To build virtue in us.
Through difficulty, patience is
    built.
Each nuisance, affliction, and
    ache,
As well as waiting on hope—
All are designed to teach us
    patience.

Our God is patient.
His Spirit produces patience
    in us.
This patience leaves room
    for God
To work in our hearts, our
    relationships.
Be patient as God is patient.

Patience originates from God.
It is part of the fruit of the
    Spirit,
Directly linked to self-
    control and
Demonstrated by Christ,
Who we should always imitate.

Our patience is pleasing
to God.

"I therefore, a prisoner for the Lord, urge you to walk in a manner worthy of the calling to which you have been called, with all humility and gentleness, with patience, bearing with one another in love, eager to maintain the unity of the Spirit in the bond of peace."

(Ephesians 4:1–3)

Patriarchs

"To them belong the patriarchs, and from their race, according to the flesh, is the Christ, who is God over all, blessed forever. Amen."

(Romans 9:5)

Men were empowered by God
To establish the nation of
Israel:
Abraham, Isaac, and Jacob.

Abraham, the father of a
multitude.
God made a covenant
with him,
Promising that his descendants
Would be a great nation.

Isaac, the fulfillment of God's
promise.
The son of Abraham,
Himself a man of great faith.

Jacob, the one who wrestled
with God,
Who changed Jacob's name to
Israel.
Father of the twelve tribes.

These three are known as the
Patriarchs of Judaism,
Their lifetimes span the
patriarchal age.

When used more widely,
Patriarchs can also refer to the
twenty men
Between Adam and Abraham.

The term sometimes also
includes
The twelve sons of Jacob,
Each one becoming the head of
a tribe.

Usually, but not always, the
Eldest son invested with this
dignity.
Authority was paternal.
The patriarch was honored
as the
Representative head of the
family,
Responsible for family
continuance.

They were seen as wise and
　　respected,
Humble, watchful,
　　self-confident—
Their advice was sought and
　　heeded.

**"And he gave him the covenant
of circumcision. And so Abraham
became the father of Isaac, and
circumcised him on the eighth
day, and Isaac became the father
of Jacob, and Jacob of the twelve
patriarchs."**

(Acts 7:8)

Paul

**"For if I preach the gospel, that
gives me no ground for boasting.
For necessity is laid upon me.
Woe to me if I do not preach the
gospel!"**

(1 Corinthians 9:16)

Born of wealth and Benjamite
　　lineage,
Stock of Israel—a Hebrew of
　　Hebrews.
Lightning-sharp mind,
Wanted to be part of the
　　Sanhedrin.

As a tentmaker, Paul paid
　　his way
With a blue-collar trade.

Feared by Christians
Because he persecuted many.
He stood watching and
　　approving
At the stoning of Stephen.
He was zealous for the law and
Ruthless in pursuit—
Until heaven's light struck him
　　down,
And he was called by our Lord
　　Jesus.

Blinded by the light,
Reborn a Christian.
He rose and was baptized,
His sin washed away.
Once a foremost enemy of
　　Christ,
He became a foremost
　　advocate and
Grew great in the Word.
Taught by the risen master
　　Himself.

For thirty years, Paul
　　proclaimed the Word,
Traversing twelve thousand
　　miles,
Endured lashes, stoning, the
　　rod, bandits,
Hunger, sleepless nights, and
　　shipwrecks.

Evangelized fifty cities and
Planted scores of churches.

Authored thirteen New
    Testament books:
Romans, 1 and 2 Corinthians,
    Galatians,
Ephesians, Philippians,
    Colossians,
1 and 2 Thessalonians, 1 and 2
    Timothy,
Titus, Philemon—
All under inspiration of the
    Holy Spirit.

Celebrated as an apostle to the
    Gentiles.
Tradition holds that he was
    beheaded
By Nero, at around age
    sixty-one.
A life well lived,
A life with a single focus:
Christ Jesus.

**"I have fought the good fight, I
have finished the race, I have kept
the faith."**

                           (2 Timothy 4:7)

Peace

**"Peace I leave with you; my peace
I give to you. Not as the world**

**gives do I give to you. Let not
your hearts be troubled, neither
let them be afraid."**

                           (John 14:27)

Common definitions:
Quietness and tranquility,
Freedom from disturbance or
    hostility.
But biblical peace is much,
    much more.

Root of this word refers to
    completeness,
Living well. It conveys a state
    of being
Both dynamic and static.

Nuances of four categories:
Wholeness of life, body,
Harmony between others,
Prosperity, success, fulfillment,
    and the
Absence of war.

While peace can be inactive, it
Relates more to ordered,
Controlled activity.
It requires wisdom,
    knowledge, and
Power that come only
    from God.
It is a blessing flowing through
The Holy Spirit.

While God is the God of
peace,
He neither slumbers nor sleeps.
As Christians, we are to
imitate Him,
Obeying His commandments,
Being active participants in this
life.

Peace is unrelated to
circumstances.
It is a goodness of life,
regardless
Of what happens around you.
We can possess peace even in
The midst of great trials.

Peace begins in a relationship
with God.
Our nature rebels against God;
Through Jesus, we cease
Our enmity with God
And embrace His gift of peace.

The peace Jesus gives
Must be received and applied
in our lives.
Only then can we have
Calm and untroubled hearts
and a
Fullness of life.

**"May the God of hope fill you with
all joy and peace in believing, so**
**that by the power of the Holy
Spirit you may abound in hope."**

(Romans 15:13)

Pentateuch

**"And God said, 'Let there be lights
in the expanse of the heavens to
separate the day from the night.
And let them be for signs and for
seasons, and for days and years.'"**

(Genesis 1:14)

Penta for "five," and *teuchos* for
"scrolls."
The Old Testament's first five
books:
Genesis, Exodus, Leviticus,
Numbers, and Deuteronomy.
Also known as the Torah,
meaning "law."

Authored by God and
Written down by Moses,
Its teachings and revelations
were
Traced from God through
Moses.
Christ Himself refers to the
Pentateuch
As the Law of Moses.

It contains historical
background:

The creation; God's choosing of
Abraham;
Israel's emergence as His
chosen people;
Laws and instructions given
On Mount Sinai. This was the
beginning
Of God's progressive revelation
to man:
Creation, fall, and promise of
redemption.

The Pentateuch provides an
overview
Of God's plan of redemption,
Providing a backdrop to all
scripture.
The promises, types, and
prophecies
Contained in these books have
Ultimate fulfillment in the
person
And work of Jesus Christ.

**"Then he said to them, 'These
are my words that I spoke to you
while I was still with you, that
everything written about me in
the Law of Moses and the Prophets
and the Psalms must be fulfilled.'"**

(Luke 24:44)

Pentecost

**"When the day of Pentecost
arrived, they were all together
in one place. And suddenly there
came from heaven a sound like a
mighty rushing wind, and it filled
the entire house where they were
sitting. And divided tongues as of
fire appeared to them and rested
on each one of them."**

(Acts 2:1–3)

The day on which the Holy
Spirit
Descended upon the apostles,
And under Peter's preaching,
Many thousands were
converted
In Jerusalem.

Also a prominent observance
In the Old Testament, coming
fifty days
After Passover and
celebrating the
Feast of Harvest or Firstfruits.
Feast detailed are found in
Leviticus 2.
Its purpose: to
commemorate the
Completion of the grain
harvest.

Looking back to the Joel 2
    prophecy,
And forward to the promise
Of the Holy Spirit in Acts 1,
Pentecost signals the beginning
Of the church age. At
    Pentecost,
The disciples witnessed the
    birth
Of the New Testament church
In the coming of the Holy
    Spirit
To all believers.

A true day of celebration
With the arrival of the Holy
    Spirit,
Miraculous speaking in
    tongues,
Bold, incisive preaching,
Listeners repenting and being
    baptized,
Three thousand souls added
To the fellowship—
In breaking of bread and
    prayers,
Apostolic signs and wonders—
A true Christian community.

**"Now when they heard this they
were cut to the heart, and said to
Peter and the rest of the apostles,
'Brothers, what shall we do?' And
Peter said to them, 'Repent and
be baptized every one of you in
the name of Jesus Christ for the
forgiveness of your sins, and you
will receive the gift of the Holy
Spirit.'"**

(Acts 2:37–38)

Persecution

**"Blessed are those who
are persecuted because of
righteousness, for theirs is the
kingdom of heaven."**

(Matthew 5:10)

A stark reality of living as a
    Christian,
All who live a godly life in
Christ Jesus will be persecuted.
Christians do not belong to the
    world,
So the world persecutes us
For being different.

The Jews were attacked by the
    Philistines,
Prophets were persecuted by
    the Jews,
Jesus was persecuted by the
    Pharisees,
And Christians persecuted by
    the Romans.
Yet, it did not end there.

Christians are still persecuted

In this fallen world.
Persecution takes the form of
Harassing, oppressing, and
    banishment.
It includes even the killing of
    Christians.
It can include ridicule,
    restrictions, and
Ostracism—but also
    imprisonment,
Torture, and death.
It is perpetrated on the basis of
    religion,
Directed at Christians, and
Results in varying levels of
    harm.

Christians can be persecuted
By governments, societies,
    friends,
And even by their families.

Persecution promotes
    fellowship
With the Lord. It develops
Endurance and maturity in
    life,
Enables believers to better
    value the
Support of true friends.
It stimulates a greater resolve
To love and comfort one
    another.
It permits an opportunity to
    pray for

Those who accuse, misuse, and
    abuse us.

**"In fact, everyone who wants to
live a godly life in Christ Jesus will
be persecuted."**

(2 Timothy 3:12)

Pestilence

**"Before him went pestilence, and
plague followed at his heels."**

(Habakkuk 3:5)

It walks in darkness,
From out of obscurity
Its sudden onset appears.
Not the name of any
Specific and unique disease
But is used to indicate any
Sudden fatal epidemic or
    disaster.
As used in scripture, it
Indicates divine visitations
Causing pain and death, and
God's judgment upon
Evil and disobedience.

Kingdom against
    kingdom, and
Famine, earthquake, and wild
    beasts,
Compare to the plagues of
Egypt.

It is noisome, hurtful, and
    causes distress
And diseases named and
    unnamed.
All signify punishment
Upon the practice of evil
With the penalty falling
Upon a whole community.

The cure—or, better yet, the
    avoidance:
Submit yourself to the Lord,
Resist Satan, trust God,
Be joyful always, and pray
    unceasingly,
Give God thanks in all
    circumstances.
Abide in the Lord.
Pray that heaven touches earth.

"There will be great earthquakes, famines and pestilences in various places, and fearful events and great signs from heaven."

(Luke 21:11)

Peter

"As Jesus was walking beside the Sea of Galilee, he saw two brothers, Simon called Peter and his brother Andrew. They were casting a net into the lake, for they were fishermen. 'Come, follow me,' Jesus said, 'and I will send you out to fish for people.' At once they left their nets and followed him."

(Matthew 4:18–20 NIV)

Simon Peter, the Rock,
Brother of Andrew—
Both fishermen by trade.
Peter was a man's man, full of
    vigor,
With a boisterous temper and
    outspoken.
A married man, a disciple of
    the Lord,
Became a bold witness.
Upon being called by Jesus, he
Simply walked away, leaving
    everything:
Fishing boats, nets, and
    accessories.
Dedicated himself to Jesus and
Was often the spokesman for
    the apostles,
For good or bad.

He was present when Jesus
    raised
The daughter of Jairus,
Present also at the
    transfiguration.
He once walked on water.
Peter rashly rebuked the Lord
To his own peril.
It was Peter who drew his
    sword

At the arrest of Jesus.
He attended the trial,
But famously denied Jesus
    three times.

He truly became a fisher
    of men.
He spoke on the day of
    Pentecost;
The church grew three
    thousand that day.
Peter healed the lame
In the name of Jesus,
Preached boldly
To the Sanhedrin,
Suffered beatings,
Yet continued his work
To preach the risen Christ.
He open the church's door
To Jew, Samaritans, and
    Gentiles.

He spent much time with
    Mark,
Who wrote the gospel of Mark
Based on Peter's time with
    Jesus.
Peter wrote two inspired
    epistles,
1 and 2 Peter.

Tradition has it that
Peter died a martyr's death,
Between AD 60 and 68—
Supposedly crucified
Upside down in Rome.

"Now when they saw the boldness of Peter and John, and perceived that they were uneducated, common men, they were astonished. And they recognized that they had been with Jesus."

(Acts 4:13)

Poor in Spirit

"Blessed are the poor in spirit, for theirs is the kingdom of heaven."

(Matthew 5:3)

A recognition of helplessness,
Realizing that, due to sin,
One has nothing,
Is nothing, and can do nothing
To deliver himself from
His calamitous state.

Demonstrated through
Biblical examples:
Abraham—"I am but dust and
    ashes";
Jacob—"I am not worthy";
Moses—"Who am I that I
Should go to Pharaoh?"
All were helpless, fallen men,
Unworthy of God's love.
All had to recognize this state
And plead for God's grace.

To be poor in spirit is opposed
To being proud, self-
    assertive, and
Self-sufficient—traits the world
Admires and praises.
The reverse of being poor in
    spirit is
Being independent, defiant,
And refusing to bow
    before God.

Being poor in spirit is to
Admit helplessness before God.
This is the first evidence of
    divine work
Of grace within the soul.
The initial awakening of faith.

"The LORD is near to the
brokenhearted and saves the
crushed in spirit."

(Psalm 34:18)

Praise

"Praise be to the name of God for
ever and ever; wisdom and power
are his."

(Daniel 2:20)

To extol in words or song,
To magnify or to glorify
While recognizing perfections,
Excellent works.

To do honor to,
To display the excellence of,
To express adoration,
    approval, and
Thanksgiving. A celebration of
The one who created and
    redeemed us.

We praise the Lord,
For He is worthy of all our
    praise.
He alone is worthy of
All adoration and approval.
Praise, the joyful thanking,
The adoration of God, the
Celebration of His goodness
    and grace.
Such praising is rightfully due
To God alone.

Scripture overflows with ways
To praise our Lord:
With musical instruments and
    singing,
With clapping hands and
    shouts of joy,
In the assembly or by ourselves,
By kneeling, standing, sitting,
Bowing down, lifting
    hands, and
Falling prostrate. We
    praise God
In all our words and actions,
For all to hear and see.

Praising God reminds us
Of His greatness,
His power, and His presence.
Praise gives us clearer awareness
Of God's blessings and grace.
Thus, we may praise Him
With all our hearts, our minds,
    our souls.

More than a natural impulse or
    delight,
Praise is a duty.
To withhold praise from God
Is to shut one's eyes to His
    presence,
To be forgetful of His
    mercies and
Unthankful for His kindness.
We are to earnestly cultivate
A habit and spirit of praise
By fixing our hearts upon
    God and
Meditating on His Word,
    works, and ways,
Dwelling upon His
    unspeakable gift—
His only begotten Son, Jesus
    Christ.

"Praise the LORD! For it is good
to sing praises to our God; for it
is pleasant, and a song of praise
is fitting."

(Psalm 147:1)

Pray

"Then you will call upon me and
come and pray to me, and I will
hear you."

(Jeremiah 29:12)

A willful act, an integral action
In a Christian's spiritual life.
It is of the heart:
Opening the heart,
Speaking the heart,
Quieting the heart,
Truly calling out to God.

In Hebrew, to pray
Refers to the act of intercession.
Moses prayed for the Israelites;
The prophets prayed for them
    as well.
The Lord heard and responded,
Showing mercy on them
Time and time again.

In Greek, to pray is to beg,
Petition, beseech—always
    to God.
As Paul prayed for the church,
Christians are endowed
With the ability to pray
For ourselves and others.

We are to pray at all times,
In all situations,
For all things, big and small.

Pray with confidence,
Pray with earnestness and zeal,
Pray for favors,
Pray for thanks,
Pray for our enemies.
Pray with the righteousness
Of Christ Jesus.

Pray in worship,
With solemnity, reverence, and
    adoration.
Pray to confess sins,
Pray for mercy,
Pray to glorify
Our heavenly Father.

**"I pray that the eyes of your heart
may be enlightened in order that
you may know the hope to which
he has called you, the riches of his
glorious inheritance in his holy
people, and his incomparably
great power for us who believe."**

(Ephesians 1:18–19 NIV)

Prayer

**"Do not be anxious about
anything, but in everything by
prayer and supplication with
thanksgiving let your requests
be made known to God. And the
peace of God, which surpasses all
understanding, will guard your**
**hearts and your minds in Christ
Jesus."**

(Philippians 4:6–7)

Prayer is not an end in itself.
It carries the design of God and
Accomplishes His purposes.
Prayer, the primary means
By which we cultivate an
Intimate relationship with
    our God.

Prayer is a direct address
    to God.
There is nothing passive
    about it.
It is communication of our
    souls
With the Lord, the
    principal way
For Christians to communicate
Our emotions and desires
    to God.
It is fellowship with God.

It is a dialogue with God.
In scripture, God speaks to us,
In prayer, we speak to God.
In prayer, we review His
    attributes,
Rehearse His mercies,
Wrestle with our doubts, and
Remind ourselves of His truth.

Prayer is more than asking God
For things. It is more than
texting Him
With a "need this" or "thanks
for that."
It is communion with God
In the splendor of His glory,
In the receiving of His care.
One of our goals in prayer
Is to grow to know our God,
Reflecting on His Word and
His creation,
And especially on His Son.

There are many forms of
prayer:
Audible or silent,
Private or public,
Formal or informal.
All prayer is to be offered in
faith
In the name of Jesus Christ.

It is seeking God's favor,
Pouring out one's soul to the
Lord,
Crying out to heaven,
Drawing near to God, and
Kneeling before the Father.
Prayer is to be continuous
And heartfelt.

No special formula,
But there are basic components:
Adoration, confession,

Thanksgiving, and
supplication.
Prayer is possible in all
circumstances.
Prayer demonstrates our
trust and
Our dependence upon God.

The greatest hindrance to
potent prayer:
The presence of
unconfessed sin.
Other hindrances:
Living according to the flesh
Rather than in the Spirit,
Praying from selfish
motivations,
Being indifferent to others'
needs.

Prayer is to be in faith,
For God does not hear a prayer
of doubt.
Effective prayer flows from
Secure belief and
understanding
Of God's character, nature,
and promises.
If we confess our sins,
God is faithful and just.

God's house is a house of
prayer.
God's people are people of
prayer.

Righteous prayer offers the
believer
A deep sense of joy and
Assurance that God is
listening and
That He is caring.

"Therefore I tell you, whatever
you ask in prayer, believe that
you have received it, and it will
be yours."

(Mark 11:24)

Preaching

"I charge you in the presence of
God and of Christ Jesus, who is
to judge the living and the dead,
and by his appearing and his
kingdom: preach the word; be
ready in season and out of season;
reprove, rebuke, and exhort, with
complete patience and teaching."

(2 Timothy 4:1–2)

God's appointed means
To proclaim the gospel,
And to instruct the church.
A connected discourse,
Joining or weaving together
Biblical concepts.
A means to exposit, explain,
and apply

The meaning of God's Word.
Not merely teaching,
But glorifying in the truth.

Preaching serves as a means of
grace
For the building up and
strengthening
Of Christ's church.
It is the Word of God
communicated
With applied relevance
To contemporary listeners,
With the whole process
Under the influence of the
Holy Spirit.

A preacher's definition is:
"Preaching is God speaking
In the power of His Spirit
About His Son
From His Word
Through a man"
(Thabiti Anyabwile).

"For if I preach the gospel, that
gives me no ground for boasting.
For necessity is laid upon me.
Woe to me if I do not preach the
gospel!"

(1 Corinthians 9:16)

Predestination

"For those whom he foreknew he also predestined to be conformed to the image of his Son, in order that he might be the firstborn among many brothers. And those whom he predestined he also called, and those whom he called he also justified, and those whom he justified he also glorified."

(Romans 8:29–30)

To determine beforehand, to
ordain,
To decide upon ahead of time.
Not a modern doctrine,
But propagated by Paul
And theologians ever since.
Predestination is God's eternal
decree
By which—and according to
His will and pleasure—He
called
Certain individuals to be
conformed
To the likeness of His Son,
That they be called, justified,
and glorified.
Essentially, God determines
Through His divine plan alone
All who receive salvation.

Although used closely with
salvation,

It is even more. It is God
Having a purpose that is
determined
Long before it is brought to
pass.
It implies that God is infinitely
capable
Of planning and
accomplishing
All He has planned.

It follows closely man's true
condition,
Which is a state of total
depravity.
Man is dead in sin,
Unable to desire or obtain
Salvation on his own.
Being blind, we cannot
Give ourselves sight.
As fallen people, we are slaves
to sin.
As Paul states, no one—
not one—
Seeks for God.

Predestination resolves our
dilemma.
Only when the Holy Spirit
Regenerates us,
Makes us spiritually alive,
Can we have faith and be
saved.
This does not eliminate our
freedom.

Anyone may accept Christ
or not.
But we, in our fallen state,
Will never choose Christ on
our own.
Those who choose Christ do so
Only through God's divine
election.
Each follows his or her heart's
desire.
A heart enslaved to sin
rejects God,
While a heart
Touched by the Holy Spirit
Chooses Christ.

The doctrine of predestination
Gives all glory to God.
He elects us,
Sends Christ to pay for our
sins,
Sends the necessary faith and
grace
To save us, sustains us to
the end.
We do absolutely nothing.
All glory to our sovereign God!

"God from all eternity
Did by the most wise and holy
counsel
Of His own will,
Freely and unchangeably
Ordain whatsoever comes to
pass"
(Westminster Confession).

"In him we have obtained an inheritance, having been predestined according to the purpose of him who works all things according to the counsel of his will."

(Ephesians 1:11)

Pride

"When pride comes, then comes disgrace, but with the humble is wisdom."

(Proverbs 11:2)

Pride: the taking of glory
For oneself, self-worship.
Included in the Hebrew word is
Arrogance, presumption, and
Cynical insensitivity to others.
It is the shifting of confidence
From God to self.
Those with pride
Are insolent toward God.

It is a failure to accept and
perceive
Our utter dependence on God.
It is a roadblock stopping many
From entering the kingdom
of God,
A type of insanity caused
By a lack of humility.

It is easier to recognize than to
    define,
Easier to recognize in others
Than in oneself.
Pride is a rebellion
    against God,
For it attributes to self,
The honor and glory,
Due to God alone.

Pride is usually at the root of
    all sin.
It caused Lucifer's fall from
    heaven;
It caused humanity's fall in the
    garden,
It has been the downfall of
    many.
The desires of the flesh—
Pride-filled passions.
The desires of the eyes—
Adultery to follow.
The pride of life—
Placing God second.
If one does not crush pride,
Pride will surely crush him.

Pride is difficult to spot.
Alarms should blare when we
Find fault in others, judge their
    faults,
Or grow occupied with how
Others view us. Pride is evident
In defensiveness toward
Challenge or rebuke,

In lack of confidence
    before God,
In pursuing others'
    attentions, and
In neglecting others.

But there is good news for the
    prideful.
Confession of pride signals
The beginning of the end for
    pride.
It signals that the war has
    begun,
And with faith in Christ,
Victory is assured.

**"For all that is in the world—
the desires of the flesh and the
desires of the eyes and pride in
possessions—is not from the
Father but is from the world."**

(1 John 2:16)

Priest

**"For it was indeed fitting that
we should have such a high
priest, holy, innocent, unstained,
separated from sinners, and
exalted above the heavens."**

(Hebrews 7:26)

First mention in scripture:
Melchizedek, priest of God
    Most High.
A priest represents himself and
    others
In things pertaining to God.
Duly authorized to minister
In sacred things,
Particularly to offer sacrifices
As mediator between people
    and God.

An office of extreme
    importance,
A position of high rank.
Indispensable sources of
Religious knowledge,
The channel through which
Spiritual life is communicated.
In ancient days,
Stood next to the monarch
In influence and dignity.
Aaron is a proper example.

The office of a priest has
A fourfold implication.
Implies divine choice—
Not elected or self-appointed,
But called of God.
Implies representation of the
    people—
Acting for people in things
Pertaining to God.
Implies offering sacrifices—
In the chief priestly duty
Of reconciling people to God,

By making atonement for their
    sins.
Implies intercession:
The priest offers up
Prayers, thanksgivings, and
    sacrifices.

Prior to Jesus, all priests
Were only dim shadows,
Obscure sketches of the
One great high priest of God,
The Lord, Jesus Christ,
    Himself.
Perfection is revealed in Christ
    as priest.
Appointed by God, the
    Father, and
Consecrated with an oath:
"You are a priest forever."
Christ was sinless;
His priesthood is
    unchangeable,
His offering of self is perfect
    and final.
His intercession is
    all-prevailing.
As God and man in one
    person,
He is the perfect mediator.

As our high priest,
Jesus is greater than all other
    priests,
Allowing us with confidence
To draw near to the throne of
    grace,

Receiving His mercy and
blessings.
He took on our humanity
So that he could become
Our merciful and faithful high
priest,
Atoning for our sins,
Helping us who are being
tempted,
Able to sympathize
With our weaknesses.

"Since then we have a great high priest who has passed through the heavens, Jesus, the Son of God, let us hold fast our confession. For we do not have a high priest who is unable to sympathize with our weaknesses, but one who in every respect has been tempted as we are, yet without sin. Let us then with confidence draw near to the throne of grace, that we may receive mercy and find grace to help in time of need."

(Hebrews 4:14–16)

Principalities and Powers

"For we wrestle not against flesh and blood, but against principalities, against powers, against the rulers of the darkness of this world, against spiritual wickedness in high places."

(Ephesians 6:12 KJV)

Principalities and powers
Rulers and darkness,
Forces and authorities—
All are designating spiritual
forces.
That vast array of evil,
Those malicious spirits,
Those who make war
Against the people of God.
Beings that wield power
In the unseen realms.

Their goal:
Steal the affections of
mankind,
Destroy God's beloved
creation.
These rulers of darkness
Tempt humanity with sin.
We battle and struggle against
them,
For they seek to corrupt us,
Desiring that we disobey God.

Powerful? Yes.
Victorious? No.
Try as they might, they cannot
Separate us from the love
of God.
They have been disarmed,
Made a public spectacle,

Triumphed over by the cross.
They are answerable
To the resurrected Christ,
Risen far above all
Principalities and powers—
They answer to Him alone.

"And having spoiled principalities and powers, he made a shew of them openly, triumphing over them in it."

(Colossians 2:15 KJV)

Prodigal

"Not many days later, the younger son gathered all he had and took a journey into a far country, and there he squandered his property in reckless living."

(Luke 15:13)

To "drive forth,"
Particularly regarding
    belongings,
Indicates a person who
Is extravagant with his or her
    possessions
To the point of reckless
    abandonment.
Today we interpret *prodigal* as
Rebellious or a runaway.

But in truth, it means
    "extravagant,"
Even extravagant
    abandonment.

The parable commonly
    referred to
As that of the Prodigal Son
Contains three real prodigals:
Younger son, an elder son,
And a loving father—
All three are extravagant.

The younger son rejected his
    father
Through a journey of
    self-discovery.
He sought pleasure
And did not need his father.
He was extravagant with what
    his father
Lovingly gave to him.

The older son rejected his
    father
Through self-sufficiency and
    morality.
He thought himself so good,
And did not need his father.
He was extravagant with
His father's blessings.

Yet the real prodigal
Was not either of the sons,
But the father himself,

Who was the most extravagant
of all.
For the father is
Extravagant with his love.
The younger son wished him
dead,
Yet the father gave him love.
The older son disrespected the
father,
But the father reminded him,
"Everything I have is yours."
The father in this story is the
prodigal.
He is extravagant with his love,
Just as our heavenly Father
Is extravagant with His love.

"Who is a God like you, pardoning iniquity and passing over transgression for the remnant of his inheritance? He does not retain his anger forever, because he delights in steadfast love."

(Micah 7:18)

Prophecy

"For no prophecy was ever produced by the will of man, but men spoke from God as they were carried along by the Holy Spirit."

(2 Peter 1:21)

In simple terms, a prediction.
Biblically, it is a message
inspired by God:
A divine revelation or
A function of the prophets,
Declaration, description,
representation
Of something future,
Something beyond human
wisdom—
To foresee, discern, or
conjecture.

The great prophecy of the Bible
Runs like a golden thread
Through its contents.
Regards the coming and the
work
Of the Messiah.
Its purpose was to perpetuate
faith in
His coming, preparing the
world
For this glorious event,
All declaring God's wisdom,
Sovereignty, and love.

The first great prophecy
Stated in Genesis 3:15,
Declared a future redeemer
And the Messiah's ultimate
victory.
God revealed His redemptive
intention

After the fall of humanity in
Eden—
The prophecy of prophecies.

**"I will put enmity between you
and the woman, and between
your offspring and her offspring;
he shall bruise your head, and you
shall bruise his heel."**

(Genesis 3:15)

Prophets

**"No prophecy of Scripture came
about by the prophet's own
interpretation of things. For
prophecy never had its origin in
the human will, but prophets,
though human, spoke from God
as they were carried along by the
Holy Spirit."**

(2 Peter 1:20–21)

A title bestowed by God.
People used by God
To communicate His message.
Prophets are the mouth
By which God speaks to us,
Communicating His mind and
will.
Also called "seers,"
Because they could "see"
Dreams and visions from God.

Credentials of a true prophet
include:
A true Israelite,
A spiritual descendant of
Abraham,
Speaking in the name of the
Lord alone.
Must call people to living in
obedience
And worship of God.
His or her predictions must
become true.

A true prophet has many
purposes:
To reveal God's nature and
attributes,
To make God's laws known to
others,
To call people back to
obedience
Of God's commands and
statutes,
To exhort the people to sincere
worship,
To warn them of divine
judgment
Upon sin, to foretell future
events
That God has willed,
To foretell the coming of the
Messiah,
To record God's dealings with
humanity,
And to record God's Word
In the holy scriptures.

The ultimate prophet is
Jesus Christ Himself.
Fulfilling all requirements
In title, word, and deed.
Predicted from the
Days of Moses,
Who spoke of the prophet to
    come.
Jesus, as a prophet, spoke of
    Himself.

Jesus not only proclaimed
The Word of God;
He *is* the Word of God.
He came to the world because
    of sin,
Proclaimed our need
To repent and believe, and
Proclaimed our pardon,
The forgiveness of sin.

**"And he said, 'Hear my words: If
there is a prophet among you, I the
LORD make myself known to him
in a vision; I speak with him in a
dream.'"**

(Numbers 12:6)

Prophets, False

**"Beware of false prophets, who
come to you in sheep's clothing but
inwardly are ravenous wolves."**

(Matthew 7:15)

One who spreads false
    teachings,
A message untrue, wrongly
Claiming to speak the Word
    of God,
False prophets speak
On behalf of false gods.
They speak only to deceive.

Rather than speak the Word of
    the Lord,
False prophets deliver messages
Originating in their own hearts
    and minds.
They not only speak lies;
They fill others with false
    hopes.

True prophets are motivated
By loyalty to God above all.
False prophets are motivated by
    self-interest,
And a desire to be popular
    among others,
Saying what people want to
    hear,
Not what God wants to
    say, and

Often speaking for financial
  reward.
They judge for a bribe,
Teach for a price, and
Tell fortunes for money.

The Old Testament penalty for
  being
A false prophet was to be put to
  death.
Jesus preached about false
  prophets,
Denying them entrance into
  heaven,
Calling them evildoers.

Adjectives for false prophets
  include:
Adulterous, treacherous,
Drunkards, wicked, liars,
Associates with witchcraft.

Believers are to be diligent in
  faith,
Devoted to Christ's teachings,
So that we can detect
False prophets and teachers.
The key is knowing
What a true prophet is like.
A true prophet's words
Will be fulfilled.
A true prophet's teachings
Are consistent with scripture.
A true prophet
Encourages righteous
  living and

Provides spiritual benefit.
A true prophet's life
Reflects a divine call.
A true prophet acknowledges
Jesus Christ as divine.

**"Beloved, do not believe every
spirit, but test the spirits to see
whether they are from God, for
many false prophets have gone out
into the world."**

(1 John 4:1)

Proverbs

**"Let the wise hear and increase
in learning, and the one who
understands obtain guidance."**

(Proverbs 1:5)

Not merely an anthology,
But the collection of
  collections, written
To give prudence to those who
  are simple,
Knowledge, discretion, to the
  young,
To make the wise even wiser.
Overflowing with biblical
  wisdom,
They discuss values, moral
  behaviors,

Life's meaning, and right
   conduct.

A book with no particular plot,
No storyline is found in its
   pages,
No principal characters.
But it is a book where wisdom
   takes
Center stage, a grand, divine
   wisdom,
Transcending history, peoples,
   cultures.
As relevant today as
Thousands of years ago.

It is a book written principally
By the wise Solomon.
It reveals the mind of God in
   matters
Both high and lofty as well
   as in
Ordinary, common, everyday
   situations.
No topic escapes his attention.
Personal conduct, sexual
   relations,
Business, wealth, charity,
Ambition, discipline, debt,
Child-rearing, character,
   alcohol,
Politics, revenge, and godliness.
All are discussed among the
   many topics—
A reminder that God is
   concerned

Not just with major events of
   life,
But also with those common,
Mundane experiences,
Those invisible moments in our
   lives.

Proverb means "to be like";
Thus Proverbs is a book of
   comparisons
Between common, tangible
   images
And life's most profound
   truths.
It consists of simple, moral
Statements and illustrations,
Highlighting and teaching
Fundamental realities about
   life,
All in the search for God's
   wisdom.
Designed to make men
   contemplate
The fear of God, living by His
   wisdom.
The sum of this wisdom is
Personified in the Lord, Jesus
   Christ.

Proverbs contains a gold mine
Of biblical theology,
Reflecting themes of scripture
Brought to the level of
Practical righteousness,
By addressing people's ethical
   choices,

Calling into question how we
Think, live, manage our daily
    lives
In light of divine truth.
More specifically,
Proverbs calls us to live
As our Creator intended us to
    live.

"The fear of the LORD is the beginning of knowledge; fools despise wisdom and instruction."

(Proverbs 1:7)

Providence

"And we know that for those who love God all things work together for good, for those who are called according to his purpose."

(Romans 8:28)

The governance of God
Whereby He cares for and
    directs
All things in the universe.
This is accomplished with love
    and wisdom,
Divine providence asserts
That God is in complete
    control.

God, the Creator of all,
Upholds, directs, disposes, and
    governs
All creatures and things
According to the glory of His
    wisdom,
Power, justice, goodness, and
    mercy.

Examples in scripture abound.
Abraham with his son,
Joseph and his brothers,
Judas Iscariot—
This providence of God and
Mysteriously balances
God's sovereignty with
People's responsibilities.

To accomplish His providence,
God primarily works
Through secondary causes—
The laws of nature and human
    choice.
Divine providence does not
    destroy
Humanity's freedom of the
    will.
It takes our freedom into
    account
And in God's infinite wisdom
Sets a course to fulfill God's
    will.

Divine providence is clearly
    taught
On every page of scripture.

It rejects all notions of luck,
 fate, chance,
For God is in control.
God governs all.
Nothing exists or happens
Outside God's providence.

The Heidelberg Catechism
 defines
God's providence as the
 almighty,
Everywhere-present power
 of God
Whereby, as it were by His
 hand,
He upholds heaven and earth
 with all
Creatures, and so governs them
That herbs and grass, rain and
 drought,
Fruitful and barren years,
Meat and drink, health and
 sickness, and
Riches and poverty—
Indeed, all things—
Come not by chance,
But by His fatherly hand.

To paraphrase John Calvin:
Ignorance of providence is
The ultimate of all miseries,
For then we are left to our own
 follies.
But the highest blessedness lies
In the knowledge and
 acceptance

Of divine providence, in
 knowing
We have an all-powerful,
 loving God
Who has a plan for us.

God not only created the
 universe
And all within it, including us,
But He continues to regulate
And sustain all things
Through the word of His
 power,
Through His divine
 providence.
All to accomplish His ultimate
 purpose,
The display of His glorious
 glory.

"If that is how God clothes the grass of the field, which is here today and tomorrow is thrown into the fire, will he not much more clothe you—you of little faith?"

(Matthew 6:30)

Psalms

"Blessed is the man who walks not in the counsel of the wicked, nor

stands in the way of sinners, nor
sits in the seat of scoffers."

(Psalm 1:1)

A song or a poem used in
worship,
Comes from the Greek "to
pluck,"
Which led to the translation,
"A song sung to harp music."
Today, regardless of the
instrument, it
Refers to a sacred song.

Often called the Psalter and
known as
Ancient Israel's national
hymnbook,
It includes 150 psalms.
The Hebrew title *Tehillim*
Translates as "praises."
It is a songbook of praises
Collected over the centuries,
Its final form completed
Around the third century BC.

The Psalter is clearly unified,
Yet it is also structured into five
books
(With these divisions
coming at
Psalms 1, 42, 73, 90, and 107).
Each section ends with a
Doxology or song of praise.

The Psalms contain an
introduction
(Consisting of the first two
psalms),
And a conclusion (the last five).
Some psalms are hymns;
There are also psalms of
lament,
Royal psalms, thanksgiving
psalms,
Wisdom psalms, and psalms of
ascent
Sung by worshipers traveling
To Jerusalem.

Authors of these psalms include
David (writing seventy-three),
Asaph (writing twelve)
And the sons of Korah (writing
eleven).
Others are written by Solomon,
Moses, Heman the Ezrahite,
And Ethan the Ezrahite.

The basic metaphor and most
pervasive
Theological concept in the
Psalms
Is the supreme kingship
of God.
To be a human being
In this world that God created
Is to be dependent on and
responsible
To God. To deny this fact
Is the root of all wickedness.

Throughout the Psalms,
We learn the importance of
    prayer and
The acknowledgment of pain,
As well as the power of
    praise and
The glory of our heavenly
    Father.
The psalms are emotional,
Written from the heart.
It is a book of encouragement
To praise God for who He is
And for what He has done.
They illuminate the greatness
Of our God.

The final verse in Psalms
    tells us:
Let everything that has breath
Praise the Lord.
Praise the Lord.

"Enter his gates with thanksgiving, and his courts with praise! Give thanks to him; bless his name! For the LORD is good; his steadfast love endures forever, and his faithfulness to all generations."

(Psalm 100:4–5)

Publican

"And as Jesus reclined at table in the house, behold, many publicans and sinners came and were reclining with Jesus and his disciples."

(Matthew 9:10)

Considered vile and degraded,
The worst of the worst in
    society,
Betrayers to their own people,
    lap dogs of conquerors.
These were the tax collectors.
Literal translation: tax farmers.
Loathed in every culture,
Rich beyond others
By collecting for themselves.

The apostle Matthew, who
    wrote a gospel,
Was first a well-known
    publican and a
Friend of thieves and of the
    corrupt.
But he was not beyond
    salvation.

Jesus befriended society's worst,
Demonstrating that all are
    capable
Of being saved.
He forgave an adulteress,
Healed lepers, and
Spoke with Samaritans.
But unbelievable in the eyes of
    many,
Jesus also befriended a
    publican—

A demonstration of His love
    for all,
Showing that if He can use
    publicans
In mighty ways for His glory,
He can use anyone.

"And the Pharisees and their scribes grumbled at his disciples, saying, 'Why do you eat and drink with publicans and sinners?'"

(Luke 5:30)

Pure in Heart

"Blessed are the pure in heart, for they shall see God."

(Matthew 5:8)

A singleness of heart
    toward God.
Marked by transparency,
An uncompromising desire
To please God with
No hypocrisy, no
    treachery, and
No hidden motives.
More than external purity of
    behavior,
It is an internal purity of soul.

The pure in heart are declared
    innocent

By the redemptive work of
    Christ.
They are being sanctified
By His refining fire.

To be pure is to be clean and
    blameless,
Unstained from guilt.
The heart is the spiritual center
    of life,
Where thoughts, desires,
    will, and
Character reside—that place
    from which
All of one's words and actions
    flow.

A pure heart comes from God,
Through the sacrifice of
    His Son
And His sanctifying work in
    our lives.
The pure in heart are those
Saved by grace and
Given a new life in Jesus.
The pure in heart desire
To be filled with the love of
    Christ
And to live in the love of God.

"Create in me a pure heart, O God, and renew a steadfast spirit within me."

(Psalm 51:10)

Rainbow

"I have set my bow in the cloud, and it shall be a sign of the covenant between me and the earth."

(Genesis 9:13)

A creation of God,
Physically caused by the
    refraction
Of the sun's rays on falling
    rain.
Appointed as a witness
Of divine faithfulness, it was
Constituted as a sign
Of the covenant.

The covenant, God's promise,
    was this:
He would never again to
    destroy the earth
With a flood.
Never again would all life be
Destroyed by a flood.
The rainbow, a sign of this
    covenant
Between God and humanity, is
A reminder to God
Of His promise to us,
For Him to see—
Whenever a rainbow
Appears in the clouds.

A promise made
Not only to humanity,
But to every living creature on
    earth.
This covenant is perpetual,
Enduring to all generations.
Never again will there be
A worldwide flood.

"Though it is a bow,
Yet without arrows,
And is not turned
Downward toward the earth,
But upward toward heaven,
And so is a token
Of mercy and kindness,
Not of wrath and anger" (John
    Gill).

A sign we delight in,
Awe-inspiring in the sky.
A symbol of God's
Faithfulness and mercy.

"Like the appearance of the bow that is in the cloud on the day of rain, so was the appearance of the brightness all around. Such was the appearance of the likeness of the glory of the Lord."

(Ezekiel 1:28)

Rapture

"Then will appear in heaven the sign of the Son of Man, and then all the tribes of the earth will mourn, and they will see the Son of Man coming on the clouds of heaven with power and great glory. And he will send out his angels with a loud trumpet call, and they will gather his elect from the four winds, from one end of heaven to the other."

(Matthew 24:30–31)

An eschatological concept
Of an end-time event
When all believers alive on
    earth,
Along with resurrected dead
    believers,
Will rise into the clouds
To meet the Lord in the air,
To be forever with Him.

A rapture in that we rise
To meet the Lord,
Like a great band of
    welcoming.
We come back with Him
For His established judgment
    and rule.

It is a common belief that
    Christ
Will ultimately return
Bodily, visibly, and gloriously,
To reign and rule forever
    with His
Resurrected and transformed
    saints.
The details of this are to be
    made known
In God's own time.
Yet much debate over
    meaning and
Scope of this rapture exists.
God's intent is not to sow
    disagreement.
Rather, the rapture should be
A comforting doctrine,
    giving us
Much hope and
    encouragement.

To this author,
There is one great, glorious
Coming of the Lord in our
    future.
He is coming once more to give
Relief to His church and
Judgment to His adversaries—
To establish His kingdom
    eternal.

We should all rejoice,
    proclaiming,
"Come, Lord Jesus!"

"For the Lord himself will descend from heaven with a cry of command, with the voice of an archangel, and with the sound of the trumpet of God. And the dead in Christ will rise first. Then we who are alive, who are left, will be caught up together with them in the clouds to meet the Lord in the air, and so we will always be with the Lord."

(1 Thessalonians 4:16–17)

Rebuke

"Preach the word; be ready in season and out of season; reprove, rebuke, and exhort, with complete patience and teaching."

(2 Timothy 4:2)

In our lives, an action
Underappreciated,
    underused—
Rebuke is a part of loving,
Even when it is unwanted.
A critical aspect
Of healthy biblical correction.
Rebuke, correction,
    admonishment is
The exposing of sin or fault.

To care well for others,
We must identify and
    expose sin,
Even when this offends
Someone we love.
Through rebuking,
We encourage, comfort, and
    build up
Our brothers and sisters in
    Christ.
This must be done with
Compassion and hope,
Speaking the truth in love.
More than just pointing
    out sin,
It is a courageous act
Of genuine love that originates
In the heart.

The church is to confront
Believers who refuse
A loving rebuke.
A sinner who persists in
    exposed sin
Is to be treated as a pagan.
Harsh words were spoken by
    Jesus
To protect the purity
Of His church, which is
Of upmost importance
    to Him.
Sinners defiling His reputation
Must be rebuked, not excused
Or overlooked.

God rebukes many:
The serpent, Cain,
Moses, Balaam, Israel,
Pharisees, Satan,
Peter, congregations,
The wind, the waves, kings,
The arrogant, sinners,
And many more.
God protects His church,
And divine rebuke protects
His glory.
To His children, this is
A loving gift of correction.
Others are exposed not just
To their sinful ways,
But also to God's wrath.

"As many as I love, I rebuke and chasten; be zealous therefore, and repent."

(Revelation 3:19 KJV)

Redemption

"In him we have redemption through his blood, the forgiveness of our trespasses, according to the riches of his grace."

(Ephesians 1:7)

Redemption, a metaphor of
Christ's achievement
Through the atonement.

The purchase back of
something lost
By payment of a ransom.
All people are guilty, for all
have sinned
And fall short of the glory
of God.
We are slaves to sin, bound for
death.
Because of God's holiness
And righteousness,
Sin must be punished.

Redemption is an act of God's
grace
By which He rescues and
restores
His people. The payment
By Christ on the cross
Is not viewed as simply
canceled,
But as paid in full. Christ's
blood
Is the ransom, the payment,
That secures deliverance
For His people from the
servitude
Of sin and death.

In a symbolic sense,
The death of Jesus on the cross
Fully pays the ransom,
Releasing Christians from
Bondage to sin and death.
Redemption is a legal term:
We are no longer legally subject

To the punishment
Our sinful nature demands.

Redemption by Christ
Provides many benefits:
Eternal life, forgiveness of sin,
Right relationship with God,
Peace with God,
The Holy Spirit to live
    within, and
Adoption into God's family.
Jesus gave Himself for us
To redeem us from all
Lawlessness and to purify
For Himself a people
For His own possession.

When we are redeemed,
We are new creations,
No longer captive to sin and
    death.
Now we are citizens of God's
    kingdom,
Anticipating our eternal home
With our heavenly Father.

"Knowing that you were ransomed from the futile ways inherited from your forefathers, not with perishable things such as silver or gold, but with the precious blood of Christ, like that of a lamb without blemish or spot."

(1 Peter 1:18–19)

Refuge

"On God rests my salvation and my glory; my mighty rock, my refuge is God."

(Psalm 62:7)

A place of safety and shelter,
Protected from danger,
Protected from distress.
A place where we can take
    cover
From storms.
Yes, a cave, a cleft in the rocks,
An underground bunker.
But there is only one true
Refuge providing peace and
    security
To calm our troubled hearts.
It is the refuge of God
And His Son, Jesus Christ.

Our heavenly refuge
Not only protects us
Against Satan's schemes and
The temptations of this world;
He protects us from
Our own sinful natures and
The consequences of
Our own sins.
God is a refuge
For His children;
He brings us peace.

Only one way to make God
  our refuge:
Ask Him.
Pour out your heart to Him;
Trust in Him.
It is by staying our minds on
  Jesus
That God keeps us in perfect
  peace.

God promises peace
That surpasses understanding,
Peace that guards hearts and
  minds
For all who look to Him
As their everlasting refuge.

"Oh, taste and see that the LORD is good! Blessed is the man who takes refuge in him!"

(Psalm 34:8)

Regeneration

"He saved us, not because of works done by us in righteousness, but according to his own mercy, by the washing of regeneration and renewal of the Holy Spirit."

(Titus 3:5)

A synonym for rebirth,
Related to "born again."
A radical change,

A transformation of heart,
A passing from death to life—
Becoming a new creature
In Christ Jesus.

A change ascribed
To the Holy Spirit.
Originates not with people,
But with God.
To be regenerated
Is to start a new life,
One that is from God
Rather from human parents.

A result of faith in Christ.
Faith, a gift of God
Through His love, is
Not a result of works,
And not our own doing;
Truly, it is a gift of God
So that no one may boast.

The only means of regeneration
Is by faith in the finished work
Of Christ on the cross.
This is no renovation or
  reformation
Or reorganization,
But a total regeneration.
The old is gone; the new is here
For eternity.

Regeneration begins
The process of sanctification,
Wherein we become

The people God intends us
to be.
Just as an infant grows and
matures,
A regenerated person grows
And matures spiritually—
In and for Christ.

Regeneration—a new life from
above.
God has done something
amazing
In our souls, giving us
Living hope through
The resurrection of Jesus
Christ.
Through our regeneration,
God has opened our eyes
To see the glory of Christ.
He has made us a new creation
In Christ.

**"Therefore, if anyone is in Christ,
the new creation has come: The
old has gone, the new is here!"**

(2 Corinthians 5:17 NIV)

Rejoice

**"Rejoice always, pray without
ceasing, give thanks in all**
**circumstances; for this is the will
of God in Christ Jesus for you."**

(1 Thessalonians 5:16–18)

To exalt, boast, express joy, or
Jump in celebration;
To delight in or
Literally to experience God's
grace.
It is to be full of cheer and
Saturated with joy.
To rejoice is also to dispel
Gloom, sorrow, silence, or
apathy.

Associated with "praise."
Being filled with joy because of
Christ
Causes one to sing praises to
His name.
To rejoice in His presence
Is to sing praises to God
And to His name.

"Rejoice always" is
A personal, present, permanent
duty
To be performed by all
Christians.
It is not our option whether
To sorrow or to rejoice;
The Lord has commanded us
To rejoice evermore.
No idleness is allowed.

To rejoice in the Lord
Is to know Christ Jesus
As our Lord and Savior,
Knowing that He gives us
Deeper, purer, sweeter,
More lasting purpose
Than anything in the world.

We rejoice in each other
For Christ's sake,
Celebrating His continuous
    work
In each of our lives,
A work He will bring to
    fruition
At His second coming.

The ability to rejoice follows
A close union with Jesus
    Christ.
We have redemption only
    in Him;
In Him, we have forgiveness of
    sins.
In Him, we are blessed
With all spiritual blessings.
He is the foundation and
    source
Of all gladness in the Christian
    life.

**"I will greatly rejoice in the
LORD; my soul shall exult in my
God, for he has clothed me with
the garments of salvation; he
has covered me with the robe of
righteousness."**

(Isaiah 61:10)

Repentance

**"The times of ignorance God
overlooked, but now he commands
all people everywhere to repent."**

(Acts 17:30)

Not mere sorrow for one's
        actions or deep remorse
        only,
But a change of mind-set,
A change of fundamental
        attitude
And outlook on life.
It is heartfelt sorrow for sin,
A renouncing of sin,
A sincere commitment to
        forsake sin and
To walk in obedience to Christ.

Like faith, repentance includes
An intellectual understanding.
We recognize that sin is wrong.
There is also emotional
        approval
Of scripture's teachings and
A personal decision to turn
        from sin,
Renouncing and forsaking it,

To lead a life of obedience to
    Christ as
Demonstration of a changed
    life.

Like faith, it is a necessity for
    salvation—
Two aspects of the one event
Of conversion. There is no true
    faith
Without genuine
    repentance and
No genuine repentance
Without true faith.
Our expressions of
    repentance are
Not relegated to a single point
    in time
Or solely to our declaration of
    faith;
It is not confined to the
    beginning
Of a Christian's life
But to an attitude of heart and
    mind
Continuing throughout our
    lives.

The first recorded words
Preached by Jesus were,
    "Repent,
For the kingdom of heaven is at
    hand."
Repentance is at the very heart
Of understanding the gospel
    message.

Without understanding, there
    is no repentance.
Repentance does not originate
    within us
But is foreign to our corrupt
    hearts.
Only through the working
Of the Holy Spirit
Can we truly repent,
For by God's grace He gives us
The inclination to repent.

Repentance is not only sorrow
    for our sins,
Not just a resolve to do better,
Not a New Year's resolution,
And definitely not a penance—
Trying to atone for one's own
    sins.
Repentance is a transformation
Of nature, a definitive turning
From evil and a resolute
    turning to God
In total obedience.
Repentance affects the whole
    person and
His or her conduct at all times,
    in all situations.

"From that time on Jesus began to preach, 'Repent, for the kingdom of heaven has come near.'"

(Matthew 4:17)

Rest

"Therefore, while the promise of entering his rest still stands, let us fear lest any of you should seem to have failed to reach it."

(Hebrews 4:1)

God's rest is in the spiritual
  realm.
It is the rest of salvation.
Faith is the key to entering
  God's rest.
For His promise is one of
  salvation
Through Jesus Christ.
He alone can provide true rest,
Through His blood shed on the
  cross
For the remission of sins.

To enter this rest,
We must depend solely
  on God,
Trusting Him implicitly,
Yielding fully to the promises
  of God
Through the free grace of His
  salvation.

Although this rest has a
  spiritual nature
Linked to the world to come,
It is also intended for this
  world.

It is the sense of security and
  peace
Flowing from
A right relationship with God,
Through obedience to His Son,
The Messiah.

Rest involves remaining
  confident,
Holding on to the truth of
  Christ,
To His sacrificial death,
Free from jumping from
One lifestyle to another,
From one fad to another.
To rest is to be grounded,
Established, rooted, and
Unmovable in Christ,
Having absolute trust and
  confidence
In God's power and care.

To enter into God's rest means
That for our lives and all
  eternity
We can lean on God,
Sure that He will never fail
  us and
That his promises are secure;
We depend on Him for
  everything.
In this relationship, we are sure
Of God's love for us
And of our love for God.

Biblical rest is not inactivity
Or idleness or sleep.
The rest God promises is
    spiritual,
Not physical.
Yet, this spiritual rest gives us
Release from life's burdens,
Freedom from worry and
    anxiety, and
Freedom from guilt and sin.
It is the ability to take time
To bask assuredly
In God's love and glory.

"Come to me, all who labor and are heavy laden, and I will give you rest. Take my yoke upon you, and learn from me, for I am gentle and lowly in heart, and you will find rest for your souls. For my yoke is easy, and my burden is light."

(Matthew 11:28–30)

Resurrection

"Jesus said to her, 'I am the resurrection and the life. Whoever believes in me, though he die, yet shall he live, and everyone who lives and believes in me shall never die.'"

(John 11:25)

Principal tenet of the New
    Testament:
The resurrection of Jesus,
Rising from death to life.
Literally, it means to stand up,
    to rise.
Death is the enemy of
    humanity
And the just punishment
    for sin.
The mortality rate for people
Is 100 percent—with no
    exceptions.
Yet Jesus's resurrection proves
His sinless character and divine
    nature.
By His divine nature,
He does more than give life;
He *is* life. Therefore,
Death has no power over Him.
Jesus confers this spiritual life
On those who believe in Him,
So they share His victory over
    death.

The resurrection witnesses
The immense power of God.
If God exists, if He created
    all and
Has power over all,
Then He has the power to raise
    the dead.
Only He can remove its sting;
Only He gains victory over the
    grave.

To believe in God
Is to believe in the resurrection.
To believe in the resurrection
Is to believe in God.

All who believe in Jesus
Will personally experience
    resurrection,
For by having the life of Jesus,
We overcome death.

The resurrection of Jesus Christ
Proves that Jesus is the Son
    of God,
The Messiah. It demonstrates
That God the Father accepted
The sacrifice of Jesus on our
    behalf.
It shows that God has the
    power
To raise us from the dead.
It guarantees that the bodies
Of believers will not remain
    dead,
But will be resurrected unto
Eternal life.

"But in fact Christ has been raised from the dead, the firstfruits of those who have fallen asleep. For as by a man came death, by a man has come also the resurrection of the dead. For as in Adam all die, so also in Christ shall all be made alive."

(1 Corinthians 15:20–22)

Revelation

"The heavens declare the glory of God, and the sky above proclaims his handiwork."

(Psalm 19:1)

An uncovering, a bringing to
    light
Of that which had been
    previously
Hidden entirely or only
    obscurely seen.
God has been pleased
In various ways at various
    times,
To make supernatural
    revelations
Of Himself, His purposes, and
    His plans.
Under the guidance of His
    Spirit,
These have been committed to
    writing
In holy scripture.
The scriptures are not merely
The record of revelation;
They are the full revelation
    itself
In written form.

231

Yet more than scripture alone,
It is God revealing Himself to
humanity
Through nature and through
The person of His Son, Jesus
Christ.
God wants us to know Him,
To know him intimately.
He has revealed His existence,
His eternal power, and His
divine nature
Through the magnificence
Of the universe and all that is
in it.
We can clearly see and
understand
That God exists and that He is
Intelligent, powerful, and
transcendent.

The Holy Spirit guided the
authors
Of scripture to record and
reveal
The attributes of God.
The Word is inspired,
profitable, and
Sufficient. It reveals
All that we need to know,
What God expects of us, and
What He has done for us.
The Bible is all-sufficient in
that
It is the inspired Word of God,
The complete and final
revelation

Of our heavenly Father.
Nothing needs to be added.

The ultimate revelation is Jesus
Christ,
Who is the radiance of God's
glory,
The exact representation of His
being—
God becoming human to
identify with us,
Set an example for us, teach us,
Reveal Himself to us,
And, most importantly, to
provide
Salvation for us on the cross.

God and His holy nature
Are no secret to us.
He has revealed Himself
In many ways, in many
times—
Through nature, through
scripture,
And especially through
His Son, Jesus Christ.

**"And the Word became flesh and
dwelt among us, and we have seen
his glory, glory as of the only Son
from the Father, full of grace and
truth."**

(John 1:14)

Revelation (Book of)

"The revelation of Jesus Christ, which God gave him to show to his servants the things that must soon take place. He made it known by sending his angel to his servant John."

(Revelation 1:1)

A book written by the apostle
    John,
While exiled on Patmos,
Giving hope and
    encouragement
To Christians suffering for
Their faith in Jesus Christ.
A reminder that God
Controls whatever happens
On this earth and in this
    universe,
Now and forevermore.

Sometimes called the
    apocalypse,
Meaning disclosure, it
Conveys the idea
Of laying bare, uncovering.
As with all scripture, it was
Given by the inspiration
    of God.
Therefore, Revelation contains
Information that God intends
To reveal to us,

Rather than to conceal
    from us.

Through imagery and
    symbols—
Of which many remain
    mysteries—
One thing is made absolutely
    clear:
Jesus Christ is Lord,
Ruler of everyone and
    everything.
Christ is in control,
And He will return
To judge the living and the
    dead.

Revelation gives
A small glimpse of heaven,
Of all the glories awaiting
    those
Who keep their robes white.

This book journeys through
The great tribulation with all
    its woes,
The fires that unbelievers
Will face for eternity.
It reiterates the fall of Satan,
The doom he and his minions
Are bound for.

We are shown the duties
Of all creatures, all people and
    angels;

We are shown the promises to
the saints
Who will live forever with
Jesus
In the New Jerusalem.

It is a sobering reminder to
Remain loyal and obedient
to God
No matter the pressure, the
difficulties—
Even until death;
To repent of sins,
To keep the commandments,
To withdraw from ungodly
ways,
To never compromise our
obedience
And loyalty to God.

Revelation is lavish in colorful
descriptions
Of the visions proclaiming the
last days
Before Christ's return, the
ushering in
Of the new heaven and new
earth.

**"Then I saw a great white throne
and him who was seated on it.
Earth and sky fled from his
presence, and there was no place
for them."**

(Revelation 20:11)

Reward in Heaven

**"Rejoice and be glad, for your
reward is great in heaven, for so
they persecuted the prophets who
were before you."**

(Matthew 5:12)

Entering eternal life with God,
Seeing God face to face,
Being like Christ—
Great is the reward in heaven!

We will be recipients of
heavenly crowns:
Glory, righteousness, gold,
Joy, and life.
All these represent the same
reward,
That of eternal life
With the Father.

All true believers will receive
The great reward
Of seeing God face to face,
The greatest motivator of all.
On this earth, our lives shall be
Loving God and neighbors,
Sharing, praying, fasting, and
Living for the reward.
We are to focus on eternal
truths,
Not on earthly vanities.
We seek the approval of our
Lord

While storing up treasures in
heaven.

A subject much discussed
Is that of different levels of
reward.
While some may have greater
capacities
As well as greater
responsibilities,
All will experience the fullness
of joy and
Pleasures forevermore.
For there in heaven
Perfect harmony will reign.
No envy, no strife—all will
Experience glorious eternal life
With God,
Never ceasing to sing:
"Holy, holy, holy,
Is the Lord God Almighty!"

"But love your enemies, and do good, and lend, expecting nothing in return, and your reward will be great, and you will be sons of the Most High, for he is kind to the ungrateful and the evil."

(Luke 6:35)

Righteousness

"In his days Judah will be saved, and Israel will dwell securely.

And this is the name by which he will be called: 'The LORD is our righteousness.'"

(Jeremiah 23:6)

The perfect holiness of Christ.
An essential attribute in the
Character of God.
God, the Father, is
righteousness (just);
Jesus Christ is the righteous
one (just);
Repenting sinners
Are declared righteous (just);
The Spirit makes them
righteous (just),
And they will be wholly
righteous (just)
In the age to come.

A simple definition is: "morally
good,"
Yet it encompasses much more:
Purity of heart, morality of life.
Righteousness includes all
That we call justice, honesty,
virtue—
All with holy affections.
When applied to God,
righteousness
Is the perfection or holiness
Of His nature.

People, by nature, are not
righteous.
Jesus became our righteousness

On the cross.
Our best efforts are as filthy
    rags.
We are unable to attain
    righteousness
On our own. Only through
Our responses to God's grace
By our believing in His Son,
His work on the cross,
Can Christ's righteousness
Be imputed to us.

**"For our sake he made him to
be sin who knew no sin, so that
in him we might become the
righteousness of God."**

(2 Corinthians 5:21)

Rose of Sharon

**"I am a rose of Sharon, a lily of
the valleys."**

(Song of Solomon 2:1)

Sharon, a plain of Palestine,
Wild and fertile, is
Home to a host of beautiful
    flowers,
A place renowned for majesty
    and beauty.

This "rose" was possibly
The cistus or rock-rose,
Which blooms in Palestine,

Known for its soothing aroma
And pain-relieving qualities.
Possibly a hibiscus,
With white, red, or pink
    flowers, or
Possibly a crocus-like flower,
The source of saffron.

Used once in scripture,
Spoken about by Solomon's
    beloved bride,
Referring to herself as
The rose of Sharon—
A term expressing beauty.

Used by many as a name for
    Jesus.
The source of this usage is
    unknown.
Possibly due to Jesus being
The spiritual pinnacle
Of beauty and splendor.
As the rose is the
Most perfect of flowers,
Jesus is totally perfect
In His nature and personality.
Although a beautiful image,
    there is
No direct biblical connection
To this symbolism.

Others interpret this rose of
    Sharon
Not as Jesus, but as His bride.
For He has perfected forever
    those

Who are being sanctified.
Also, He presents us to Himself
A glorious church, not having
    a spot
Or a wrinkle or any such thing.

It is a beautiful image,
A name to employ for
Majesty, beauty, healing
    power—
The rose of Sharon.

"The wilderness and the dry land shall be glad; the desert shall rejoice and blossom like the crocus."

(Isaiah 35:1)

Sabbath

"Remember the Sabbath day, to keep it holy."

(Exodus 20:8)

The fourth commandment is
An order to be obeyed,
Blessed and made holy
By our heavenly Father
From the creation of the world
Until the resurrection of
    Christ.
Now called the Lord's Day, it
Shall continue to the end of the
    world,

As the Christian Sabbath.

The Sabbath was made for
    humanity,
Not humanity for the Sabbath.
It is not a burden we must
    conform to,
But a delight that we can enjoy.

God gave the nation of Israel
A day of rest for their benefit,
To recover from a week's labor,
To recall His goodness and
    grace.
It is a command bound to
The holiness of God.
Adam was expected to obey
    this command,
As are all generations, in every
    society.
All are to keep the Sabbath
As an everlasting ordinance to
    the Lord.

As we keep the Sabbath,
We celebrate the rest and peace
We have in Jesus Christ
And look forward to the day
Of eternal rest in God our
    Father.

Many opinions about "rest":
Unnecessary commerce and
    labor, and
Commerce for the sake of
Merchandising ought to cease.

Three categories are considered
Acceptable: Worship,
Preservation of life, and acts of
 mercy.
Activities of enjoyment and
 pleasure that honor the
 Lord, turn our thoughts
 to God,
Are not banned but
 encouraged.
We are to cease from the
Works, words, and thoughts
Related to our worldly
 employments.
A day to keep holy unto the
 Lord;
Not only should we rest from
 such activities, but it is a
 day of public and private
 exercise of worship,
Giving all glory to our Lord
 and Savior.

**"For in six days the LORD made
heaven and earth, the sea, and all
that is in them, and rested on the
seventh day. Therefore the LORD
blessed the Sabbath day and made
it holy."**

(Exodus 20:11)

Sackcloth

**"I clothe the heavens with
blackness and make sackcloth
their covering."**

(Isaiah 50:3)

Sackcloth, a course material,
Usually made of black goat's
 hair,
Possibly of camel hair,
Or of hemp, cotton, or flax.
It is rough, abrasive, itchy, and
Uncomfortable to wear.

Being clothed in sackcloth
Holds many meanings,
Somewhat similar but each
 unique.
Worn by those in mourning,
Worn as an act of
 repentance and
An act of humility.
Also worn as act of austerity,
Leading a simple lifestyle,
Removed from the frills
That make life complicated.

Sackcloth is an outward sign
Of one's inner condition.
Demonstrates one's grief,
Repentance, austerity.
Wearing sackcloth does not
Move God to act or intervene,

But sackcloth represents the
humility
To which God responds.

Although the physical
Donning of sackcloth is
Not practiced today,
We must don it spiritually,
To mourn, to humble
ourselves, and
To repent of our fallen nature.
For God looks favorably on
Those who are poor and
contrite
In spirit and heart.
Sackcloth is a spiritual tool.
God knows the challenges we
face and
Expects us to rend
Our hearts before Him,
Trusting Him in all things.

"Woe to you, Chorazin! Woe to you, Bethsaida! For if the mighty works done in you had been done in Tyre and Sidon, they would have repented long ago, sitting in sackcloth and ashes."

(Luke 10:13)

Sacrament

"Peter replied, 'Repent and be baptized, every one of you, in the name of Jesus Christ for the forgiveness of your sins. And you will receive the gift of the Holy Spirit.'"

(Acts 2:38)

Holy signs and seals
Of the covenant of grace,
Instituted by God, the
Outward and visible sign
Of inward and spiritual grace.

Visible signs of Christ
And His work of redemption,
Seals of the covenant of grace,
Marking the believers
As belonging to Christ.
They represent the spiritual
reality
Of our union to Christ.

Two sacraments ordained by
Christ are:
Baptism and the Lord's Supper.
Both are instituted by God,
Ordained by Christ.
Both are signs pointing to
Something greater than
ourselves:
Christ and His redemptive
work.
Both are seals,
Sealing the covenant of grace
Upon the believer,
Marking the believer as
Belonging to Christ.

Sacraments are signs and seals
Used by the Holy Spirit
To identify us with Christ and
with
The salvation He accomplished
for us.
They are physical, visible,
touchable,
Representing the spiritual
reality
Of Christ and our salvation
through
Faith. The Holy Spirit is the
link
Between the sacraments
And the spiritual realities
Of forgiveness of sins,
Our new lives in Christ.
When we participate in the
sacraments,
We testify to our faith in God's
promises
Before a watching world.

"Now as they were eating, Jesus took bread, and after blessing it broke it and gave it to the disciples, and said, 'Take, eat; this is my body.' And he took a cup, and when he had given thanks he gave it to them, saying, 'Drink of it, all of you, for this is my blood of the covenant, which is poured out for many for the forgiveness of sins.'"

(Matthew 26:26–28)

Sacrifice

"I appeal to you therefore, brothers, by the mercies of God, to present your bodies as a living sacrifice, holy and acceptable to God, which is your spiritual worship."

(Romans 12:1)

A symbol of our desire to
repent, to dedicate our lives
to God.
It is a symbol of holiness,
Not punishment.
It is tied with love, mercy,
Humility, and justice. It is a
symbol
Of communion with God,
A sign of drawing near, coming
closer.
Thus, the purpose of a sacrifice
Is to gain intimacy with God
By bringing Him a cherished
gift.

The sacrifices of old, bloody
or not,
Had no value or efficacy in
themselves.

They were only the shadow
Of good things to come,
Pointing believers forward
To the coming of the great
    high priest,
Who, in the fullness of time,
Was offered once for all
To bear the sin of many.
Those sacrifices belonged to a
Temporary economy, a system
Of types and emblems.
They served their purposes
But now have passed away.

Thus, with the
    once-for-all-time
Sacrifice of the Lamb of God,
Those today who are in Christ
    Jesus
By virtue of saving faith
Are to offer ourselves
    completely
To the Lord.
We become a living sacrifice by
Not being conformed to this
    world,
But by renewing our minds
Through the power of God's
    Word.
We are to hear, read, study,
Memorize, and meditate on
    scripture,
Giving all praise and glory
    to God.

"Through him then let us continually offer up a sacrifice of praise to God, that is, the fruit of lips that acknowledge his name."

(Hebrews 13:15)

Salt of the Earth

"You are the salt of the earth. But if the salt loses its saltiness, how can it be made salty again? It is no longer good for anything, except to be thrown out and trampled underfoot."

(Matthew 5:13)

Many interpretations of this,
Since salt is such a well-known
    item,
Cherished by all in the ancient
    world.
Roman soldiers were paid in
    salt.
Greeks considered it divine.
Mosaic law required all
    offerings
To contain salt.

Perhaps as salt gives food
A rich-and-pleasant taste,
Christians are to give a good
    flavor
To the lives of those we
    encounter.

Our conduct shows the fruit of
the life
To which God has called us.

Possibly means Christians are
to serve
As preservatives, stopping
moral decay
In our sin-infected world.
The spiritual health and
strength
Of Christians can counteract
The corruption in this world,
Inhibit sin's power to destroy
lives,
And create opportunities for
the gospel
To be proclaimed and received.

Exact meaning is not specified;
Perhaps it is a general sense of
value
And usefulness. Since salt was
important,
Christian ministries are
important.
As salt has an impact,
Christians are to have an
influence
On this world we live in.

A beautiful image,
One that comes with a
warning:
If it loses its flavor,

It is no longer good for
anything.
The meaning is not that we
Could lose our salvation,
For salt does not lose it
saltiness.
If we let sin gain control of us
And live according to the flesh,
We become contaminated;
We need to confess our sins,
And let the Lord restore us
To the purpose for which we
are called.

"You shall season all your grain offerings with salt. You shall not let the salt of the covenant with your God be missing from your grain offering; with all your offerings you shall offer salt."

(Leviticus 2:13)

Sanctification

"Now may the God of peace himself sanctify you completely, and may your whole spirit and soul and body be kept blameless at the coming of our Lord Jesus Christ. He who calls you is faithful; he will surely do it."

(1 Thessalonians 5:23–24)

To be gradually transformed
    in heart, mind, will, and
    conduct, conforming more
    and more
To the will of God,
To the image of Christ—
Until at death we are made
Perfect in holiness.

Sanctify means "to make holy."
It is a progressive work
Of God and of people,
Making us increasingly
Free from sin and
More like Christ
In our actual lives.

God's part is in freeing us
From sinful habits,
Forming Christ in us
In affections, disposition, and
    virtues.
It is convincing the believer
Of the helplessness of our
    sinful natures,
Convincing us of our need for
    Christ, and
Enabling us to live unto
    righteousness.

Humanity's part has three
    responsibilities.
First, seek the Lord in
An active, earnest, and
    persistent way;
We must want to be sanctified.

Second, believe that God
Can deal with our sins,
That He has freed us from sin's
    authority.
Third, partake actively in the
    means
Of Christian growth—
Prayer, study, discipline.

Our God is a faithful God;
Those He calls, he will sanctify.
God will sanctify us;
He will keep us blameless,
Making us increasingly to
Abound in love.
Regardless of how slowly
Or how imperfect we feel,
He will do it.

"But we ought always to give thanks to God for you, brothers beloved by the Lord, because God chose you as the first fruits to be saved, through sanctification by the Spirit and belief in the truth."

(2 Thessalonians 2:13)

Satan

"How you have fallen from heaven, morning star, son of the dawn! You have been cast down to

**the earth, you who once laid low
the nations!"**

(Isaiah 14:12)

Simply put: Satan is our enemy.
Satan opposes God and
Opposes all God's people.
Satan is behind
Every evil scheme on this
    planet:
Idolatry, cults, and false
    religions.
Desperate to be worshiped, he
Desires to destroy God
And the kingdom of heaven.

Satan is more than you think.
His heavenly name was Lucifer,
The shining one,
The morning star.
The model of perfection,
Created as a cherub and
Full of wisdom,
Perfect in beauty.
Present with God in Eden,
Ordained, and anointed
    by God
As the mighty heavenly
Angelic guard.

Satan became arrogant,
Full of pride in his beauty and
    status.
Wanted a throne higher than
    God's.

Not content in his
    position, and
He rebelled against God,
Lost the battle, and was cast
    out of heaven—not in a
    fall, but a shove.
He didn't go alone; he dragged
    along
At least one-third of all the
    angels.
Exactly when is a mystery—
It was after creation, sometime
    before
The temptation of Adam
    and Eve.

Satan became ruler of our
    world.
He is the prince of the power
    of the air.
He is an accuser, a tempter, and
    a deceiver.
His very name means
    "adversary" or
"One who opposes."
His title, "the devil," means
    "slanderer."

Never to be underestimated,
He is a tempter.
He tempted Jesus in the
    wilderness.
He has much power,
Blinding the minds of those
Who do not believe.

His purpose is to steal, kill, and
destroy.
He is desperate; he is
dangerous.
He is desperate to be
worshiped and
Desperate to destroy.
He is a serpent and a dragon
Who will be defeated.

Satan does all in his power
To oppose God and His
followers,
Yet his destruction is assured.
He knows his time is limited.
His final destiny is sealed:
An eternity in the lake of fire.

"And the devil who had deceived
them was thrown into the lake of
fire and sulfur where the beast and
the false prophet were, and they
will be tormented day and night
forever and ever."

(Revelation 20:10)

Savior

"For unto you is born this day in
the city of David a Savior, who is
Christ the Lord."

(Luke 2:11)

A person who saves and
rescues, delivering others
from harm.
One true Savior only: Jesus
Christ,
Who truly saves us
Not from worldly danger
But from the wrath of God.

Since we all have sinned,
And since sin contradicts God's
Perfect and holy character,
We deserve judgment
from God—
Who is perfectly just,
Unable to allow sin to go
unpunished.
Because He is eternal and
infinite,
Only eternal and infinite
punishment
Is sufficient for sin.
The only fitting penalty:
Eternal death.

Hence, we need a Savior,
Someone who will pay the
penalty,
For it must be paid.
We need someone to save us
From this wrath of God,
His eternal punishment.
We need a Savior,
And there is only one—
He who lived a perfect sinless
life,

Lived the life we were meant
   to live,
He who died on the cross—
A death we deserved to die.
We are the sinners,
Jesus is our Savior.
It is Jesus who saves.

"Who saved us and called us to a holy calling, not because of our works but because of his own purpose and grace, which he gave us in Christ Jesus before the ages began, and which now has been manifested through the appearing of our Savior Christ Jesus, who abolished death and brought life and immortality to light through the gospel."

(2 Timothy 1:9–10)

Scripture

"Now we have received not the spirit of the world, but the Spirit who is from God, that we might understand the things freely given us by God. And we impart this in words not taught by human wisdom but taught by the Spirit, interpreting spiritual truths to those who are spiritual."

(1 Corinthians 2:12–13)

Sacred writings inspired by
   God to perpetuate His
   revealed will.
Referred to as the oracles
   of God.
The scriptures are
   God-breathed,
The source of truth on which
We can base our lives.
Its words are inerrant and
   infallible—
Not only without error,
But incapable of error.
Scripture makes good
On all its claims.

Jesus Himself equates scripture
As God's Word.
The term was used in the New
   Testament
Signifying the definite
   collection
Called the Old Testament.
Thereafter, it was enlarged by
   the Spirit
Until we now possess
A completed scripture—
Old and New Testaments,
Both accurately preserved,
Passed down from
Generation to generation.

"Inspired by God"
Refers to the fact that God
Divinely influenced human
   authors

Of scripture, so that what they
wrote
Is the very Word of God.
This inspiration extends
To the very words themselves,
Not just concepts or ideas.
All scripture is God-breathed.
All its words, not just its
doctrines,
Are inspired—each and every
word,
From Genesis to Revelation.

There is nothing that can be
Added or subtracted from
scripture.
For in them, God has revelated
Everything that His people
Are to believe concerning God,
And what duty
God requires of man.

**"And how from childhood you
have been acquainted with the
sacred writings, which are able
to make you wise for salvation
through faith in Christ Jesus. All
Scripture is breathed out by God
and profitable for teaching, for
reproof, for correction, and for
training in righteousness, that the
man of God may be competent,
equipped for every good work."**

(2 Timothy 3:15–17)

Seeing God

**"Blessed are the pure in heart, for
they shall see God."**

i

The greatest blessing of all.
Heavenly, awe-inspiring,
glorious,
And oh, so personal!
It is to have a relationship
with God
Through faith in Jesus Christ.

It is trusting Christ, being
delivered
From spiritual blindness and
darkness.
It is experiencing God through
faith,
Beholding His wonders that
were
Previously invisible.

It is seeing God in all things—
Not by chance or coincidence
But only the hand of God.
It is recognizing the sovereignty
Of our Father in heaven.

To see God is to live
blissfully and
Reverently in the awareness
That God is with us always.

It is to know Him, to love
Him, and
To desire to please Him.

Sin blurs and blocks our
sight and
Our spiritual vision.
It blinds us to God's presence.
Our iniquities separate us
from God;
He hides His face from us
And will not hear us.
God, through Christ, has
promised
To deliver us from this
blindness.

His promise is not just for the
present,
But for eternity.
God is preparing the moment
When we shall enter His
presence
And truly see Him face to face.

"As for me, I will be vindicated
and will see your face; when I
awake, I will be satisfied with
seeing your likeness."

(Psalm 17:15)

Self-Control

"For the grace of God has
appeared, bringing salvation for
all people, training us to renounce
ungodliness and worldly passions,
and to live self-controlled, upright,
and godly lives in the present age."

(Titus 2:11–12)

Fruit of the Spirit,
One of the famous nine,
Last but definitely not least,
As important as the first—
It could be called climactic.
It is one of the first
Characteristics of leaders.

Self-control presumes that
Something in us needs
controlling
And that there is a way
To control it.
Self-control embraces
Both mind and emotions,
Both our external and internal
states,
Both behavior and sentiments.

Self-control has a path,
Beginning with the heart,
Flowing to the mind, and
Then revealed in actions.
This path is full of obstacles—
Desires, lusts, passions—

A path fraught with challenges.

Self-control is a direct gift
From the Holy Spirit.
This gift cannot be passively
    received,
But must be acted upon—
A gift to unwrap and live out.
Our self-control glorifies God
As we release control to Christ.

Self-control refers to
    temperance and
Involves moderation and
    constraint and
The ability to say no to earthly
    desires.
It is controlling all thoughts,
Words, and actions.
True self-control
Is God working within us.

This godly characteristic is
Not an easy one to master.
It is much more than mere will
    power and
Requires yielding to the Holy
    Spirit,
Abiding in God's Word, and
Constantly being in prayer.
Only then may it truly shine
    forth.

A gift we are to practice
In order to master control

Of this beast of our sinful
    passions
Includes not being a slave to
    wine,
Abstaining from sexual
    immorality, and
Not living according to the
    flesh.
We must practice turning to
    the source
Of true change and real power.

This source is not inward
But upward.
It is admitting our
    inadequacies,
Repenting of our evil ways,
Trusting in God's
    promises, and
Acting in faith that He will
    do it
In us and through us.

**"For this reason I remind you to
fan into flame the gift of God,
which is in you through the laying
on of my hands, for God gave us a
spirit not of fear but of power and
love and self-control."**

(2 Timothy 1:6–7)

Seraphim

"I saw the Lord sitting upon a throne, high and lifted up; and the train of his robe filled the temple. Above him stood the seraphim."

(Isaiah 6:1–2)

A title meaning "fiery ones,"
In allusion to their
Burning love for God.
Angelic beings with human
    form,
Described as having six
    wings—
Two covering their faces,
Two covering their feet, and
Two used to fly
About the throne of God.
They sing His praises
With powerful voices,
Calling special attention
To His glory and majesty.
At the sound of their voices,
The doorposts and thresholds
    shook and
The temple filled with smoke.

Seraphim also serve
As agents of purification,
As when they touched
Isaiah's lips with a hot coal.
Then said, "Your guilt is taken
    away
And your sins atoned for."

The Seraphim are similar
To other holy angels,
Being perfectly obedient to
    God and
Focusing on worshiping Him
    constantly.

"And one called to another and said: 'Holy, holy, holy is the LORD of hosts; the whole earth is full of his glory!'"

(Isaiah 6:3)

Sermon on the Mount

"Seeing the crowds, he went up on the mountain, and when he sat down, his disciples came to him. And he opened his mouth and taught them."

(Matthew 5:1–2)

Taught on a mountain side,
    it is
The most famous sermon ever.
    It was
Addressed to Christ's disciples,
Teaching them how to live a
    life
Dedicated and pleasing
    to God,
Free from hypocrisy and
Full of love and grace

And wisdom and discernment.
Augustine called it a perfect
    standard
For the Christian life.
It is an exposition of Christian
    ethics.

This sermon is Jesus Christ's
Lengthiest discourse in
    scripture
And the best known, though
    probably
The least understood and
    obeyed
In modern times. Although
    directed
To His disciples and believers,
    it was
Designed to teach the
    multitude
What is involved in
Repentance and following
    Christ.
Includes an evangelistic
Element for unbelievers.
Contrasts true and false
    ethics and
True and false piety.
Exposes religious hypocrisy,
Teaches the necessity
Of entering by the narrow
    gate, and
Warns of the deadly dangers
Of false teachers.
The Sermon on the Mount
Tells believers that they must

Be different from the world.

The Sermon on the Mount
Starts off powerfully with
The Beatitudes,
Followed by teachings on
Salt and light,
Fulfillment of the law,
Murder, adultery, divorce,
Oaths, an eye for an eye,
Loving your enemies,
Giving to the needy,
How to pray (including
The Lord's Prayer),
How to fast,
Treasures in heaven,
Worrying, judging others,
Asking and seeking and
    knocking,
The narrow and wide gates,
False prophets, and
The foolish and wise builders.
A collection of subjects,
All applicable to the Christian
    life.

A sermon to read often,
A sermon to meditate upon,
A sermon to cherish, and
A sermon to live.
Words from the Master
    Himself.

**"And when Jesus finished
these sayings, the crowds were**

astonished at his teaching, for he was teaching them as one who had authority, and not as their scribes."

(Matthew 7:28–29)

Seven Deadly Sins

"There are six things that the LORD hates, seven that are an abomination to him: haughty eyes, a lying tongue, and hands that shed innocent blood, a heart that devises wicked plans, feet that make haste to run to evil, a false witness who breathes out lies, and one who sows discord among brothers."

(Proverbs 6:16–19)

Seven vices,
Negative qualities of character,
Which, when left unchecked,
Results in a host of other sins
    and death.
First delineated by
Pope Gregory the Great and
Later expounded by Thomas
    Aquinas.

These seven sins are:
Pride—an unrealistic sense of
    one's self-worth.
Envy—a feeling that you
deserve another person's possessions, success, virtues, or talents.
Lust—a selfish focus on sex and sexual pleasure with someone other than your spouse.
Gluttony—excessive desire for eating and drinking.
Anger—excessive, improper desire to exact revenge.
Greed—strong desire for possessions.
Sloth—a lack of effort while facing a necessary task, causing it to go undone or be done badly.
Are these according to scripture?
Yes and no.
Proverbs 6 contains a list
Of seven things that are
An abomination to God—
But not identical to the list
    above.

Those seven sins in
    Proverbs 6—
Haughty eyes—a sign of pride.
Lying tongue—speaking falsehoods with intention to deceive.
Shed innocent blood—the killing of a person not judged guilty of any capital crime.

Heart that devises wicked plans—thoughts of wickedness, evil feelings, and designs.

Feet that make haste to run to evil—a willingness to commit all manner of sin with greediness.

A false witness who breathes out lies—bearing false witness or lies against one's neighbor.

Sows discord among brothers—by whispers, slanders, and false flatteries that causes disharmony.

In the final analysis,
No sin is more "deadly" than any other.
All sin results in death.
To be guilty of even one sin
Is to be condemned as a lawbreaker.

Praise be to God
That Jesus Christ took the penalty
For all our sins, including
The "seven deadly sins."
By the grace of God,
Through faith in Christ,
We can be forgiven.

"For whoever keeps the whole law but fails in one point has become guilty of all of it."

(James 2:10)

Shaken

"When I felt secure, I said, 'I will never be shaken.'"

(Psalm 30:6)

To be shaken is to not stand firm,
To be easily moved, not hold true,
Or to be defeated.
Many ways to voice the idea:
Turn one's faith from God
To false idols, especially self;
Self-confidence, pride;
Pride, carelessness, and self-dependence.

An aim of Satan,
Who wants us all to be shaken,
Especially amid our blessings
Of health, wealth, family,
Contentment, and victories.

Enjoyments beget confidence.
Confidence brings forth carelessness.
Carelessness gives opportunity for

Satan to work unseen.
The only defense is:
Never be shaken in our faith.
Hold true to the gospel
Regardless of blessings or
    curses.
Pray continuously.

To be shaken is
The arrogance of godless
    confidence.
The mistake of a good person
Who needs correction,
The unwarranted confidence
Of a doubtful soul.

Being shaken is forgetting to
    depend
Upon our true God—
Obviously not good.
We must keep focus on
    our God,
Never doubting Him,
Always giving praise and
    thanks,
Knowing that He blesses us
As well as tests us.
Stand with Christ,
Never to be shaken.

"Put on the whole armor of God, that you may be able to stand against the schemes of the devil."

(Ephesians 6:11)

Shepherd, Good

"I am the good shepherd. I know my own and my own know me, just as the Father knows me and I know the Father; and I lay down my life for the sheep."

(John 10:14–15)

A beautiful image.
A reference to the Lord's
    inherent
Goodness, righteousness, and
    love.
Not just *a* shepherd, but *the*
    shepherd,
Unique in character—

Patiently tending his flock,
Especially those prone to
    wandering,
Going astray, and turning to
    their own ways. This flock
    is subject to danger:
Thieves, wolves, storms,
And themselves.

The good shepherd
Patiently endures for the flock's
    welfare,
Subjecting Himself to grave
    danger—
To protect those He truly loves.
David fought lions and bears,
Defending his father's flock

As a shepherd boy.
Christ laid down His own life
On the cross,
Making salvation possible
For all who come to Him in
     faith.

As helpless creatures,
We require a shepherd.
We are easily frightened, easily
     confused,
And easily follow false idols.
We are dependent on the Lord
To shepherd us,
Protect us, and
Care for us,
Night and day.

As the good shepherd,
He not only protects and
     guides us,
Searching for us when we are
     lost
But He also provides for our
     needs:
Food, water, rest,
Safety, and direction.
We lack nothing,
For He knows exactly what we
     need.

Listen closely,
Hear His voice.
His sheep know Him,
For He gives eternal life,
So that we never perish.

He knows each one by name.

"For thus says the Lord GOD: Behold, I, I myself will search for my sheep and will seek them out. As a shepherd seeks out his flock when he is among his sheep that have been scattered, so will I seek out my sheep, and I will rescue them from all places where they have been scattered on a day of clouds and thick darkness."

(Ezekiel 34:11–12)

Signs and Wonders

"So Jesus said to him, 'Unless you see signs and wonders you will not believe.'"

(John 4:48)

One adjective of biblical
     signs is:
Supernatural.
They are tokens,
Something by which another
Thing is shown or represented.
Possibly a motion, action, or
     word,
For sure, a miracle—
An event, an appearance,
Intended as proof positive,
Of something else.

Often desired by people
To prove that God exists,
To prove that Jesus was God,
To prove the Word of God,
To quench the doubts
Of those of little faith.

The gospel is the power
Of God unto salvation,
Not signs and wonders.
Jews demand signs;
Greeks seek wisdom;
The faithful preach Christ
    crucified.
Sign-seeking is easily a
    diversion
From the power of the Word
When coming from a resistant
    heart and
An unwillingness to believe.

When signs and wonders
Are witness to His Word,
They are not in competition
Or against or over the Word.
They are divine witnesses to the
Value, truth, necessity, and
The centrality of the Word,
Of Christ crucified.

Signs and wonders
Are not the saving word of
    grace;
They do not save.
They are not the power of God
Unto salvation,

They do not transform the
    heart.
There is one warning to all:
They can be imitated by Satan.

Yet God at times uses signs and
    wonders
To shatter the shell of
    disinterest,
To shatter the shell of
    skepticism,
To shatter the shell of false
    religion.
They can help the fallen heart
To fix its gaze on the gospel,
On Christ crucified.

"God also testified to it by signs, wonders and various miracles, and by gifts of the Holy Spirit distributed according to his will."

(Hebrews 2:4 NIV)

Sin

"For there is no distinction: for all have sinned and fall short of the glory of God, and are justified by his grace as a gift, through the redemption that is in Christ Jesus, whom God put forward as

a propitiation by his blood, to be received by faith."

(Romans 3:22–25)

At is simplest, sin is a deviation
From what is good and right.
It is missing the mark,
Failure to achieve intended
    results,
Failure to glorify God, or
A lack of reverence
    toward God.
Sin includes everything
That is unacceptable to God.
Anything wrongly related to
    God is sin.
Sin provokes God's wrath,
For He hates sin.
Sin calls God's character into
    question.

The Bible describes sin in the
    negative:
Lawlessness, disobedience,
    impiety,
Unbelief, darkness, falling
    away,
Weakness,
    unrighteousness, and
Faithlessness.

Sin is transgressing the law
    of God,
Rebellion against God
    Himself.

People became sinners by
    nature
Through Adam's act of
    disobedience.
We are sinners not because
    we sin,
But we sin because we are
    sinners.
We are sinful at birth,
Sinful from the time we are
    conceived.

There is original sin
As a result of Adam's
    disobedience—
The sinful tendencies,
    desires, and
Dispositions in our hearts
With which we are all born.
There is imputed sin,
Where we are regarded
As having sinned in Adam
Such that we are guilty
Of his sinful act as well.
There is personal sin,
Sin committed daily
As a result of our fallen nature,
From seemingly innocent
    untruths
To murder.
All sin is condemned by God's
    justice,
For all sin is sin against God—
And therefore infinitely serious.

Sin has far-reaching
consequences:
Separation from God's love,
A quenching of the Holy Spirit;
It removes our heavenly joy,
Takes away excitement in the
Lord,
Robs us of peace,
Hinders fellowship with
God, and
Loses confidence in prayer.
The just penalty of sin is death,
Physical as well as spiritual
death.

Yet through all this there is
hope,
For our God is merciful.
Through the sacrifice and
suffering
Of our Lord Jesus Christ,
All sin has been nailed to the
cross.
Past, present, and future sins
Have been forgiven through
His sacrifice,
Through our faith in Him.
We are redeemed through His
blood
According to the riches
Of His grace.

"For the wages of sin is death, but the gift of God is eternal life in Christ Jesus our Lord."

(Romans 6:23)

Six Days

"For in six days the LORD made heaven and earth, the sea, and all that is in them, and rested on the seventh day. Therefore the LORD blessed the Sabbath day and made it holy."

(Exodus 20:11)

Six twenty-four-hour periods?
Six years?
Maybe millennia?
Old earth, new earth?
Many theories abound.
The one fact holds true:
God did the creating.

Some interpret these days
Through the experience
Of general revelation,
Based on scientific
observations.
Others interpret through
scripture,
Holding fast to God's Word
As it was written for us.
Whatever view is decided
upon,

It must not conflict with
    scripture
Or be illogically forced upon it.

Evolution theory remains a
    theory,
Omitting God and ignoring
    scripture,
Guessing on science.

Many different takes on earth's
    origin: theistic evolution,
Gap theory, apparent-age
    theory,
Scientific creationism,
Twenty-four-hour
    interpretation, and
Historical creationism,
To name a few.

Historically, and still holding
True to this day, Genesis
    speaks
Of a literal twenty-four-
    hour day.
Yet both the young-earth
And old-earth interpretations
Rely on certain assumptions.
The case for how to interpret
The true meaning of *day*
Can be credibly made on both
    sides.
But we must let
Scripture interpret scripture.

These conflicting theories
Must never permit us to
Diminish the importance of
What Genesis teaches us.
God is the Creator.
The universe and all it
    contains,
Including you and me, was
Created by God. Without
    doubt,
He is our Creator.

**"For every house is built by
someone, but the builder of all
things is God."**

(Hebrews 3:4)

Slave

**"Slaves, obey your earthly masters
in everything; and do it, not only
when their eye is on you and
to curry their favor, but with
sincerity of heart and reverence
for the Lord."**

(Colossians 3:22)

Someone subject to involuntary
    servitude, legally owned as
    property
By another person,
Bonded to service without
    wages.

The slavery discussed in
scripture
Is not based on color or
nationality;
There are no modern parallels.
Slavery in Israel was not the
cruel system
Of Greece, Rome, and later
nations.
In general, the treatment of
slaves
Along with a slave's rights,
Made for a tolerable life
In difficult times,
Much like the life of a soldier
Or of a lower-class worker.
Masters were instructed
To not rule over them
ruthlessly and
To supply them with
What is right and fair.
Freedom was possible
In a number of ways.

Yet slavery is slavery
And is never condoned by
scripture.
It is spoken of as part
Of the fabric of society.
The gospel in its spirit and
genius
Is always hostile to slavery
In every form.
The purpose of the Bible is to
point
To the way of salvation,

Not to reform society.
Yet through the love, mercy,
And grace of God,
We are to love our neighbors,
Thus transforming how people
Treat each other—
As one in Christ Jesus.

This biblical image
Of a slave or bondservant
Grew to great importance
To Christians then and now.
We are called to be
Slaves of Christ Jesus,
Dedicated to Jesus
As our one master,
In His service for eternity.

"Masters, treat your bondservants justly and fairly, knowing that you also have a Master in heaven."

(Colossians 4:1)

Sodom and Gomorrah

"Then the LORD said, 'Because the outcry against Sodom and Gomorrah is great and their sin is very grave, I will go down to see whether they have done altogether according to the outcry that has

come to me. And if not, I will
know.'"

(Genesis 18:20–21)

Two evil cities,
Notorious for flagrant sin.
Destroyed by God with a rain
Of fire and brimstone.
A cautionary example
Of the destructive
Consequences of sin.

Cities of many sins—including
Rampant homosexuality
    among men.
God sent two angels
To find ten innocent persons
Within the city walls.
Ten were not found.
Abraham's nephew, Lot, was
    able
To flee, along with his wife
And two daughters.

Then the Lord rained down,
Burning sulfur on
Sodom and Gomorrah.
He destroyed all life,
Men and women,
Along with all
Vegetation on the plain.

Lot's wife disobeyed
The angel's instruction
Not to look back.
She turned into a pillar of salt

For identifying with
The people of Sodom.
This is a vivid warning
    from God.

Yes, Sodom and Gomorrah
Gave themselves up to
Sexual immorality and
    perversions,
The most likely primary reason
For their destruction.
But their sins extended much
    further.
Clearly, the general wickedness
Of these two cities was great,
Including a lack of hospitality
Shown by their residents.
These prideful people
Who delighted in cruelty,
Neglected any form of
Social justice.

God, the righteous judge,
Condemned these cities.
Although their sins of pride,
Sexual immorality,
Inhospitality, and cruelty
Were committed against
Men and women,
Their sins were ultimately
A direct offense against God.
All sin is an offense to God.

To this day,
The plain where Sodom and
    Gomorrah

Were located remains a desolate
    wasteland.
Sodom and Gomorrah serve
As a powerful example
Of God's hatred toward sin,
Of His wrath against sin.

**"Behold, this was the guilt of
your sister Sodom: she and her
daughters had pride, excess of
food, and prosperous ease, but
did not aid the poor and needy.
They were haughty and did an
abomination before me. So I
removed them, when I saw it."**

(Ezekiel 16:49–50)

Son of God

**"Long ago, at many times and
in many ways, God spoke to our
fathers by the prophets, but in
these last days he has spoken to us
by his Son, whom he appointed the
heir of all things, through whom
also he created the world. He is the
radiance of the glory of God and
the exact imprint of his nature,
and he upholds the universe by
the word of his power."**

(Hebrews 1:1–3)

Jesus Christ, the Son of God—

A title of nature, not of office.
Denotes His equality with the
    Father and
Asserts His true and proper
    divinity.
The second person of the
    trinity,
Because of His eternal relation
To God, the Father,
Is truly the Son of God.
He did not become God's Son
Upon His incarnation,
For He was with God
In the beginning.
Through Him, all things were
    made.
And when the set time had
    fully come,
God sent His Son,
Born of a woman, born under
    the law.

Jesus is God's Son
In the sense that He is God
Made manifest in human form,
Conceived in the virgin Mary
By the Holy Spirit.
This was confirmed by God
    Himself
Upon Jesus's baptism,
When His voice spoke from
    heaven:
"This is my beloved Son
In whom I am well pleased"—
Not only designating Jesus
As the Messiah,

But speaking personally
As a pleased Father to His Son.

Although Jesus never directly
Called Himself the Son
    of God,
The devil did,
The demons did,
The disciples did,
The centurion did,
The angels did,
And His Father in heaven did.

To be the Son of God
Means that Jesus is God—
No mere man
Or high-ranking angel.
He was not only a prophet,
    but had
The divine essence of God
From all eternity.
As the Son of God
Our salvation appeared.

"While he was still speaking, a bright cloud covered them, and a voice from the cloud said, This is my Son, whom I love; with him I am well pleased. Listen to him!"

(Matthew 17:5)

Son of Man

"I saw in the night visions, and behold, with the clouds of heaven there came one like a son of man, and he came to the Ancient of Days and was presented before him. And to him was given dominion and glory and a kingdom, that all peoples, nations, and languages should serve him; his dominion is an everlasting dominion, which shall not pass away, and his kingdom one that shall not be destroyed."

(Daniel 7:13–14)

A double meaning in this title.
    It commonly refers to a
    human being, but also to
    the exalted heavenly One.
    Jesus is both divine and
    human—
Two natures, one person.

Conceived of the Holy Spirit,
Born of the virgin Mary.
As the Son of Man,
Jesus was truly a human being.
Although He was fully God,
He was also fully man—
A mystery to our finite minds.

A messianic title,
The promised deliverer,

The Lord of the Sabbath,
Fulfillment of prophecy.
This Son of Man in
The book of Daniel
Is a heavenly figure,
Revealing the origin,
Majesty, and dignity
Of the one who will rule
Forevermore.
The title was used extensively
By Jesus Himself.

As the Son of Man,
Jesus was not just a human
    figure,
But an exalted figure.
Jesus was always subtle
When referring to Himself,
Calling Himself the Son
    of Man.
He was saying
That He is a human being,
Fully understanding all
Our pains and needs.
But for those with ears to hear,
He was also actually claiming
His role as redeemer—
A fitting title for the Son
    of God,
Who became incarnate
In the person of Jesus Christ.

"And he said, 'Behold, I see the heavens opened, and the Son of Man standing at the right hand of God.'"

(Acts 7:56)

Sons of God

"Blessed are the peacemakers, for they shall be called sons of God."

(Matthew 5:9)

Referenced in both the
Old and New Testaments.
In the Old Testament, it
Possibly refers to angels—
At times, to bad angels, but
At other times, to good angels.
Not always well defined.
Some could be fallen angels
Who impregnated women.
Some could be good angels,
Those who shouted for joy
    to God.

In the New Testament,
It refers to people, not angels,
Those who trust in God.
Not sons of God by nature.
For by nature,
All are children of wrath.
People become sons of God
    in the
Regenerative, adoptive sense,
By acceptance of Jesus Christ
As Lord and Savior.

The benefits are numerous in
scripture:
Sons of God receive God's love,
Objects of His fatherly care.
God comforts those He calls
His sons;
He also chastens those He
accepts as sons.
As sons, we are heirs of God,
Coheirs with Christ.
Our promise of life is
Rooted in being sons of God.

Evidence of being sons of God:
Those led by the Spirit,
With childlike confidence
in God,
Having a love of brothers and
sisters, and
Obedience to God's
commands.

Being adopted as sons of God
Is a reality. It is a deep, strong,
Full-hearted reality.
This is not a loosely used term.
If you have trusted Christ
As your Lord and Savior,
Then you are adopted into
God's family.
You are one of the sons of God.

**"For all who are led by the Spirit
of God are sons of God. For you
did not receive the spirit of slavery
to fall back into fear, but you have
received the Spirit of adoption
as sons, by whom we cry, 'Abba!
Father!'"**

(Romans 8:14–15)

Songs of Ascent

**"In my distress I called to the
LORD, and he answered me."**

(Psalm 120:1)

A special group of psalms,
Also called pilgrim songs, the
Songs of Ascent were used for
travelers
On their way to Jerusalem
For the yearly festivals.
Each with a unique theme,
Each offered encouragement.

Psalm 120: God's presence
during distress.
Psalm 121: Joyful praise to the
Lord.
Psalm 122: Prayer for
Jerusalem.
Psalm 123: Patience for God's
mercy.
Psalm 124: Help comes from
the Lord.
Psalm 125: Prayer for God's
blessing upon His people.

Psalm 126: The Lord has done
  great things.
Psalm 127: God's blessing on
  our efforts.
Psalm 128: Joy for those who
  follow God's ways.
Psalm 129: A cry for help to
  the Lord.
Psalm 130: A prayer of
  repentance.
Psalm 131: Surrender as a child
  to the Lord.
Psalm 132: God's sovereign
  plan for His people.
Psalm 133: Praise of brotherly
  fellowship and unity.
Psalm 134: Praise to God in
  His temple.

Contained much value
In believers' lives then,
And they still do today.
Three major truths:
Joy in providence—
These psalms record
Many accounts of God's
Goodness, provision,
  sustenance.
Joy in salvation—
These psalms capture
The victory over our
Helpless condition of sin
Through God's grace.
Joy of worship—
These psalms emphasize
Worship of God,

A passion to revere God
For His saving works in us.

As believers,
We are on spiritual journeys
With the Lord.
These psalms were written
To accompany us,
Giving us security
In God, our Father,
During our trying journeys
Of uncertainty, danger, and
  temptations.
They are psalms of
  encouragement.

"Lift up your hands to the holy place and bless the LORD!"

(Psalm 134:2)

Sovereignty (God's)

"I know that you can do all things, and that no purpose of yours can be thwarted."

(Job 42:2)

Simply put, God is in control,
Total control—the ultimate
  source
Of all power and authority
Over all in existence.

God's counsel will stand.
He does all He pleases.
God is not limited
By anything outside Himself,
Nothing can thwart His will.

God is in control of this world.
Nothing happens by random
    chance;
Neither are things left to their
    own devices
Independently of Him.
God rules the world,
The entire universe,
All of creation.

God chose a people for Himself
Before the foundation of the
    world.
He is not dependent upon us;
He elected to set His love
    upon us.
He chose us for redemption in
    Christ,
Despite ourselves.
And because of that choice,
He will never let us go.

God remains in control
Even when we face
Evil, suffering, and injustice.
While God is not evil's author,
He does permit it.
Everything happens
According to God's definite
Plan and foreknowledge.

He uses our difficult
    circumstances
To work for our good
And His glory.

If people were in control,
All would be in chaos,
For we live in a fallen world;
We are a fallen people.
God's sovereignty is
An immense comfort for us,
A source of strength for us—
Knowing God is sovereign.

"A man's steps are from the LORD; how then can man understand his way?"

(Proverbs 20:24)

Spiritual Gifts

"There are different kinds of gifts, but the same Spirit distributes them. There are different kinds of service, but the same Lord. There are different kinds of working, but in all of them and in everyone it is the same God at work. Now to each one the manifestation of the Spirit is given for the common good."

(1 Corinthians 12:4–7)

Spiritual gifts,
Granted as an act of God's
    grace, are
Not based on our worthiness or
    abilities.
Given according to
God's sovereign choice.
Given by the Spirit of God,
As part of our new lives
Granted to us in Christ Jesus.
Given to faithful followers
To serve God
For the benefit of His people,
For His glory.

Many ways of classifying them,
Many different lists—
But only two main categories:
Speaking gifts and
    administering gifts.

Speaking gifts include:
Prophecy: boldly proclaiming
    God's truth.
Teaching: making clear the
    truth of God's Word.
Exhortation: motivating others
    to action, application, or
    purpose.
Shepherding: overseeing,
    training, feeding, and
    coaching.
Evangelism: passionately
    leading others to the saving
    knowledge of Christ.

Ministering gifts include:
Mercy: identifying with,
    comforting those in need.
Serving: providing practical
    help, both physically and
    spiritually.
Giving: releasing material
    resources to further the
    work of the church.
Administrating: organizing,
    managing, promoting,
    leading.

There are also the miraculous
    gifts:
Apostleship, tongues,
    interpretation,
Miracles, healing.
And the enabling gifts: faith,
Discernment, wisdom, and
    knowledge.

All spiritual gifts are given
For a purpose.
We are to use these gifts
According to the character
    of God
And His revealed will,
With simplicity, diligence,
    cheerfulness.
All gifts are given so that
In all things
God may be praised
Through Jesus Christ.

"In order that in everything God may be glorified through Jesus Christ. To him belong glory and dominion forever and ever. Amen."

(1 Peter 4:11)

(See also **Fruit of the Spirit**.)

Steadfastness

"For this very reason, make every effort to supplement your faith with virtue, and virtue with knowledge, and knowledge with self-control, and self-control with steadfastness, and steadfastness with godliness, and godliness with brotherly affection, and brotherly affection with love."

(2 Peter 1:5–7)

A word meaning
"To endure patiently, to
    persevere"—
An essential principle
In the Christian character.
It is a cleaving to God,
Letting the storms rage as
    they may.
It is resting and abiding in
    Jesus
Through the severest trials of
    life.

A firm, fixed, settled decision
To abide by biblical doctrines.
One who is steadfast is
Unmovable in the Word, who
Continually moves forward
To fulfill his or her duty—
Who is completely, utterly
    dependable.
Steadfastness resists Satan,
Resists all indifferent feelings,
Focusing on doing one's
    obligation
At whatever the cost.

Scripture is full of examples of
    those
Steadfast, those faithful
    to God,
Showing forth God's abiding
    presence
And sustaining grace,
Testifying to the power of
    faith,
Bearing witness to the
One mightier than Satan.
Joseph, maligned and
    persecuted,
Preserved his virtue and
    integrity.
David, hunted like a beast of
    prey,
Remained faithful to God.
Daniel, cast into the lion's den
Remained true in allegiance
    to God.

Job, deprived of worldly
   possessions,
Maintained his love for his
   Lord.
Many Christians,
Falsely accused of dreadful
   crimes,
Did not waver in their faith.

Jesus was the supreme example
Of steadfastness. He was
   decisive
For our benefit in all His
   action,
Regardless of consequences.
He was unwavering
In carrying out the Father's
   will.
He was determined to finish;
Failure was not an option.
   He was
Steadfast to the cross and
   beyond.

"May the Lord direct your hearts
to the love of God and to the
steadfastness of Christ."

(2 Thessalonians 3:5)

Stewardship

"By the Holy Spirit who dwells
within us, guard the good deposit
entrusted to you."

(2 Timothy 1:14)

The doctrine of stewardship
Expresses our relationship
   to God.
It identifies God as owner,
And humanity as manager.
Began at creation and
   continues throughout our
   history.
Essentially, stewardship is
   about
Exercising our God-given
Dominion over His creation,
Reflecting the image of
Our Creator, God, in His care,
Responsibility, maintenance,
Protection, and beautification
Of His creation.
It is utilizing and managing
All resources that God provides
For the glory of God
And the betterment of
His creation.

The Christian is responsible
Not only for the material
   blessings
Provided by God,
But also for the spiritual gifts

Given through the Holy Spirit.

Our stewardship of creation
Involves the caretaking
Of the environment and
    animals,
As well as of our families
And our communities.
Being a good steward in this
    world
Is one way of expressing
Our love for God and
Our gratitude to Him.

This stewardship required of us
Is not a result of our
Own powers or abilities.
The strength, inspiration,
And growth in the
Management of our lives
Must come from God
Through His Holy Spirit.
Otherwise, our labor
Is in vain, being acts of
Self-righteousness, without
    virtue.

Stewardship defines our
Practical obedience
In the administration
Of everything under our
    control.
It is the consecration of
Ourselves and our possessions
To God's service.
It is recognizing not only

God's ownership of all,
But God's control of all.
We are under His constant
    authority
As we manage His affairs.
It is acknowledging that
We are not our own,
But that we belong to Christ,
Who gave Himself for us.

**"As each has received a gift, use
it to serve one another, as good
stewards of God's varied grace."**

(1 Peter 4:10)

Tabernacle

**"And let them make me a
sanctuary, that I may dwell in
their midst."**

(Exodus 25:8)

The center of worship by the
    people of Israel
During their wilderness
    journey.
It was later replaced by
    Solomon's temple.

A dwelling place, tent,
    residence—
A sanctuary for God to
    dwell in.
A small reflection of

God's heavenly home.
The tabernacle,
The focus of ancient Israel,
Was the place where God's
    presence
And His glory dwelt.
From Egypt to the Promised
    Land, it was
A portable tent,
Moving as God led
His people through the desert.
It contained the ark of the
    covenant,
Aaron's rod, and the tablets of
The Ten Commandments.
Entry was restricted to high
    priests only,
And then, only once a year
On the Day of Atonement.

Its physical structure is detailed
In Exodus 27:9–19.
It is full of symbolism,
Though we must exercise care
In expending too much
Energy in speculation.
Yet some aspects are apparent.
The white curtains are the
    purity of God.
Blue speaks of God's
    transcendence.
Purple speaks of His royalty.
Red is the blood that must be
    shed.
Gold, silver speak of the riches

Of the divine kingdom and its
    blessings.
The bronze laver: is a necessity
Of being cleansed from sin.
The bronze altar was the
    judgment
Of God for sin.
The table of showbread is the
    spiritual
Nourishment of God.
The golden lampstand is God,
    the light
Of the world.
The incense altar is Christ
    interceding prayer for His
    people.
The ark of the covenant: God's
    promises
With His people.
All are foreshadowing Christ
As the Word became flesh
And dwelt among us.

As Christ's Spirit dwells in
    believers,
They represent the living
    temple of God.
God dwells with us and is
    present in us.
God has chosen to dwell
With His people
In a much more personal
    manner,
In the Word who became flesh:
Jesus came to earth to
    tabernacle with us.

DIVINE MUSINGS

Now, to meet God,
Talk with God, and
    worship God,
We no longer come to
A building or a tabernacle
Made with human hands;
We come to Jesus,
The temple of God.

We, as the church,
Are the body of Christ, and
    therefore
The temple, the tabernacle,
In which God is pleased to
    dwell
Permanently and powerfully
Through the Holy Spirit.

Our human bodies are
The temple of God,
The tabernacle of God,
The dwelling place of God.
God's glory can shine
    through us
By our obedience
To His commandments,
Through our love for one
    another.

"Do you not know that you are God's temple and that God's Spirit dwells in you? If anyone destroys God's temple, God will destroy him. For God's temple is holy, and you are that temple."

(1 Corinthians 3:16–17)

Temple (of Herod)

"Thus says Cyrus king of Persia: The LORD, the God of heaven, has given me all the kingdoms of the earth, and he has charged me to build him a house at Jerusalem, which is in Judah."

(Ezra 1:2)

Following the destruction
Of Solomon's temple,
For four hundred years,
Many built up a second temple.
Only when Herod took
    control,
After slaughtering many
    priests,
Did he renovate this temple.
Not only a restoration,
But a major expansion.

It was substantial,
Made of marble and gold,
Taller than fifteen stories,
Built on exact location
Of Solomon's temple—
The world's largest
Religious site by far.

273

It was here that Jesus
Debated with the scholars.
Possibly in its highest corner
Is where Satan took Jesus.
Here was the courtyard
Where Jesus drove out
The money changers.
And here the widow donated
Her last two mites.
On the west side,
The court of the women,
Where Mary brought
Baby Jesus for His
Presentation.

The temple contained
The Holy of Holies,
As in Solomon's temple,
But minus the ark and the
    tablets of
The Ten Commandments.
Entrance was protected by the
    veil,
The veil that had torn from top
    to bottom
At the death of Jesus.

Herod's temple stood until
    AD 70.
Four Roman legions destroyed
    this temple,
With fires so hot they melted
    the gold
Which seeped between the
    stones,
Causing Roman soldiers

To tear the temple apart
Stone by stone.
This fulfilled Jesus's prophecy
That there would not be left
One stone upon another.

"And Jesus entered the temple and drove out all who sold and bought in the temple, and he overturned the tables of the money-changers and the seats of those who sold pigeons."

(Matthew 21:12)

Temple (of Solomon)

"Then Solomon began to build the house of the LORD in Jerusalem on Mount Moriah, where the LORD had appeared to David his father, at the place that David had appointed, on the threshing floor of Ornan the Jebusite."

(2 Chronicles 3:1)

A house for the Lord,
A magnificent temple in
    Jerusalem,
The crowning achievement
Of Solomon's reign—
The Temple of Solomon was
    constructed on Mount
    Moriah,

The site where God appeared
To his father David.
Begun in 966 BC.

A massive structure
By any measurement.
The highest point being
Twenty stories—207 feet.
All material was prepared off
   site,
So not a hammer,
ax, or any iron tool
Was heard in the house.
This temple replaced
The portable tabernacle
Used during the
Wilderness wandering.
No expense was spared.

Upon completion, Solomon
Invited all to come for
Prayer and sacrifice and
Petitions to God
To heed their prayers.
The predominate mode of the
Temple's divine service
Was sacrifice to God,
The giving up of
Items of value:
Animal life, grain,
Wine, and money.

The temple contained
A room bare of furniture,
Called the Holy of Holies.
It housed the two tablets

Of the Ten Commandments
Inside the ark of the covenant.
All this was lost at its
   destruction
By the Babylonians in 586 BC.

"Hear in heaven your dwelling place and do according to all for which the foreigner calls to you, in order that all the peoples of the earth may know your name and fear you, as do your people Israel, and that they may know that this house that I have built is called by your name."

(1 Kings 8:42–43)

Temptation

"Watch and pray that you may not enter into temptation. The spirit indeed is willing, but the flesh is weak."

(Matthew 26:41)

Solicitation to that which is
   evil.
   It is a trial of being
Faithful or unfaithful to God.
A challenge of choosing
Between fidelity or infidelity
To the Word of God.

Temptation is an invitation
to sin.

A Christian's life a constant
struggle,
Beset by temptations to sin.
Result of our fallen nature,
Always encouraged by Satan,
The great tempter.
Temptation in itself is not
sinful;
Only when we allow it
To become action or thought
Does it become sin.

Satan tempts Christians
By trying to crush us under
hardships,
Urging us to fulfill natural evil
desires,
Making us complacent and
careless,
Misrepresenting God to us,
Creating false ideas of
God's truth and will.
Satan is constantly on the
prowl,
Always striving to drive a
wedge
Between God and His
children.

Yielding to temptation results
in sin
Such as pride, greed, and envy
Taking root in our hearts,

Replacing the fruit of the Holy
Spirit
With the dross of the flesh, and
Making idols of things not
of God.

The best defense against
temptation is
Knowing the Word of God.
As Jesus quoted scripture
To silence Satan's lies,
We, too, should store
His truth in our hearts and
minds.
Jesus instructed us to watch
and pray,
Not to enter temptation.
Never hesitate to flee
At temptation's first sight,
As Joseph did with Potiphar's
wife.
Temptation is unavoidable,
Yet as our faith strengthens
We are ever more prepared
To douse Satan's flaming
arrows.

**"And lead us not into temptation,
but deliver us from the evil one."**

(Matthew 6:13)

Transfiguration

"And he was transfigured before them, and his face shone like the sun, and his clothes became white as light."

(Matthew 17:2)

Upon the mountain high,
A glimpse of Christ's glory was
Revealed to Peter, James, and
     John.
Parallels Moses at Sinai and
Revealed Jesus's divine nature,
A manifestation of His glory.
A reinforcement for the
Faith of those apostles,
A demonstration to them that
     Jesus
Was who He said He was.
Also present were three
     heavenly witnesses—
Moses, Elijah,
And the voice of God.
Transfiguration in Greek means
     literally
"To transform, to change
Into another form."
It also refers to changing the
     outside
To match what is inside.
Jesus's true character was
     previously
Hidden from the world;
This transfiguration was

A glimpse to a trusted few
Of His true nature,
Attesting to His Sonship,
Confirmed not just by His
     image
But by the voice of God.

Jesus's face shines
With the brilliance of the sun;
His garments become
Dazzlingly bright,
His true nature is revealed in
     glory.
What had previously been
     hidden
Is made manifest to the
Privileged disciples.
It was revealed in the gospels
Of Matthew, Mark, and Luke.

Encouragement was necessary
To the apostles that all
Was proceeding exactly as
God had planned,
That suffering for Christ's sake
Would be worthwhile.
The transfiguration provided
Such encouragement and
     assurance,
This taste of His boundless
     glory.

"He was still speaking when, behold, a bright cloud overshadowed them, and a voice

from the cloud said, 'This is my beloved Son, with whom I am well pleased; listen to him.'"

(Matthew 17:5)

Transgressor

"Therefore I will divide him a portion with the many, and he shall divide the spoil with the strong, because he poured out his soul to death and was numbered with the transgressors; yet he bore the sin of many, and makes intercession for the transgressors."

(Isaiah 53:12)

One who knowingly takes a
    false step—a violator of a
    command,
One who is morally delinquent,
    a sinner.
It is one who goes beyond
Or overpasses any rule
Prescribed for civility or
    morality.
A violator of law,
Ignores principles of decency,
    rebelling against the Word
    of God.
In our fallen state, you and I
Are transgressors,
Violators of the law, sinners.

Whether inherited sin through
    Adam,
Or individual trespasses
Against God's law,
We are all transgressors at
    heart.

Major errors are not required
To be classified as a
    transgressor.
Any sin wins you the name.
God abhors all sin,
Whether major or minor.
Cheating on a test,
Cheating on a spouse—
One is not profoundly worse
Than the other.
Size is irrelevant when it comes
To our salvation.
Break any commandment, and
You are a lawbreaker,
Guilty of sin—
A transgressor.

The apostle Paul tells us that
We have all sinned and
Fallen short of God's glory.
All have sinned; all are
    transgressors.
It demands the need of God's
    forgiveness,
To judge us according to
Jesus's goodness and
    righteousness,
Not our own,

For we possess none.
We are transgressors.

"Whoever is wise, let him understand these things; whoever is discerning, let him know them; for the ways of the LORD are right, and the upright walk in them, but transgressors stumble in them."

(Hosea 14:9)

Treasures in Heaven

"But lay up for yourselves treasures in heaven, where neither moth nor rust destroys and where thieves do not break in and steal."

(Matthew 6:20)

We lay up treasures in heaven,
By using for His glory
Whatever worldly possessions
God has bestowed on us:
Time, talents, creativity,
Material wealth, energy, and
Even our lives.
Use them strategically,
    sacrificially
To serve others in love and
To advance God's kingdom
For God's glory.

Fallen people constantly

Desire permanence and
    security
In this world,
Seeking worldly treasures
Instead of seeking the
Truth and God's kingdom,
The treasures in Christ.
Sinful people all too often
Settle for a counterfeit.

As pilgrims in this world,
We are mere stewards
Of all our gifts and possessions,
And we must give an account.
We are not the owners of these
    things.
We are not to cling to them,
Or let them become
The center of our lives.
We are not to be governed by
    them,
But to govern them.
We are to hold them loosely,
Use them not just for ourselves,
But especially for the benefit
Of others and those less
    fortunate.

The treasures of heaven
Begin with the Father,
Made possible by His Son,
Enacted by His Holy Spirit.
The treasures are
Immeasurable, unsearchable.
We are to treasure the Lord
    Jesus,

For when He is our treasure,
We commit our resources
To His work in this world.
We are then truly serving
The Lord, Jesus Christ.

Living sacrificially is storing up
Treasures in heaven.
When we serve God
By serving the body of Christ,
We store up treasure in heaven.

The applause of people,
Working for our own glory,
Is storing treasures
In the here and now.
It is receiving payment in full
For temporary pleasure—
All to decay and rot.

Treasures in heaven
Far outweigh any trouble or
    pain
We may face on Earth.
We can serve the Lord
    wholeheartedly,
Knowing that our reward
Will be abundantly gracious.

We may store up these
Treasures in heaven
In many ways—
Not only by rightly using
Our material possessions,
But also by faithfully
Enduring persecution,

Loving our enemies,
Forgiving our neighbors,
Sharing the gospel,
Praying in secret, and
Serving the Lord and His
    people.
It is living and loving
Like Jesus.

"Sell your possessions, and give to the needy. Provide yourselves with moneybags that do not grow old, with a treasure in the heavens that does not fail, where no thief approaches and no moth destroys. For where your treasure is, there will your heart be also."

(Luke 12:33)

Tree of Good and Evil

"And the LORD God commanded the man, saying, "You may surely eat of every tree of the garden, but of the tree of the knowledge of good and evil you shall not eat, for in the day that you eat of it you shall surely die."

(Genesis 2:16–17)

A tree in the garden of Eden,
A garden created to meet all
    needs—

A garden of paradise.
A place for Adam and Eve
To care for God's creation,
To live rich, full lives
In harmony with God,
In communion with Him.

Yet communion without choice
Is no communion at all.
A garden, regardless of its
    beauty,
Is still a prison without a gate.
The Tree of Good and Evil is
    the gate,
Located within the reach of
    Adam.
Along with this tree came one
    order:
Do not eat of this fruit.

The fruit was not to be eaten;
This gate was not to be opened.
The tree was not evil,
Neither was it cursed or
    imbued with sin.
It did not impart knowledge,
But the act of eating its fruit
Was an act of rebellion,
An act contrary to God's
    character,
Causing humanity to desire
    itself,
Rather than desiring God.
It was dependence on God
Versus independence of
    humanity.

God placed a temporary
    prohibition
Upon His children,
Who were set to grow
Wise, mature, and free
By way of obedience.
They were to judge between
Good and evil.
The tree was the instrument
To train them in this.
But by disobedience,
By eating of its fruit,
They seized the opportunity
By way of rebellion.
Yes, they did judge
Between good and evil,
But their judgment was flawed
And proved fatal.

They forfeited communion
    with God
By departing through the gate.
Yet God, their Father, so loved
    them
That He offered His only Son
To bring them back to His
    garden—
The new heaven and earth.

**"For God knows that when you eat
from it your eyes will be opened,
and you will be like God, knowing
good and evil."**

(Genesis 3:5)

Tree of Life

"And the LORD God said, 'The man has now become like one of us, knowing good and evil. He must not be allowed to reach out his hand and take also from the tree of life and eat, and live forever.'"

(Genesis 3:22)

A tree in the garden of Eden
Whose fruit imparts eternal
    life.
Created to enhance and sustain
Humanity's physical life.
Planted by God
In the middle of the garden
Alongside the Tree of
    Knowledge
Of Good and Evil.

Adam and Eve were
Banished from the garden
So as not to eat of this tree.
For doing so in their fallen
    state
Would condemn them to live
Eternally in a cursed world.
Eating of this tree would
Have prolonged their lives
    indefinitely,
Dooming them to live forever
In sorrow and toil,
Without hope of escape.

Christ is at times signified
By the Tree of Life,
For He is not only the author
Of natural and spiritual life
But also the giver of eternal
    life.
As Christ is in the midst
Of His people,
The Tree of Life is in the midst
Of the garden.

This tree of eternity
Will stand in the middle
Of the holy city,
The new Jerusalem,
Bearing twelve crops of fruit,
Yielding its fruit every month.
Its leaves used for the
Healing of the nations.
In this eternal state,
The curse will be no more.
Access to this blessed tree
    will be
Reinstated once more.
Darkness is to be forever
    banished, and
Eden is to be restored.

"He who has an ear, let him hear what the Spirit says to the churches. To the one who conquers I will grant to eat of the tree of life, which is in the paradise of God."

(Revelation 2:7)

Trinity

"Go therefore and make disciples of all nations, baptizing them in the name of the Father and of the Son and of the Holy Spirit."

(Matthew 28:19)

A name in the singular,
Three in the body:
Father, Son, and Holy Spirit.
One in essence,
Yet three in person,
Each fully God.

Although a true mystery—
Three in one, one in three—
It is no contradiction.
One in essence,
Three in persons,
Each being fully divine.

No inferiority is implied.
All three are identical in
    attributes,
Equal in power, love, mercy,
Justice, holiness, and
    knowledge.
There is total unity among the
    three,
For God is one.

This one God is
The subject of all divine
    revelation,

Self-disclosed in the trinity.
The Father, from whom all
Revelation proceeds,
The Son, who mediates and
Incarnates that revelation, and
The Spirit, who applies
That revelation to men.

God reveals Himself as
The triune God.
When we meet the one God,
We immediately meet the
    three.
Meeting the three, we meet
    the one.
Regardless of distinct roles,
Each intertwined to make one.

Divine salvation involves the
    trinity.
All three work in perfect unity
To rescue sinners.
The Father chooses,
The Son redeems those chosen,
And the Spirit regenerates
Those chosen and redeemed.
One saving purpose,
One saving plan,
One saving enterprise.

The three persons—each
Not part of God, but
    fully God,
Equally God. Within God's
One undivided being exists an

Unfolding into three
    relationships,
Interpersonal relationships
    signified
By the Father, Son, and Holy
    Spirit.
The Lord, our God, the Lord
    is one.

"But when the Helper comes, whom I will send to you from the Father, the Spirit of truth, who proceeds from the Father, he will bear witness about me."

(John 15:26)

(See also **Godhead**.)

Trustworthy

"Moreover, it is required of stewards that they be found trustworthy."

(1 Corinthians 4:2)

Faithful, reliable, and secure.
Quality of truthfulness and
    dependability,
Binding oneself to keep
    promises
For people. Trusting is not
    faith;
It is a result of faith.

An attribute of God,
For He is dependable,
The same yesterday as today
And forevermore.
He will never abandon us,
Never forsake us.
His promises are sure,
His Word is truth.

God created us,
Laid aside His power
To become one of us,
Allowed people to have
Power over Him,
Forgave us as we killed Him,
Died the death we deserved,
Rose again to save us from
    death,
Prepared a place for us in
    heaven, and
Gave us His Spirit to guide us.
He is totally trustworthy!

Recognizing His
    trustworthiness,
Surrendering our lives to Him,
Allows us to experience all
The sweet joys and blessings
He lays upon us.
Moreover, this removes our
Worries about tomorrow,
The stress we experience today,
And opens peace and joy
On a daily basis.

And he who was seated on the throne said, "Behold, I am making all things new." Also he said, "Write this down, for these words are trustworthy and true."

(Revelation 21:5)

Truth

"What is truth?" retorted Pilate. With this he went out again to the Jews gathered there and said, "I find no basis for a charge against him."

(John 18:38 NIV)

Pilate's eternal question.
There is so much that truth
    is not.
It is not what makes people feel
    good,
Not simply what is believed,
Not what is understandable,
Not what the majority
    agrees on.
Not subjective, relative, or
    dependent
Upon circumstances.

In Greek, it means to
    "un-hide,"
Conveys the idea that truth
Is always there,
Available for all to see.

In Hebrew, it means
    "firmness,"
"Constancy," and "duration,"
Implies an everlasting
    substance,
Something to rely upon.
Truth is unique.
It is the way things really are—
Any other viewpoint is
    incorrect.
A clear distinction.

The biblical definition of
    truth is:
That which is consistent with
    God's
Mind, will character, glory, and
    being.
It is the self-expression of God.
It flows from God.
It is the way things really are,
For God declared it so and
Made it so.
God is the author, source,
Determiner, governor, arbiter,
Ultimate standard, and final
    judge
Of all truth.

The Word of God is truth—
Not just nuggets of truth, but
Pure, unalterable, and
    inviolable truth
That cannot be broken.

Pilate had his answer
But was blind to it;
He was staring directly
At the origin of all truth,
Christ Jesus Himself.

"Jesus answered, 'I am the way and the truth and the life. No one comes to the Father except through me.'"

(John 14:6)

Unconditional Love

"In this the love of God was made manifest among us, that God sent his only Son into the world, so that we might live through him. In this is love, not that we have loved God but that he loved us and sent his Son to be the propitiation for our sins."

(1 John 4:9–10)

Loving someone irrespective
Of that person's behavior;
Acceptance of others
Without their meeting any
    conditions;
Having affection for someone
Without establishing
    limitations.

God sent his beloved Son,
Demonstrating unconditional
    love
By His death on the cross for
    our sins.
God forgives us of our sins
Through His sacrificial love
    for us.
God's wrath was satisfied
By this act of unconditional
    love.

This love of God is
A love that initiates,
Not a love in response, which
Positively makes it
    unconditional.
There is no earning or meriting
This love of God;
He offers it unconditionally
To save His people from their
    sins.
Christ died for us at our worst,
Amid our sins,
When we were totally
    unlovable.

He calls us to have
The same love for others,
As He has for us—
Not an emotional love,
But a sacrificial love.
Loving others is a matter
Of the will and the volition,
Not the emotions.
We are to love one another

As He loved us.
He commanded an action,
Not a feeling.
Making a sacrifice to love
    another
Offers a glimpse of the depth
Of God's love for us.

When we exercise
    unconditional love
To our neighbors in spite of
    their
Lack of lovability,
The Spirit shines through us,
God is glorified, and
The world sees Christ in us—
Sees love unconditional.

"A new commandment I give to you, that you love one another: just as I have loved you, you also are to love one another. By this all people will know that you are my disciples, if you have love for one another."

(John 13:34–45)

Valley

"Even though I walk through the valley of the shadow of death, I will fear no evil, for you are with me; your rod and your staff, they comfort me."

(Psalm 23:4)

Many a valley exists in
    scripture:
The Valley of Shaveh,
The Valley of Gerar, and the
Valley of Baca.
Yet we all have our own valleys:
The valley of despair,
The valley of uncertainty, and
The valley of fear.
These spiritual valleys, these
Places of darkness, are
Places of hopelessness and
Places of trials and tribulations.

Yet valleys are also places
Of new insights and
    understandings.
They alter our perceptions
Of the world and of God.
The Lord is the ultimate
    teacher,
And teaching is what He does
In our valleys.

In the valley, remember:
You belong to God.
Remember God's Word
And put your trust in it.
Expose your doubts.
Draw on God's strength.
Learn to walk in the Lord.
Learn to be still in the Lord.

Know that there is a purpose
For being in this valley.

Although valleys are dark
    places,
They are places of new sight,
Places to experience
The comforting and healing
    power
Of the Holy Spirit.
They are not places to fear,
For they are part of our walk to
    glory.
Difficult, yes, but hopeless, no.
Valleys are impartial,
Inevitable, and purposeful.
Our pain, our trials, our
    journeys
Will not be wasted.

In the valley,
In our times of afflictions,
Treasure the Lord.
Draw close to Him,
Talk to Him through
    prayer, and
Keep walking by faith.
And above all else,
Praise Him continuality.

Scripture doesn't promise
The absence of valleys or
The absence of shadows.
It does promise the continuing
    presence

Of our shepherd
Amid those valleys.

"Blessed be the God and Father of our Lord Jesus Christ, the Father of mercies and God of all comfort, who comforts us in all our affliction, so that we may be able to comfort those who are in any affliction, with the comfort with which we ourselves are comforted by God."

(2 Corinthians 1:2–4)

Vanity

"Vanity of vanities, says the Preacher, vanity of vanities! All is vanity."

(Ecclesiastics 1:2)

Literally, "vapor,
        breath"—therefore,
Meaningless, empty, futile.
Never alone, its baggage
    includes
Pride, jealousy, envy,
Strife, haughtiness, and
    confidence.
It devalues what is
    important and
Elevates the trivial.

Wait for the Lord

It is self-absorbed and
idol-oriented.
Self, the root of all vanity, is
An enemy of the Holy Spirit,
A destroyer of faith.

It describes life apart from
God, with
No ultimate significance,
and is
Consequently valueless.
It describes the condition
Of human life without God.

Riches, health, power, even
wisdom—
All forms of vanity without
faith,
To live outside faith in Christ
Jesus
Is the vanity of vanities,
Life without meaning.
All will vanish, return to dust.
Without the blood of Christ,
All is worthless,
All is vanity.

"For what gives you the right to make such a judgment? What do you have that God hasn't given you? And if everything you have is from God, why boast as though it were not a gift?"

(1 Corinthians 4:7 NLT)

"Wait for the LORD; be strong, and let your heart take courage; wait for the LORD!"

(Psalm 27:14)

Hebrew word means "wait,"
"To bind together."
In Greek, it means "to stay in
a relationship, abide, be
present, stand."
Waiting is not being spiritually
idle,
But it is productive in nature.
It is binding, remaining, being
present.
It is about relationship and
intimacy.

Christians wait for the Lord
To act, to save, to answer
prayers,
To provide for needs, to renew
strength,
To reveal His glory, to
return—for
His glorious return.
We wait on Him because He
is God.
He can accomplish what we
cannot
Because we are helpless
without Him.

It is not like a waiting room,
Where time stands still and
Where action is nonexistent,
But a time of confident
    expectation
Based on knowledge, trust, and
    confidence.
It is seeking the Lord through
Studying His Word,
Spending time in prayer,
Meditating on who God is.
It involves actively growing in
    Christ,
Seeking His counsel.
It involves resting in God's
    timing
While taking care
Of our responsibilities.
It is about trusting God
In His faithfulness and
    goodness.

Waiting for the Lord
Brings you closer to God.
You will have no shame;
You will be blessed
With increase perseverance,
Character, and hope.
You will experience the Lord's
    goodness,
Receiving answers to prayers,
Obtaining promised
    blessings, and
Gaining new strength—
Enjoying God's mercy.

Wait for the Lord,
And I say once again,
Wait!

"Even youths shall faint and be weary, and young men shall fall exhausted; but they who wait for the LORD shall renew their strength; they shall mount up with wings like eagles; they shall run and not be weary; they shall walk and not faint."

(Isaiah 40:30–31)

Wilderness

"They did not say, 'Where is the LORD who brought us up from the land of Egypt, who led us in the wilderness, in a land of deserts and pits, in a land of drought and deep darkness, in a land that none passes through, where no man dwells?'"

(Jeremiah 2:6)

Areas in the Holy Land,
Particularly in the southern
    part,
With little rainfall and few
    people.
Biblical wilderness is similar
To the modern word *desert*,

Yet not with dunes, but rocks.
It is sometimes called "tamed"
    deserts,
Containing oases and some
    grass,
Where shepherds could drive
Their sheep for pasture.

It is historically connected
    with the
Wanderings of the Hebrews
After their escape from Egypt
And remembered as
A great and terrible wilderness.

Place where David fled from
    Saul and the location of the
    temptation of Jesus.
Usually, it is a place feared
    for its
Preying beasts, snakes,
    scorpions,
And possibly even demons.

The wilderness is not restricted
    to a locale
But is also a spiritual state in
    which
A believer endures discomfort
    and trials,
Often with intense
    temptation and
Spiritual attacks.
Emotional burdens may press
    down,
The flesh may cry for relief.

They are hard pressed on every
    side—
But with God, they are not
    crushed;
They are perplexed, but not in
    despair;
They are persecuted, but not
    abandoned;
They are struck down, but not
    destroyed;
All this is demonstrating the
All-surpassing power of God.

The wilderness is an unpleasant
    place.
Yet, just as God created the
    garden,
He created the wilderness—
Times of trials and pressure,
Where our faith is tested.
Our God of grace is ever
    with us,
Even in the wilderness.
Even there, He can refresh us;
Even there, He can renew us.

"And he was in the wilderness forty days, being tempted by Satan. And he was with the wild animals, and the angels were ministering to him."

(Mark 1:13)

Wisdom

"Blessed are those who find wisdom, those who gain understanding."

(Proverbs 3:13)

The blessed ability to discern or
  judge
What is true, right, and
  lasting, is
A gift from God,
A moral as well as an
  intellectual quality.
More than mere knowledge,
It is the ability to discern,
The inclination to choose
That which is pleasing to God,
Along with the surest path
Of attaining it.

God alone naturally
Encompasses wisdom.
His essence includes wisdom
Along with power, truth, and
  love.
Wisdom is His character,
And He shares this wisdom
With His people.

Wisdom is the application
Of knowledge.
Knowledge is knowing the
Ten Commandments;
Wisdom is obeying them.

Wisdom begins and ends
With fearing the Lord,
Having a deep, abiding, and
  holy
Reverence for the Lord and His
  Word.
True wisdom is found
In obedience to God,
By praying and asking for it.

Characteristics of a wise person
  include:
Humility, obedience, and
  discernment.
Wisdom includes a renewing of
  the mind,
Enabling you to discern God's
  will,
And then aligning your life
  with it.
Only through God's wisdom
Is true contentment possible,
When through our words and
  deeds
We give all glory to God.

"But the wisdom that comes from heaven is first of all pure; then peace-loving, considerate, submissive, full of mercy and good fruit, impartial and sincere."

(James 3:17)

Wisdom Literature

"Blessed is the one who finds wisdom, and the one who gets understanding."

(Proverbs 3:13)

Teachings about life,
   virtue, and
The very nature of God.
Five books in scripture:
Job, Psalms, Proverbs,
Ecclesiastes, and Song of
   Solomon.
Also knows as poetical books
For their abundant use
Of Hebrew poetry.
They emphasize the
   understanding and
The attaining of wisdom
For all areas of life,
Including our relationships
With God and our neighbors.

Written by various authors—
Not necessarily prophets or
   priests,
But by sages and elders—
Focusing on practical aspects
Of how to live and
The intellectual challenges that
   arise
When contemplating human
   experience.
Job's author is unknown;

The psalms have various
   writers,
David being the most notable.
Proverbs, Ecclesiastes,
And the Song of Solomon are
   attributed
Primarily to Solomon.

Job is the study in human
   suffering
And the sovereignty of God.
Psalms is a collection of songs
For worship of God.
Proverbs is a study in
   wisdom and
Short, wise sayings.
Ecclesiastes is an essay on
The meaning of life.
Song of Solomon is a touching
   portrait
Of love and affection within
   marriage.

These are wonderful books
   designed
To stimulate the imagination,
Inform the intellect,
Capture the emotions, and
Direct the will.
Deserving of meaningful
Reflection and contemplation.
Instructions in righteousness,
Showing what it means to
   please God.
Ultimately, Christ is our
   wisdom,

Yet God gives us not only
   His Son,
But also the wisdom of His Son
To deal with our daily
Successes and failures.
He alone will make us wise.

"If any of you lacks wisdom, let him ask God, who gives generously to all without reproach, and it will be given him."

(James 1:5)

Worship

"Therefore let us be grateful for receiving a kingdom that cannot be shaken, and thus let us offer to God acceptable worship, with reverence and awe."

(Hebrews 12:28)

A lifestyle, not a moment in
   time.
It is rendering proper homage
To God alone. Our lives are
To be dedicated to the worship
   of God.
True worship is constant:
Inner praise to God expressed
   in prayer,
Expressed in song, service, and
   giving, and

Expressed in living.

True worship is not a matter
Of taste, style, or culture.
It is more concerned with what
   God thinks,
Than with what we think.
It is worshiping God in spirit
   and truth,
For God is spirit,
God is truth.

True worship is
Listening to the Word of God.
Our attitude must be:
"Speak, Lord, for your servant
Is listening," not "Listen, Lord,
For your servant is speaking."

True worship is
   Christ-centered,
For He is the center of worship.
He is our great high priest,
Our mediator, our sacrifice,
Our hope, our joy, our
   peace, and
Our Savior.
This is done by offering
Our bodies and minds,
Through praise,
Through gifts,
Through a contrite heart, and
Through boldly speaking
The Word.

True worship is
Wholehearted and full-bodied.
Worship runs like a thread
From Genesis to Revelation.
It is not confined to what
Takes place in church or in
    open praise.
It is the acknowledgment
    of God,
Of all His power and glory,
In all our thoughts and actions.
The highest form of worship
Is obedience to Him and His
    Word.
To properly do this,
One must know God.

True worship is to glorify and
    exalt God,
To show our loyalty and
    admiration
To our Father.

"I appeal to you therefore,
brothers, by the mercies of God,
to present your bodies as a living
sacrifice, holy and acceptable
to God, which is your spiritual
worship."

(Romans 12:1)

Worthy

"As a prisoner for the Lord, then, I
urge you to live a life worthy of the
calling you have received."

(Ephesians 4:1)

Two ideas in this word:
Having weight and a sense of
    becoming.
Much more than merely
Possessing merit or value
Or deserving or virtuous.

Having weight that is balanced:
In doctrine—one's walk,
And in truth—one's life.
Only when these are in
    balance,
Are we walking worthy
According to scripture.
Doctrine and truth,
To balance with practice,
With how one lives.
Only then can we be worthy.

A sense of becoming is
An idea of matching.
One's doctrine and one's
    practice
Must never clash, but must
    always match.
Doctrine is the basic garment
Of Jesus's way of life.
The way we're to live

GEORGE THOMAS YAPUNCICH

Is to complement His garment,
To complement His life.
Only then can we be worthy.

To be worthy of God
Is to be in balance with His
    truth and
To complement His life.
To walk worthy of the Lord
Is to walk in a way that
The Lord deserves from us,
Not in a way that
We deserve from the Lord.
It is acting in a way that
    demonstrates
How worthy, able, and gracious
Our Lord truly is.

Walking worthy means
Being in step with the Lord,
Walking in the shadow of His
    grace.
It is making choices
Reflecting God's heart and His
    will.
It requires a teachable heart.
Walking worthy means
We know Jesus Christ as our
    Savior.
Walking worthy is not
For the faint of heart,
But for the born-again soul.

**"So as to walk in a manner worthy
of the Lord, fully pleasing to him:
bearing fruit in every good work
and increasing in the knowledge
of God."**

(Colossians 1:10)

Wrath

**"For the wrath of God is revealed
from heaven against all ungodliness
and unrighteousness of men, who
by their unrighteousness suppress
the truth."**

(Romans 1:18)

Referring not to people's anger
But to an emotion of God.
God's wrath is an expression
We cannot fully define.
Like His love, it is
    incomprehensible;
So is His wrath.

As God is holy,
He completely distances
    Himself
From sin, evil, and corruption.
He maintains purity,
Rejects, fights against, and
    destroys
All that offends or attacks
His holiness and love.

296

God's wrath is always seen
In defense of His attributes
Of love and holiness,
His righteousness and justice.
Hence His wrath is just.
It is biblical.
It is His intense hatred of sin.
It is to be feared.
It is satisfied in Christ's
　　sacrifice
On the cross.

The wrath of God is His
Eternal abhorrence
Of all unrighteousness.
It is the holiness of God
Stirred into activity against sin.
It is not malicious retaliation,
But divine justice against evil.
Divine wrath is God's
Righteous anger and
　　punishment
Provoked by sin,
Inseparably linked with His
　　glory.

God's wrath is just.
It is to be feared.
It is consistent throughout
　　time.
It is love in action against sin.
It is fully satisfied through
　　Christ.

**"Since, therefore, we have now
been justified by his blood, much
more shall we be saved by him
from the wrath of God."**

(Romans 5:9)

Yoke

**"And now, whereas my father laid
on you a heavy yoke, I will add to
your yoke. My father disciplined
you with whips, but I will
discipline you with scorpions."**

(1 Kings 12:11)

Physically, a wooden crosspiece
Fastened over the necks
Of animals to share a load
As they pull together.
Scripturally, a metaphor
Describing the weight
Of a task or obligation.

Breaking a yoke
Symbolized freedom from
　　oppression,
Or possibly the phase of a new
　　life.
An easy yoke meant
One's burden was not heavy,
Inferring that Christ would be
Pulling with us.

This imagery also used
To discourage Christians
From entering into intimate
Dealings with unbelievers:
"Do not be yoked together
With unbelievers."
To be yoked together
Is a binding relationship that is
Difficult to break.
Christians should not be
Yoked to this world.

The yoke of the Pharisees
Is the burdensome yoke
Of self-righteousness,
Legalistic law-keeping—
A heavy burden indeed!
Only Jesus gives rest from
The heavy burden of
Trying to earn salvation.
It is in Jesus that Christians
Find rest for their souls.

This is true because Jesus
Carried the burden we were to
    carry.
His perfect obedience is
Applied to us through faith.
Our burdens are lifted.

"Take my yoke upon you, and learn from me, for I am gentle and lowly in heart, and you will find rest for your souls. For my yoke is easy, and my burden is light."

(Matthew 11:29–30)

Zion

"On the holy mount stands the city he founded; the LORD loves the gates of Zion more than all the dwelling places of Jacob. Glorious things of you are spoken, O city of God."

(Psalm 87:1–3)

Meaning fortification,
The idea of being raised up as a
    mountain.
Refers to one of three places:
The hill in ancient Jerusalem,
The city of Jerusalem itself,
And the dwelling place of God.

In addition to a physical place,
Zion is also used in a spiritual
    sense.
In the Old Testament, it
Refers to Israel as God's people.
In the New Testament, it
Refers to God's spiritual
    kingdom—
The heavenly Jerusalem.

Yes, it is a physical place
As well as spiritual,
Yet is continually being built
In the heart of every believer
Who walks with the Lord
    obediently,
Growing in wisdom and peace.

"Those who trust in the LORD are like Mount Zion, which cannot be moved, but abides forever."

(Psalm 125:1)

INDEX TO SCRIPTURAL REFERENCES

Genesis 1:1—Creation, Earth, Genesis

Genesis 1:3—Omnipotent

Genesis 1:6–7—Firmament

Genesis 1:14—Pentateuch

Genesis 1:27—Genesis, Man

Genesis 2:7—Adam, Man

Genesis 2:16–17—Tree of Good and Evil

Genesis 2:24—Marriage

Genesis 3:5—Tree of Good and Evil

Genesis 3:6—The Fall

Genesis 3:15—Enmity; Prophecy

Genesis 3:22—Tree of Life

Genesis 3:24—Cherub

Genesis 6:4—Nephilim

Genesis 9:13—Rainbow

Genesis 12:1–3—Abraham

Genesis 14:18–20—Melchizedek

Genesis 15:6—Abraham

Genesis 17:7—Covenant

Genesis 17:10—Circumcision

Genesis 18:20–21—Sodom and Gomorrah

Exodus 3:9—Character of God

Exodus 3:10—Exodus

Exodus 3:14—God

Exodus 3:15—Names of God

Exodus 8:20—Exodus

Exodus 12:14—Passover

Exodus 12:26–27—Passover

Exodus 16:15—Manna

Exodus 20:3–4—Idolatry

Exodus 20:8—Sabbath

Exodus 20:11—Sabbath, Six Days

Exodus 20:17—Covet

Exodus 23:19—Firstfruits

Exodus 25:8—Tabernacle

Exodus 25:30—Bread of Presence

Exodus 26:33—Curtain (of the Temple)

Exodus 33:9—Character of God

Leviticus 2:13—Salt of the Earth

Leviticus 19:18—Golden Rule, Neighbor

Leviticus 20:26—Leviticus

Leviticus 22:32—Hallowed

Leviticus 23:26–27—Day of Atonement

Leviticus 24:8—Bread of Presence

Numbers 6:24–26—Numbers

Numbers 12:6—Prophets

Numbers 13:32–33—Nephilim

Deuteronomy 5:18—Adultery

Deuteronomy 8:3—Daily Bread

Deuteronomy 8:15—Deserts

Deuteronomy 10:12—Fear of God

Deuteronomy 16:13–15—Feast of Tabernacles

Deuteronomy 21:17—Birthright

Deuteronomy
23:5—Curse
Deuteronomy 31:7–8—
Deuteronomy
Joshua 9:23–24—Curses
Judges 2:16—Judges
1 Samuel 8:4–5—Judges
1 Samuel 16:13—David
1 Kings 8:42–43—
Temple (of Solomon)
1 Kings 12:11—Yoke
1 Chronicles
16:36—Amen
2 Chronicles 3:1—Temple
(of Solomon)
Ezra 3:1—Temple (of
Herod)
Job 31:11–12—Lust
Job 42:2—Sovereignty
Psalm 1:1—Blessing,
Psalms
Psalm 11:6—Fire and
Brimstone
Psalm 12:6—Infallible
Psalm 16:11—Joy
Psalm 17:15—Scripture
Psalm 18:2—Fortress
Psalm 19:1—Firmament,
Revelation
Psalm 23:2—Green
Pastures
Psalm 23:4—Conquerors,
Valley
Psalm 23:6—Goodness
Psalm 24:4—Fear
Psalm 24:7–9—King
Psalm 27:11—Inherit the
Earth
Psalm 27:14—Wait for
the Lord
Psalm 30:6—Shaken

Psalm 34:8—Refuge
Psalm 34:18—Poor in
Spirit
Psalm 47:1—Joy
Psalm 51:1—Mercy
Psalm 51:5—Original Sin
Psalm 51:10—Pure in
Heart
Psalm 62:1–2—David
Psalm 62:7—Refuge
Psalms 83:18—Jehovah
Psalm 87:1–3—Zion
Psalm 89:14—Justice
Psalm 91:2—Fortress
Psalm 94:2—Deserving
Psalm 99:5—Exalt
Psalm 100:4–5—Psalms
Psalm 103:19—Kingdom
of God
Psalm 119:160—Old
Testament
Psalm 120:1—Songs of
Ascent
Psalm 125:1—Zion
Psalm 134:2—Songs of
Ascent
Psalm 138:2—Names of
God
Psalm 139:7–10—
Omnipresent
Psalm 147:1—Praise
Psalm 148:1–2—Angels
Proverbs 1:5—Proverbs
Proverbs 1:7—Proverbs
Proverbs 3:9—Firstfruits
Proverbs 3:13—Wisdom,
Wisdom Literature
Proverbs 6:16–19—Seven
Deadly Sins
Proverbs 11:2—Pride

Proverbs
15:3—Omnipresent
Proverbs 16:6—
Faithfulness, Fear of
God
Proverbs 16:9—Free Will
Proverbs
20:24—Sovereignty
Proverbs
31:11–12—Marriage
Ecclesiastics 1:2—Vanity
Song of Solomon 2:1—
Lily of the Valley,
Rose of Sharon
Song of Solomon
6:3—Beloved
Isaiah 6:1–2—Seraphim
Isaiah 6:3—Character of
God, Seraphim
Isaiah 9:2—Darkness
Isaiah 9:6—Incarnation
Isaiah 12:2—Jehovah
Isaiah 14:12—Satan
Isaiah 25:6—Banquet
Isaiah
28:16—Cornerstone
Isaiah 35:1—Rose of
Sharon
Isaiah 40:3—John the
Baptist
Isaiah 40:28—Nature of
God
Isaiah 40:30–31—Wait
for the Lord
Isaiah 40:31—Hope
Isaiah 46:13—Israel
Isaiah 50:3—Sackcloth
Isaiah
53:12—Transgressor
Isaiah 55:8–9—Nature
of God

Isaiah 61:10—Rejoice
Jeremiah 2:6—Wilderness
Jeremiah 9:23–24—
    Know God
Jeremiah
    17:7–8—Blessing
Jeremiah 17:14—Heal
Jeremiah 19:5—Baal
Jeremiah
    23:6—Righteousness
Jeremiah
    26:11—Deserving
Jeremiah 29:11—Hope
Jeremiah 29:12—Pray
Jeremiah 32:17—Creation
Ezekiel 1:28—Rainbow
Ezekiel 11:19—Heart of
    Flesh
Ezekiel 16:49–50—
    Sodom and
    Gomorrah
Ezekiel 34:11–12—
    Shepherd Good
Daniel 2:20—Praise
Daniel 7:9—Ancient of
    Days
Daniel 7:13–14—Son of
    Man
Daniel 7:21–22—Ancient
    of Days
Hosea 14:9—Transgressor
Joel 2:28—Minor
    Prophets
Micah 5:2—Bethlehem
Micah 7:18—Prodigal
Nahum 1:7—Minor
    Prophets
Habakkuk
    3:5—Pestilence
Matthew 1:21—Jesus

Matthew
    2:1–2—Bethlehem
Matthew 3:11—Baptism
Matthew
    4:17—Repentance
Matthew 4:18–20—Peter
Matthew 5:1–2—Sermon
    on the Mount
Matthew 5:3—Poor in
    Spirit
Matthew 5:4—Comfort,
    Mourn
Matthew 5:5—Inherit the
    Earth, Meek
Matthew 5:6—Hunger
    for Righteousness
Matthew 5:8—Pure in
    Heart, Seeing God
Matthew 5:9—Sons of
    God
Matthew
    5:10—Persecution
Matthew 5:12—Reward
Matthew 5:13—Salt of
    the Earth
Matthew 5:16—Matthew
Matthew 5:28—Lust
Matthew 6:9—Hallowed,
    Lord's Prayer
Matthew 6:10—Earth
Matthew 6:11—Daily
    Bread
Matthew
    6:11–12—Debtors
Matthew 6:13—
    Temptation, Lord's
    Prayer
Matthew
    6:17–18—Fasting
Matthew 6:20—Treasures
    in Heaven

Matthew 6:28–29—Lily
    of the Valley
Matthew
    6:30—Providence
Matthew 6:33—Hunger
    for Righteousness
Matthew
    7:1–2—Judgment
Matthew 7:15—Prophets
    False
Matthew 7:12—Golden
    Rule
Matthew 7:13–14—
    Narrow Gate
Matthew 7:20—Fruit of
    the Spirit
Matthew 7:28–29—
    Sermon on the
    Mount
Matthew 8:11—Heaven
Matthew
    9:4—Omniscient
Matthew 9:9—Matthew
Matthew 9:10—Publican
Matthew
    10:2–4—Apostle
Matthew 10:28—Hell
Matthew 11:28–30—Rest
Matthew 11:29–30—Yoke
Matthew 12:18—Beloved
Matthew 13:35—Parables
Matthew 16:16—Messiah
Matthew 16:18—Church
Matthew
    17:2—Transfiguration
Matthew 17:5—
    Transfiguration; Son
    of God
Matthew 21:12—Temple
    (of Herod)

Matthew 22:1–2—Banquet
Matthew 22:12–14—Kingdom of Heaven
Matthew 22:37–38—Love the Lord
Matthew 22:37–40—Love your Neighbor
Matthew 23:12—Exalt
Matthew 24:36—Angels
Matthew 24:30–31—Rapture
Matthew 24:32—Fig Tree
Matthew 26:26–28—Sacrament
Matthew 26:41—Flesh (Is Weak), Temptation
Matthew 27:51—Curtain (of the Temple)
Matthew 28:19—Trinity
Matthew 28:19–20—Great Commission
Mark 1:4—Deserts, John the Baptist
Mark 1:13—Wilderness
Mark 3:13–15—Apostle
Mark 4:33–34—Parables
Mark 7:21–22—Evil
Mark 11:21–22—Fig Tree
Mark 11:24—Mark, Prayer
Mark 12:29–31—Deuteronomy
Mark 16:9—Mary Magdalene
Luke 2:10–11—Advent
Luke 2:11—Christ
Luke 2:37—Fasting
Luke 4:18—Blindness, Blood
Luke 5:30—Publican

Luke 6:35—Reward
Luke 6:36—Mercy
Luke 6:37—Luke
Luke 8:1–3—Mary Magdalene
Luke 10:13—Sackcloth
Luke 12:33—Treasures in Heaven
Luke 13:24—Narrow Gate
Luke 14:27—Cross
Luke 15:13—Prodigal
Luke 17:20–21—Kingdom of God
Luke 21:11—Pestilence
Luke 24:6–7—Christ is Risen
Luke 24:44—Old Testament, Pentateuch
John 1:12—Children of God
John 1:14—Incarnation, Revelation
John 1:41—Messiah
John 2:14—Money Changers
John 3:3—Born Again
John 3:16—Covenant of Grace, Faith, Gospel
John 4:48—Signs and Wonders
John 6:35—Bread of Life
John 6:39—Last Days
John 6:48–51—Bread of Life
John 6:49–51—Manna
John 7:37–38—Feast of Tabernacles
John 8:41—Fornication

John 10:14–15—Shepherd Good
John 11:25—Resurrection
John 13:23—John
John 13:34–45—Unconditional Love
John 14:6—Truth
John 14:26—Holy Spirit
John 14:27—Peace
John 15:8—Fruit of the Spirit, Glory
John 15:26—Trinity
John 17:3—Eternal Life
John 17:17—Inspired
John 18:28—Truth
John 19:30—Passion of Christ
Acts 1:8—Luke, Great Commission
Acts 2:1–3—Pentecost
Acts 2:23—Foreknowledge
Acts 2:37–38—Pentecost
Acts 2:38—Heart of Flesh, Sacrament
Acts 4:13—Peter
Acts 7:8—Patriarch
Acts 7:56—Son of Man
Acts 14:23—Elder
Acts 17:30—Repentance
Acts 26:17–18—Darkness
Romans 1:18—Wrath
Romans 1:20—Godhead
Romans 2:4—Forbearance, Kindness
Romans 2:17–21—Jew
Romans 2:28–29—Jew
Romans 3:20—Law
Romans 3:22–24—Justification

Romans 3:22–25—Sin
Romans 3:25—Atonement
Romans 4:24–25—Justification
Romans 5:8—Passion of Christ
Romans 5:9—Wrath
Romans 5:12—Adam, Death (Physical), Original Sin
Romans 5:15–17—The Fall
Romans 6:15–16—Law
Romans 6:17–18—Free Will
Romans 6:22—Bondservant
Romans 6:23—Death (Spiritual), Eternal Life; Justice, Sin
Romans 8:6–7—Flesh (Is Weak)
Romans 8:12–13—Debtors
Romans 8:14–15—Sons of God
Romans 8:16–17—Children of God
Romans 8:28—Providence
Romans 8:29–30—Predestination
Romans 8:30—Glorification
Romans 8:37—Conquerors
Romans 9:5—Patriarchs
Romans 9:6—Israel
Romans 11:4—Baal

Romans 12:1—Sacrifice, Worship
Romans 15:5—Harmony
Romans 15:13—Holy Spirit, Peace
Romans 15:5—Church, Harmony
1 Corinthians 1:9—Call
1 Corinthians 1:18—Cross
1 Corinthians 2:12–13—Scripture
1 Corinthians 3:16–17—Tabernacle
1 Corinthians 4:2—Trustworthy
1 Corinthians 4:7—Vanity
1 Corinthians 7:18–19—Circumcision
1 Corinthians 9:16—Paul, Preaching
1 Corinthians 10:31—Glory
1 Corinthians 11:23–26—Lord's Supper
1 Corinthians 11:26—Lord's Supper
1 Corinthians 12:4–7—Spiritual Gifts
1 Corinthians 12:9—Omnipotent
1 Corinthians 13:4–6—Love
1 Corinthians 13:6—Evil
1 Corinthians 13:13—Love
1 Corinthians 15:3–4—Gospel
1 Corinthians 15:20–22—Resurrection

1 Corinthians 15:22—Death (Physical)
2 Corinthians 1:2–4—Valley
2 Corinthians 1:3–5—Comfort
2 Corinthians 3:18—Glorification
2 Corinthians 4:4—Blindness
2 Corinthians 5:17—Regeneration
2 Corinthians 5:21—Righteousness
2 Corinthians 9:6–8—Generosity
Galatians 3:26—In Christ
Galatians 4:9—Know God
Galatians 5:19–21—Idolatry
Galatians 5:22–23—Faithfulness, Fruit of the Spirit
Galatians 6:1—Judgment
Ephesians 1:7—Blood, Redemption
Ephesians 1:11—Predestination
Ephesians 1:18–19—Pray
Ephesians 2:1–3—Enemy
Ephesians 2:19–21—Cornerstone
Ephesians 4:1—Worthy
Ephesians 4:1–3—Call, Patience
Ephesians 4:32—Kindness
Ephesians 5:3—Adultery

Ephesians
4:4–6—Baptism
Ephesians 6:11—Shaken
Ephesians
6:12—Principalities
Philippians
1:1–2—Deacon
Philippians 2:9–11—Jesus
Philippians
4:5—Gentleness
Philippians 4:6–7—
Anxiety, Prayer
Colossians 1:10—Worthy
Colossians
1:15—Birthright
Colossians 2:6–7—In
Christ
Colossians 2:9—Godhead
Colossians
2:9–10—Christ
Colossians 2:13—Death
Spiritual
Colossians
2:13–14—Forgiveness
Colossians
2:15—Principalities
Colossians
3:12—Humility
Colossians 3:12–13—
Forbearance,
Forgiveness
Colossians
3:14—Harmony
Colossians 3:22—Slaves
Colossians 4:1—Slaves
1 Thessalonians
4:3—Fornication
1 Thessalonians
4:16–17—Rapture
1 Thessalonians
5:16–18—Rejoice

1 Thessalonians 5:23–
24—Sanctification
2 Thessalonians 1:9—Hell
2 Thessalonians
2:13—Sanctification
2 Thessalonians
3:5—Steadfastness
2 Thessalonians
3:17—Epistle
1 Timothy 3:13—Deacon
1 Timothy 6:15—King
1 Timothy
6:18–19—Generosity
2 Timothy 1:2—Jesus
Christ
2 Timothy
1:14—Stewardship
2 Timothy
1:6–7—Self-control
2 Timothy 1:7—Fear
2 Timothy
1:9–10—Savior
2 Timothy
3:12—Persecution
2 Timothy
3:15–17—Scripture
2 Timothy 3:16—Old
Testament
2 Timothy 3:16–17—
Infallible, Inspired
(Divinely)
2 Timothy
4:1–2—Preaching
2 Timothy 4:2—Rebuke
2 Timothy 4:7—Paul
2 Timothy
1:9–10—Savior
Titus 2:11–12—Self-
Control
Titus 3:5—Regeneration

Hebrews 1:1–2—Last
Days
Hebrews 1:1–3—Son of
God
Hebrews 1:2—Heir
Hebrews 1:3—Majesty
Hebrews 2:4—Signs and
Wonders
Hebrews 3:4—Six Days
Hebrews
3:7–9—Numbers
Hebrews 4:1—Rest
Hebrews 4:14–16—Priest
Hebrews
5:5–6—Melchizedek
Hebrews
6:11–12—Patience
Hebrews 7:26—Priest
Hebrews 7:27—Leviticus
Hebrews 8:6—Covenant
of Grace
Hebrews 9:11–12—Day
of Atonement
Hebrews 9:15—Covenant
Hebrews 9:22—Blood
Hebrews 9:28—Advent
Hebrews 11:1—Faith
Hebrews 12:28—Worship
Hebrews 13:15—Sacrifice
James 1:1—Bondservant
James 1:5—Wisdom
Literature
James 1:21—Meek
James 2:8—Neighbor
James 2:10—Seven
Deadly Sins
James 3:17—Wisdom
James 4:2—Covet
James 4:4—Enmity
James 4:6—Humility

1 Peter: 1:1–2—
  Foreknowledge
1 Peter 1:3—Christ is
  Risen
1 Peter 1:3–4—Heir
1 Peter 1:18–19—
  Redemption
1 Peter 1:23—Born Again
1 Peter 2:24—Heal,
  Atonement
1 Peter 3:8—Love Your
  Neighbor
1 Peter 3:15—Gentleness
1 Peter
  4:10—Stewardship
1 Peter 4:11—Spiritual
  Gifts
1 Peter 5:1–4—Elder
1 Peter 5:7—Anxiety
1 Peter 5:8—Enemy
1 Peter 5:13—Mark
2 Peter 1:5–7—Goodness,
  Steadfastness
2 Peter 1:16—Majesty
2 Peter
  1:20–21—Prophets
2 Peter 1:21—Prophecy
2 Peter 2:3—Money
  Changers
2 Peter 3:1—Epistle
2 Peter 3:13—Heaven
1 John 1:5—God
1 John 1:9—Confession
1 John 2:1—New
  Testament
1 John 2:16—Pride
1 John 3:19–20—
  Omniscient
1 John 4:1—Prophets
  False

1 John 4:9–10—
  Unconditional Love
1 John 4:15—Confession
1 John 4:19—Love the
  Lord
3 John 4—John
Jude 1—Jesus Christ
Jude 6—Angels (Fallen)
Revelation 1:1—
  Revelation (Book of)
Revelation 2:7—Tree of
  Life
Revelation 2:11—Death
  (Second)
Revelation 3:19—Rebuke
Revelation 4:8—Cherub
Revelation 7:17—Green
  Pastures
Revelation 12:9—Angels
  (Fallen)
Revelation 20:10—Satan
Revelation 20:11—
  Revelation (Book of)
Revelation 21:1–2—New
  Jerusalem
Revelation 21:4—Mourn
Revelation
  21:5—Trustworthy
Revelation 21:8—Death
  (Second); Fire and
  Brimstone
Revelation 22:3—New
  Jerusalem
Revelation
  22:20–21—Amen

ABOUT THE AUTHOR

George T. Yapuncich is a pastor, missionary, teacher, mentor, husband, father, part-time farmer, and retired international businessman. He is the author of Righteousness Unleashed, a verse-by-verse commentary on the book of Romans.

George spent his career traveling and living around the world, and has lived in South America, Africa, and Europe, as well as Texas, Florida, and his home state of Montana. He earned a degree in science from Montana State University and a masters of divinity degree from Reformed Theology Seminary in Florida. George has served in various ministerial positions, including being pastor of an international church in Rio de Janeiro.

He is married to his wife of over thirty-seven years and resides on a small farm in the mountains of Brazil, where he preaches part time, tends the land, and writes. They have six children, many grandchildren and great-grandchildren.

Printed in the United States
by Baker & Taylor Publisher Services